Prism of Life Long Education

By the same editor
Spectrum of Life Long Education

ABOUT THE EDITOR

Dr. Rameshwari Pandya received her B.Sc., B.Ed. from Lady Irwin College, New Delhi and her M.Sc., M.Ed. and Ph.D. in Home Science from The Maharaja Sayaji Rao University Baroda in 1994. She is the recipient of Shrimati Leelaben Shah Gold Medal for her academic excellence. She is the Head of the Department of Extension and Communication, Faculty of Family and Community Sciences.

She has published more than 150 research papers, peer- reviewed papers and several technical reports. Her work has been published in different Professional Journals of repute and has authored many handbooks and booklets. She has to her credit, more than 25 books. She is the In-Charge of "PRAGATI" the Urban Extension Centre. She has successfully conducted many training programmes and has participated in many Seminars, Conferences, and Workshops at National and International level.

Her professional activities include membership on the Board of Studies, Senate and Faculty Board. Recently she is elected member in the Syndicate of the University.

She has successfully completed several projects and has recently completed a major project funded by Indian Council of Social Science Research (ICSSR) on "Promotion of Communal Harmony". She has been involved in Teaching, Research and Extension. She is an active member of several professional organizations.

Prism of Life Long Education

Edited by
Rameshwari Pandya

CONCEPT PUBLISHING COMPANY PVT. LTD.,
NEW DELHI-110059

ISBN-13: 978-81-8069-923-8

First Published 2013

Published and Printed by

Concept
Since 1974

Concept Publishing Company Pvt. Ltd.
A/15-16, Commerical Block, Mohan Garden
New Delhi - 110059 (India)
T : 25351460, 25351794, F : 091-11-25357109
E : publishing@conceptpub.com, W : www.conceptpub.com
Editorial Office : H-13, Bali Nagar, New Delhi-110015, India

Cataloging in Publication Data--*Courtesy:* D.K. Agencies (P) Ltd. <docinfo@dkagencies.com>

Prism of life long education / edited by Rameshwari Pandya.
p. cm.
Contributed articles.
Includes bibliographical references and index.
ISBN 9788180699238

1. Continuing education—India. 2. Continuing education—India—Gujarat. 3. Education—Social aspects—India. 4. Education—Social aspects—India—Gujarat. I. Pandya, Rameshwari.

DDC 374.954 23

Dedicated
to
my Teachers

Preface

This book has been prepared to serve as a reference book for students and teachers teaching Non-formal Education, Adult Education, Extension Education, Community Development programmes in Agricultural Colleges and Universities in India. This book is written primarily to meet the Indian situation.

This book is a result of the work done by different scholars, academicians, research workers and change agents. Editor has knitted them together and given its present form. Issues addressed in this book are related to Extension, Adult and Non-formal Education. The students get first-hand experience in the field during their extension work, working with different target group like children, women, elderly, disabled etc.

We all will agree that there is a growing body of knowledge in the social sciences that should have application in the real world. The material in this book is the result of an effort to bring together best information both in terms of the selection and the treatment of the subject matter contained herein. Here the author has edited several papers—theoretical and empirical—of Eminent Scholars from different parts of the country. Different topics covered are—Folk Media, Health Education, Computer Literacy, Consumer Education, ICT, CSR, Environment Education, Health and Nutrition and Case studies as well as success stories are incorporated.

In recent years a number of research studies have taken place on Life Long Education, however there is still lack of reliable data on different aspects of Non-formal and Adult Education.

Different topics are taught in the curriculum of the undergraduate college students who are getting trained as developmental practitioners. The idea of writing this book came to my mind while teaching these students the diverse themes so that one can clearly see and understand different colours, shades and hues of Life Long Education.

It is sincerely hoped that this book will prove to be informative and useful both as a text and a reference book.

Rameshwari Pandya
Vadodara

Acknowledgements

I am grateful to many people who have contributed significantly to the successful compilation of this book. My gratitude to them cannot be expressed in few lines.

I am thankful to all the contributors for this edited version. Their quick response has made this work transformed in the shape of this book.

It is my pleasure to offer my sincere loving thanks to all my friends and well-wishers who have extended their kind help, encouragement, unforgettable supporting attitude and cheerful company.

I would also like to express my gratitude to all the faculty members of the department of Extension and Communication, Faculty of Family and Community Sciences, The M.S. University of Baroda, Vadodara, Gujarat. It was a pleasure working with the authors who contributed to this book.

I cannot express in words, the moral support, inspiration, encouragement, love and never ending help given by my husband Dr. Mahesh Pandya without which this work would not have attained its present format. I would also wish to place on record my affection to my sons Siddharath and Shrikant who spared me from all parental obligations.

At this important moment of life, I wish to remember my parents who had always been an eternal source of inspiration and guidance to me.

Rameshwari Pandya
Vadodara

Contents

List of Contributors

Dr. Rameshwari Pandya, Head, Department of Extension and Communication, Faculty of Family and Community Sciences, The Maharaja Sayajirao University of Baroda, Vadodara, Gujarat.

Prof. Farzana Alim, Dean, Faculty of Agricultural Sciences, Chairman, Department of Home Science, Aligarh Muslim University, Aligarh, Uttar Pradesh.

Dr. Jagdish Solanki, Associate Professor, Faculty of Social Work, The Maharaja Sayajirao University of Baroda, Vadodara, Gujarat.

Dr. Sunita Nambiyar, Associate Professor, Faculty of Social Work, The Maharaja Sayajirao University of Baroda, Vadodara, Gujarat.

Dr. Nirmala Kumari, Associate Professor, University Department of Industrial Relations and Personnel Management (I.R.P.M), T.M. Bhagalpur University, Bhagalpur, Bihar.

Dr. Neerja Jaiswal, Associate Professor, Department of Family and Community Resource Management, Faculty of Family and Community Sciences, The Maharaja Sayajirao University of Baroda, Vadodara, Gujarat.

Ms. Ami Shah, Research Scholar, Department of Family and Community Resource Management, Faculty of Family and Community Sciences, The Maharaja Sayajirao University of Baroda, Vadodara, Gujarat.

Dr. Rekha K. Talmaki, Associate Professor, Department of Economics, SNDT College, Churchgate, Mumbai.

Dr. Santosh Tikoo, Head, Department of Home Science, Arya P.G.College, Panipat, Haryana.

Dr. Poonam Tewari, Research Officer, G.B. Pant University of Agriculture & Technology, Pantnagar, Uttarakhand.

Dr. Jagdish Gupta, Principal, Arya P.G.College, Panipat, Haryana.

Ms. Arpita Sharma, Research Scholar, Deptt. of Agricultural

Communication, G. B. Pant University of Agriculture & Technology, Pantnagar, Uttarakhand.

Dr. Surya Rathor, Associate Professor, Deptt. of Agricultural Communication, G. B. Pant University of Agriculture & Technology, Pantnagar, Uttarakhand.

Dr. Varsha Parikh, Assistant Professor, Department of Extension and Communication, Faculty of Family and Community Sciences, The Maharaja Sayajirao University of Baroda, Vadodara, Gujarat.

Ms. Leena Chauhan, Research Scholar, Department of Extension and Communication, Faculty of Family and Community Sciences, The Maharaja Sayajirao University of Baroda, Vadodara, Gujarat.

Prof . Uma Joshi, Dean, Faculty of Family and Community Sciences, The Maharaja Sayajirao University of Baroda, Vadodara, Gujarat.

Ms. Dimple Saluja, Research Scholar, Department of Extension and Communication, Faculty of Family and Community Sciences, The Maharaja Sayajirao University of Baroda, Vadodara, Gujarat.

Ms. Jagrati Vadnekar, Research Scholar, Department of Extension and Communication, Faculty of Family and Community Sciences, The Maharaja Sayajirao University of Baroda, Vadodara, Gujarat.

Dr. Anee Kurvilla, Associate Professor, Department of Foods and Nutrition, Faculty of Family & Community Sciences, The Maharaja Sayajirao University of Baroda, Vadodara, Gujarat.

Ms. Shivani R. Bhatt, Research Scholar, Department of Foods and Nutrition, Faculty of Family & Community Sciences, The Maharaja Sayajirao University of Baroda, Vadodara, Gujarat.

Mr. Udit Digal, Project Fellow, UGC-DSA, Faculty of Social Work, The Maharaja Sayajirao University of Baroda, Vadodara, Gujarat.

Prof. M.N. Parmar, Dean, Faculty of Social Work, The Maharaja Sayajirao University of Baroda, Vadodara, Gujarat.

Ms. Krutika Muley, Research Scholar, Department of Extension and Communication, Faculty of Family and Community Sciences, The Maharaja Sayajirao University of Baroda, Vadodara, Gujarat.

Ms. Chandani Jhadhav, Research Scholar, Department of Extension and Communication, Faculty of Family and Community Sciences, The Maharaja Sayajirao University of Baroda, Vadodara, Gujarat.

Ms. Shridha Chokshi, Research Scholar, Department of Extension and Communication, Faculty of Family and Community Sciences, The Maharaja Sayajirao University of Baroda, Vadodara, Gujarat.

Introduction

Right to Education has become a matter of international concern as well as gaining prominence in national development efforts, as education is fundamental to the national progress. Despite far-reaching changes in policy and programming aimed at improving the standard of life in India, the last decade has seen mixed results in terms of its achievements as far as Life Long Education is concerned. It is increasingly discussed in the academics and government as a sort of panacea to current educational and social problems.

The book contains 16 chapters each touching a specific area in the field of Life Long Education contributed by expert on the subject, which provides deep insights into the interface between different facets of education, development and innovation.

This is the result of invaluable research and reference work on the subject. It sheds light on different experiments and efforts being made, and offers an insight into the ground reality and also experimental accounts of how such projects have achieved excellent results. Each Chapter enhances our understanding of broad range of issues in Life Long Education in Indian context. The focus is not simply on describing situations or the unmet needs of education, but also to offer examples of positive solutions and successful initiatives. The projects described in the book are drawn from different areas like health, environment, women education, consumer education, computer literacy, corporate social responsibility, folk media and tribals upliftment. Interestingly, the common thread bindings these projects and making the "prism of Life Long Education" a comprehensive book. It assists readers in critically evaluation and choosing those methods that have highest probabilities of yielding benefits for their special population. Crafting and implementing plans for Life Long Education is impossible without a clear understanding and clearly defined instructional methods and strategies. This is an indispensable book for the social scientists and a wide spectrum of population in India and abroad. The book will be useful to Panchayat functionaries, development workers, teachers and students of universities involved in fieldwork and people who are working for the development of the communities in rural and urban slums.

1

Folk Media in Development Communication

Rameshwari Pandya and *Varsha Parikh*

Folk means people in general or mass. Folk includes the culture which already exists or is present and which is not new. It means whatever the culture or tradition people have their attitude, beliefs, values, skills, thinking etc. Any medium when used to give knowledge, information and entertainment for a specific purpose it becomes media. So, folk media means using cultural folk things which already exists to provide knowledge and information to the people then it becomes folk media. Folk Media are also termed as "TRADITIONAL" and "INDIGENOUS" performing arts generally referred to the aspects of culture found in Agrarian Society. They are the community's own channels which are more effective for diffusing messages. It consists of a culture of face to face interaction which is direct communication an oral traditional transmission with immediate feedback having a strong sense of group solidarity, homogeneity and a set of conventional ways and understanding. These traditional performing arts are woven in the lives of India. Folk media the ancient form of art are very close to the hearts of the people. Their appeal is universal and they provide direct understanding at the personal level. Folk media are popular with the rural or peasant people of a country (Nettle & Myers, 1976), although Rhodes (1966) believed that folk media exists in all classes of society. Sometimes, the folk are considered a particular ethnic group or nationality (Nettle & Myers, 1976). To Park (1967), folk media is part of folk culture and the culture's lore, including its ballads and stories, is passed down by word of mouth from generation to generation. Different folk cultures, sometimes referred to as folk communities developed in isolated areas where they did not have any outside contact. The people within these communities worked to preserve their traditional cultural values.

The aims therefore of 'local' or 'traditional' media are:

- To bring about cohesion among groups;
- To mobilise local resources; and
- To solve problems of large and small groups.

The very diversity of folk traditions in India stands in the way of using it as a vehicle for mass communication. Even a mere description of the various folk traditions of India would require several thick volumes. Suffice it to say, rural India is a treasure trove of folk art, theatre, music and dance and kinds of combinations of these four. Every region has its own folk art form that is immensely popular and relevant in that area. There are several types and variations of a single form—the "Bhavai" of Kutch is distinguishable from the "Bhavai" of Saurashtra and so on. This high degree of variation even within a small geographical area stands in the way of using a particular folk art from being used for an entire region. The different popular folk media in the country are:

1. Tamasha and Pawada (Dance, Drama and Ballad) of Maharashtra.
2. Nautanki—of North India
3. Yaksha Gana—of Karnataka
4. Jatra—of Bengal and Orissa
5. Terrukuthu—(A Street Theatre) of Tamil Nadu
6. Bhavai—(Folk drama-play) of Gujarat
7. Keertana, Ballad forms, Folk music, Riddles as well.
8. Puppetry—classified in *four* types.
   (a) Rod puppets—from West Bengal
   (b) Shadow puppets—Andhra Pradesh, Karnataka, Kerala, Orissa.
   (c) Glove/Hand puppets—Orissa, Kerala and Tamil Nadu.
   (d) String puppets—from Rajasthan and Gujarat. (Kathputlies).

Being ancient forms of art, the folk media is very close to the hearts of the people; its appeal is universal and its understanding direct and at the personal level. Various research studies show that folk traditions are uniformly popular regardless of the educational, social and financial standing of any community.

Advantages of Folk Media over Electronic Media

Folk media being the media of the people, as it has been with them for centuries and now they have become a part of their life. Folk media always have their own languages so it represents their true culture so they understand it well as they easily associate with the gestures, music and rhythm. This characteristic of folk media develops familiarity whereas in the case of electronic media like Radio and Television, the sender and receiver are unable to develop personal touch. The folk media are less expensive and government can use this art form to convey the developmental messages for extending non-formal education as well as life-long education. Folk media has added advantage over electronic media as cost of developing the folk media into an effective communication tool is cost-effective. They do not require electricity transmitters, receivers as well as technical experts.

Moreover, folk media have the background, myths and legends which are part of their own region. The folk media have high appeal, this leads to maximum participation as people actively participate in the communication process. Effective communication is foundation stone for developing human relationship which is to exchange knowledge and thoughts. The communication is also referred as to exchange of knowledge, skills and attitudes between people and social groups as communication leads to movement of knowledge. The objective of developmental communication is to bring about desirable change in the behaviour of the people thus the folk media has a great significance over electronic media.

As a fundamental principle of human communication is that the transfer of ideas most frequently occurs between a source and receiver who are alike or similar this feature makes folk media most appropriate media. With folk media it is possible to get immediate and constant feedback and the communicator can use the reaction of the receiver as a check for the own effectiveness or the future action. The folk media has a high credibility as rural people perceive it as trustworthy so it can be very effectively used for conveying developmental messages and people can be persuaded to act as change agents for adoption of innovation.

Department of Home Science Extension and Communication, Baroda: Sharing Experiences

In the Department of Home Science Extension and Communication, Faculty of Home Science, Baroda, we have realized that majority of the world population is still lagging far behind in development, with the advent of technology and other faster forms of communication media, unfortunately the Indian folk media have been decaying. At this juncture one has to think as an educationist for the practicability of such media when there is often shortage of electricity, prevailing illiteracy rate, the explosion of population, the type of culture we majority of us belong to, as well as the acceptance of messages and transfer through these media.

The Department of Home Science Extension and Communication, Baroda is covering extension as a major component like teaching research and extension under its curriculum for undergraduate and postgraduate students. On the other hand, department has its communication thrust area which aims to prepare students in designing and utilizing various communication strategies for development purpose. It trains students to develop variety of strategies using folk media and electronic media, for variety of target groups inclusive rural and urban masses to impart several development messages. Department of Home Science Extension and Communication also undertakes different activities like organizing seminars, symposia, debates on folk media, organizing field trips for students to make them study different folk media. Through its dynamic and comprehensive learning experiences, students acquire skills and knowledge essential in use of folk media. This leads them to use folk media to reach the disadvantaged groups and impart different educational messages related to environment, girl child, reproductive health, communal harmony, human rights, and women's empowerment and so on.

Different Types of Folk Media

Various folk media viz., Bhavai, Street play, Puppet-play, Role-play and Drama have been extensively used by the students under the guidance of the teachers to achieve different aims, i.e. course to course and level to level. Each of the above-mentioned folk media in use are varying in their nature. It is described as follows:

Bhavai

It is a folk form of Gujarat. It is very live performing art with right amount of music, dance and drama to make the content understandable and interesting. It is a flexible traditional theatre of Gujarat. It has perfect combination of actions and words. The word "Bhav" means life and "vai" means records. Bhavai has a balance between music, dance and drama. Prose and poem are woven with each other to give socially useful messages. Here besides other characters Ranglo-Ranglee and Vidushak (Joker) plays the main role of change-agent who disseminates information effectively. The treatment of message is completely determined by them in terms of degree of effectiveness in emphasizing the message and impact of message on viewers/ listeners as they have a direct contact with viewers. They sing the riddles, dance and dramatize the dialects with, music—Bhungai, Manjira and Dholak. After every important idea the music is played and Ranglo-Ranglee dance in a circular way and the dialogue are continued. They reflect the colourful life of Gujarat with traditional costumes and dialects.

Street Play

Any drama performed in the open, if not actually on the street corner, can be called a street play. Street play in India emerged primarily as a means of resistance, a form of protest during the British rule. After independence it continued to fight against the economic and social oppression of people. The themes of street plays always keep a close touch with popular mass movements. Street play in general was evolved as one of the most popular media to take issues of social relevance to the people. Street play is an effective tool to educate the large sections of India, which are poor, illiterate and underprivileged. The street play is performed in the courtyard, streets or at the important key places, near a busy place. They have pre-written scripts, practiced well by the actors for the performance on the streets. Street plays emphasize body language, dialogue directed straight at the audience and on the involvement of the audience, it is effective due to the personal contact between the audience and the actors. They are characterized by vivid portrayal of real events, popular languages, and minimal properties. The street plays are direct linked with the lives of the people and they set the audience thinking.

Puppet Play

From the different types of puppets, mainly glove puppets have been used by the majority of the students. Simple and suitable stories which contains plenty of conversation, action and incidents are thought of to be presented in the puppet plays. Even the suspense for maintaining the interest of the audience is also kept in mind. The story or the subject of the puppet play which has an appeal for all the age groups and also a story for entertainment and sometimes a story that presents a problem and its solutions are selected. Our experience is because the puppets have large eyes, loud music, coloured clothing and by changing voice each puppet sounds differently. There is synthesis of so many skills in puppetry that everyone finds a place for his or her own particular interests. This unique quality of puppet play has helped us in spreading developmental messages and helped in life-long education.

Role Play

It is unrehearsed, spontaneous form of dramatization. It has been mainly used to provide a free situation in which a student spontaneously performs what he/she feels, thinks and imagines about a particular role under specific conditions. The learner or a role player tries out real-life or fantasy-life characters or situations that he knows or imagines. It has no script or set dialogues, they make up their parts as they go along. The audience then attempts to apply the implications of the performance to the situation or problems being considered. The role play is a way of creating, identifying and clarifying conflicting views and feelings. It creates a situation in which immediate problems can be tackled directly without putting individuals on the spot. Students express personal feelings and deal with sensitive personal problems under the guise of representing someone else of "taking a role". Discussion after role play helps in discovering the cause of human behaviour.

Drama

A well written drama with clear central theme is planned and accordingly, performed for various issues. Drama mainly aims to prepare more than teaching important ideas to the beneficiaries of all ages. It has been used to pose new questions for them to think about.

It is planned to use drama mainly to sensitize women and children regarding various problems, which starts the currents in the minds of the beneficiaries. Overall, it has been found that these popular folk media have attracted the attention of the people, i.e. educated and uneducated irrespective of age, sex, caste and religion. These media have been found effective media for masses during the extension work mainly due to its indigenous, practically convenient, interesting, local, cheaper than modern mass media as well as participative nature, where the messages are easily digested by the people from deprived rural and urban slum communities.

Curriculum Scope for Using Folk Media by the Department

Above-mentioned folk media have been used mainly in the extension, i.e. urban and rural field work the programmes to obtain lower and higher level of cognitive objectives as well as also affective objective to certain extent, i.e. traditional media used have not been restricted just to reach the masses, but also shown its effectiveness to change attitudes and practices of the people. Various theoretical courses viz., Non-formal education in Home Science, Software in folk media, Development journalism give learning experiences to the students to design the script/writing part of the folk media whereas courses like Methods of teaching in Home Science, Workshop in Adult education and in Non-formal education, Community health recreation, Field work and others provide opportunities to the students to apply their theoretical concepts at the field level. Hence, wide platform for students to use these media have been available pertaining to developmental issues, they have been used to transmit information, transfer knowledge, to educate, to persuade, to entertain, to influence values and to address taboos, to change behaviour and lifestyles of the underprivileged sections of the society especially women and children from urban slums and rural areas of Vadodara, Gujarat.

Thrust Areas Covered through Use of Folk Media

While using folk media various developmental areas viz., gender equality, environment, human rights, health, literacy, rights of vulnerable groups, entrepreneurship, women's empowerment, communal harmony, awareness regarding HIV/AIDS, population explosion and many more topics have been dealt with.

Performances using different folk media are conducted at various places of urban, rural and tribal areas. It has been staged in an open-air theatre, on Panchayat office, or in street, near temple, near water taps, at key leader's house, under the tree etc. It has been also experimented in formal classroom set-up in different rural schools.

Effectiveness of Folk Media

Bhavai, role-play and drama themes have been mainly centred around social issues and aimed at poking fun at the hypocrisy of the society. It has been used mainly at the field level to improve social, educational, cultural conditions of the society. These media use have been proved effective in changing the attitudes and behaviour of the people, about some social issues like ills of the society, such as the dowry, marriage of an old man to a young girl, ill treatment to women, girl's education, gender bias, income generating activities, awareness regarding HIV/AIDS, Communal harmony and so on. The themes of street plays always keep a close touch with popular mass movements. Street play in general was evolved as one of the most popular media to take issues of social relevance to the people. Yadav (1992), studied the effectiveness of street play in communicating how women are discriminated in Indian society. The sample was 113 students of a Gujarati school. Tiwari (1997), carried out a study on Nutrition Education on Anemia through Video and folk songs among adolescent girls of Thar deserts (Rajasthan). Sovani (1998), conducted a study on the effectiveness of communication strategies on environmental pollution and its effects on health for the low socio-economic groups of families in the selected communities of Baroda. Pai (2001) carried out an experimental study to find out the effectiveness of booklet and video film on street play. Bhatt (2001) studied the effectiveness of strategy consisting of videoed Bhavai, flash cards and discussion for teaching social studies to the primary school students of Baroda. Street play was also found less expensive and more effective compared to other forms of traditional media. Its effectiveness was found due to the personal contact between the audience and the actors. Moreover, it also provided a scope for improvisation according to the nature of the audience. Themes like environment cleanliness, importance of girls' education, problems of the aged, problems of working women, gender discrimination and so on were largely covered by the students through street play. It has been found that puppets have unlimited possibilities in a village for entertainment, education, self-expression and social action. The rural audience comes for entertainment but goes away with a new idea and message. The urban poor, illiterate and socio-economically deprived masses also benefited a lot through puppet plays. The persuasive themes for illiterate persons viz., cleanliness, food habits, moral education were found good with children's groups, whereas topics such as social taboos, sex discrimination, mother-in-law daughter-in-law relationship and income generation were found suitable for young and adult women. Besides these, topics like Community improvement, Nutrition, Small family, Social evils—Dowry, Heavy expenses at family and social occasions such as first pregnancy, Superstitions, Women development, Social justice for women, Practices harmful to public health, Consumer awareness, need for Economic independence of women, Parents' role in habit formation of children, Illiteracy, women's enemy, Health and Hygiene were also extensively experimented in the various programmes of rural and urban extension work conducted at undergraduate and postgraduate level.

Folk media, i.e. of the people, for the people, and by the people were found very effective communication strategy for the developmental issues especially dealing with different types of groups. As the language and dialects are of people's own, it increases intelligibility. The familiarity of language, gestures, music, rhythm makes these media them acceptable widely, by providing credibility and enhancing attentiveness amongst the rural folks. In most folk forms, audience participation has been integral part as per its original planning. Therefore, greater and better understanding of message, audience participation with quick responses and reactions were availed during many of the programmes.

In the tribal region viz., Kawant, Bodeli, Chota Udaipur, i.e. another corner of the Gujarat also these forms could prove its credibility and effectiveness. In these areas for the sensitive themes like HIV/AIDS, girls' education local folk forms along with above-mentioned folks were successfully used and achieved the goals.

Although basic form and structure of various folk art forms have remained the same or have changed very slightly, but over the period, the message conveyed have always changed with the times. Even urban extension experiences also revealed urbanites' tendency far from truth to view the folk media as an outmoded, unchanging, and an extremely rigid form of mass media. Overall, folk media can be the only answer to the need for development. As the in-built characteristics of folk media is that they are community based using their language representing natural art of the people and they are less expensive but very powerful in convincing people and thus can act as a tool for conveying developmental messages to the people of rural and urban masses. It is proved that cultural affinity of the media provide easy accessibility, creating an environment, building a congenial and absorbent climate.

Recommendations to Strengthen Folk Media Component

1. We need to provide encouragement to the master craftsman who are used to conventional media and methods, so that they can be used as the change agents.
2. Non-Governmental Organizations are also to be adequately supported, to share responsibility towards preservation, dissemination and documentation of cultural heritage and folk media.
3. A network of institution is necessary to set high standards for training, support and strengthening of folk media.
4. Involvement of Panchayati Raj Institutions and NGOs in the development and utilization of folk media.
5. Setting up of folk art groups comprising students, functionaries and local youths with the help of talented folk artists.
6. Different institutes should be equipped with adequate human resources such as qualified and competent teachers who have both theoretical insight and practical knowledge of folk media then only they will be able to give correct training to the students who in turn will act as change agents.
7. Suitable steps may be taken to utilize the services of other forms of media to reach the target groups. Folk songs/stories have to be printed in the form of booklets and widely circulated.
8. Preparation of video-cassettes on the basis of scripts prepared through workshops. Documentation of these scripts to be done for wider publicity and use by different agencies, individual for motivation and training.
9. Using folk media to eradicate illiteracy and banish poverty.

10. Securing help of NGOs and encouraging them to work in this field.
11. Enlisting and enrolling volunteers to act as 'Master Trainers'.
12. Alternative media forms such as folk theatres, puppetry etc. need to be widely encouraged, especially where existing electronic and print media have no or limited outreach.
13. Reaction of the target group after exposure to the folk media must be much more extensively researched and analyzed.
14. There should be 'Resource Centres' at the Central and State levels for identification, collection, dissemination and documentation of materials related to Folk media.

References

Agarwal, J.C. (2000). *Principles, Methods and Technique of Teaching*, Vikas Publishing House, New Delhi.

Bhatt, K. and Joshi, U. (2001). Use of Folk Media for Formal Education, Dissertation (M. Sc.), The M.S.U. Baroda, Vadodara, Gujarat.

Das, A. (1997). *Effectiveness of Folk Media in Mass Communication*, Communicator, UMC, New Delhi.

Dhama, O.P. and Bhatnagar, O.P. (1994). *Education and Communication for Development*, Oxford and IBH Publishing, New Delhi.

Gupta, V.S. (2000). *Communication and Development*, Concept Publishing, Company (P) Ltd., New Delhi.

Joshi, U. (2002). *Media Research*, Authors Press, Delhi.

Kumar, A. (1999). *The Print and Other Folk Media*, Anmol Publications Pvt. Ltd., New Delhi.

Kumar, K. (1999). *Mass Communication in India*, Jaico Publishing House, Delhi.

Mathur, K.B. (1990). *Communication for Development and Social Change*. Allied Publishers, Lucknow.

Pai, R. (2001). Comparative Study on Effectiveness of Two Communication Media in Teaching Selected aspects of Street Play to the Students of Faculty of Home Science, Dissertation (M.Sc.) The M.S.U. Baroda, Vadodara, Gujarat.

Pandey, G. (1999). "Traditional Media and Development", *Communicator*, IIMC, New Delhi.

Rafi, K. (1984). "Communication for Alternative Development", *Development Dialogue*, Vol. 1-2. 14.

Shah, A. and Joshi, U. (1992). *Puppetry and Folk Dramas*, Sterling Publishers Private Ltd., New Delhi.

Sovani, K. (1998). Effectiveness of Communication Strategies on Environmental Pollution and its Effects on Health for the Low Socio-Economic Groups of Families in the Selected Communities of Baroda city. Dissertation (M.Sc.), The M.S.U. Baroda, Vadodara, Gujarat.

Tiwari, P. (1997). Nutrition Education on Anaemia through Video and Folk Songs among Adolescent Girls of Thar deserts (Rajasthan), Dissertation (M.Sc.), The M.S.U. Baroda, Vadodara, Gujarat.

2

Women Health: Need of the Hour

Farzana Alim

India ranks 115 in the Human Development Index of 2001 (UNDP, 2001). According to the 2001 Census, overall literacy has increased to 65.38 per cent (Census of India, 2001). The overall life expectancy is 62.9 yrs., for males 63.6 yrs. and females 64.9 yrs. (United Nations Population Division, 2000). The fact that the typical female advantage in life expectancy is not seen in India suggests there are several problems with women's health. Indian women have high mortality rates, particularly during childhood and in their reproductive years.

The health of Indian Women is intrinsically linked to their status in society. Research on women's status has found that the contributions Indian women make to families are often overlooked, and instead they are viewed as economic burdens. A report commissioned by the United Nations Resident Co-coordinator in India (Menon-Sen and Shivakumar, 2001) titled 'Women in India: How free? How equal?' raises several disturbing issues concerning the current status of women in India. Data from the Census of India 2001 and the Human Development Report 2001 also corroborate them. Although the absolute number of females has grown 21.79 per cent in the last decade, the male-female ratio is still lower than it was 100 years ago.

Further, Indian women have low levels of both education and formal labour force participation. They typically have little autonomy, living under the control of first their fathers, then their husbands, and finally their sons (Horowitz and Kishwar, 1985;

Chatterjee, 1990; Desai, 1994; The World Bank, 1996). All of these factors exert a negative impact on the health status of Indian women. As a nation what we need to understand is that the health of families and communities are tied to the health of women—the illness or death of a woman has serious and far-reaching consequences for the health of her children, family and community. While targeted policies and programmes have enabled women to lead healthier lives, significant gender-based health disparities remain. With limited access to education or employment, high illiteracy rates and increasing poverty levels are making health improvements for women exceedingly difficult like reproductive health, violence, nutritional status, unequal treatment of boys and girls, HIV/AIDS etc.

Health related challenges continue. Many of the modest gains in women's health realized in recent decades are now threatened or have been reversed due to war, economic instability and the HIV/AIDS epidemic. Basic health care, family planning and obstetric services are essential for women—yet they remain unavailable to millions. Gender-equitable approaches to health are needed to enable women's full participation in the planning and delivery of health services.

India, in the words of Amartya Sen, has to account for some 25 million 'missing women'. The average Indian woman bears her first child before she is 22 years and has little control over her own fertility and reproductive health. In 1998-99, only 48 per cent of married women in the reproductive age group used any form of contraception (World Population Monitoring, 2000). This figure is much lower (30%) in poorer states like Uttar Pradesh and Bihar. The HIV/AIDS epidemic in India is spreading rapidly and increasingly will affect women's health in coming years. The highest rates of infection are found in population groups with certain high risk behaviours (i.e. sex workers, intravenous drug users, and sexually transmitted disease patients). However, infection also is increasing in the general population. For example, HIV seroprevalence among pregnant women in the state of Tamil Nadu quadrupled between 1989 and 1991 from 0.2 to 0.8 per cent (U.S. Bureau of the Census, 1995). The epidemic is fuelled by both married and unmarried men visiting sex workers who have high rates of infection. Migrant workers and truck drivers are important components for the spread of HIV. Despite the alarming growth of the epidemic, most women in India have little knowledge of AIDS. Even among those who had heard of the disease, there are many misconceptions about modes of transmission. Indian women could benefit from a strengthened national HIV/AIDS education programme and intervention programmes targeting groups most susceptible to HIV infection. The silver lining amongst the grey clouds is that though slowly but surely, realization has begun to dawn over the community regarding this. People now understand that nearly all maternal deaths are preventable through timely prenatal and postnatal care, skilled birth attendance during delivery and the availability of emergency care to deal with complications. The health benefits of spacing and limiting births for mothers and children with family planning services are well stressed upon. Millennium Development Goal 5 focuses on reducing the Maternal Mortality Ratio (MMR) by 75 per cent between 1990 and 2015 and ensuring universal access to reproductive health by 2015. Government efforts in the form of NRHM (National Rural Health Mission) RCH, EAG etc. are commendable the **goals to be achieved by NRHM.**

National Level

- Infant mortality rate to be reduced to 30/1,000 live births.
- Maternal mortality ratio to be reduced to 100/1,00,000.
- Total fertility rate to be reduced to 2.1.
- Upgrading community health centres to Indian Public Health Standards.
- Engaging 2,50,000 female Accredited Social Health Activists (ASHAs) in 10 states.

Community Level

- Availability of trained community level worker at village level, with a drug kit for general ailments.
- Health Day at Anganwadi level on a fixed day/month for provision of immunization, ante/postnatal check-ups and services related to mother and child health care, including nutrition.
- Improved access to universal immunization through induction of auto disabled syringes, alternate vaccine delivery and improved mobilization services under the programme.
- Improved facilities for institutional delivery through

provision of referral, transport, escort and improved hospital care subsidized under the Janani Suraksha Yojana (JSY) for the Below Poverty Line (BPL) families.

Concept of ASHA (Accredited Social Health Activist) is in forefront. ASHA will take steps to create awareness and provide information to the community on determinants of health such as nutrition, basic sanitation and hygienic practices, healthy living and working conditions, information on existing health services, and the need for timely utilization of health and family welfare services. She will counsel women on birth preparedness, importance of safe delivery, breast-feeding and complementary feeding, immunization, contraception and prevention of common infections including reproductive tract infection/sexually transmitted infection and care of the young child. She will arrange escort/accompany pregnant women and children requiring treatment/admission to the nearest pre-identified health facility, i.e. Primary health centre/Community health centre/First Referral Unit.

Role and Integration with Anganwadi

Organizing Health Day once/twice a month. On health day, the women, adolescent girls and children from the village will be mobilized for orientation on health related issues such as importance of nutritious food, personal hygiene, and care during pregnancy, importance of antenatal check-up and institutional delivery, home remedies for minor ailment and importance of immunization etc.

AWWs will inform ANM to participate and guide organizing the health days at Anganwadi centre. ASHA will support the AWW in mobilizing pregnant and lactating women and infants for nutrition supplement. She would also take initiative for bringing the beneficiaries from the village on specific days of immunization, health check-ups/health days etc. to Anganwadi centres.

Auxiliary Nurse Midwife (ANM) will Guide ASHA in Performing the Following Activities

She will hold weekly fortnightly meeting with ASHA and discuss the activities undertaken during the week/fortnight. She will guide her in case ASHA had encountered any problem during the performance of her activity. ANMs will inform ASHA regarding date and time of the outreach session and will also guide her for bringing the beneficiary (pregnant and lactating mothers) to the outreach session.

She will use ASHA in motivating the pregnant women for coming to the sub-centre for initial check-ups. She will also help ANMs in bringing married couples to sub-centres for adopting family planning. ANMs will educate ASHA on danger signs of pregnancy and labour so that she can timely identify and help beneficiary in getting further treatment.

The well-known **RCH (Reproductive and Child Health)** approach is in keeping with the evolution of an integrated approach to the programme aimed at improving the health status of young women and young children which has been going on in the country namely family welfare programme, universal immunization programme, oral rehydration therapy, child survival and safe motherhood programme and acute respiratory infection control etc.

Highlights of the RCH Programme

The programme integrates all interventions of fertility regulation, maternal and child health with reproductive health for both men and women.

Facilities of obstetric care, MTP and IUD insertion in the PHCs level are improved. IUD insertion facilities are also available at sub-centres.

The programme aims at improving the outreach of services primarily for the vulnerable group of population who have been, till now, effectively left out of planning-process, e.g. special programme is taken up for urban slums, tribal population and adolescents; NGOs and voluntary organizations are involved in a much larger way to improve outreach.

Panchayati Raj functionaries have a central role in determining the need of the local population for RCH services generally and for contraceptives particularly under the target free approach. While the care components are the same for all districts, the weaker districts get more support and sophisticated facilities are proposed for relatively

Table 2.1:

Family planning	Child Survival and Safe Motherhood component
Client approach to health care	Prevention/Management of RTI/STD/AIDS

advanced districts. On the basis of crude birth rate and female literacy rate, all the districts have been divided into three categories.

Interventions in all Districts

- Child Survival interventions, i.e. immunization, Vitamin A (to prevent blindness), oral rehydration therapy and prevention of deaths due to pneumonia.
- Specially designed RCH package for urban slums and tribal areas.
- RTI/STD clinics at District Hospitals (where not available).
- Facility for safe abortions at PHCs by providing equipment, contractual doctors etc.
- Adolescent health and reproductive hygiene.

Interventions in Selected States/Districts

- Screening and treatment of RTI/STD at sub-divisional level.
- Emergency obstetric care at selected FRUs by providing drugs.
- Essential obstetric care by providing drugs and PHN/Staff Nurse at PHCs.
- Facility of referral transport for pregnant women during emergency to the nearest referral centre through Panchayat in weak districts.

Essential Obstetric Care

Essential obstetric care intends to provide the basic maternity services to all pregnant women through: (1) Early registration of pregnancy (within 12-16 weeks), (2) Provision of minimum three antenatal check-ups by ANM or medical officer to monitor progress of the pregnancy, (3) Provision of safe delivery at home or in an institution, (4) Provision of three postnatal check-up to monitor the postnatal recovery.

Emergency Obstetric Care

Complications associated with pregnancy are not always predictable; hence, emergency obstetric care is an important intervention to prevent maternal morbidity and mortality.

24 Hour Delivery Services at PHCs/CHCs

To promote institutional deliveries, provision has been made to give additional honorarium to the staff to encourage round the clock delivery facilities at health centres.

Medical Termination of Pregnancy

MTP is a reproductive health measure that enables a woman to opt out of an unwanted or unintended pregnancy in certain specified circumstances without endangering her life, through MTP Act, 1971. The aim is to reduce maternal mortality from unsafe abortions.

Control of Reproductive Tract Infections (RTI) and Sexually Transmitted Diseases (STD)

Under the RCH programme, the component of RTI/STD control is linked to HIV and AIDS control. It has been planned and implemented in close collaboration with National AIDS Control Organization (NACO). NACO will provide assistance for setting up RTI/STD clinics at the district level.

Immunization

The Universal Immunization Programme (UIP) became a part of CSSM programme in 1992 and RCH programme in 1997. It will continue to provide vaccines for polio, tetanus, DPT, DT, measles and tuberculosis.

EAG (Empowered Action Group)

An Empowered Action Group has been constituted in the Ministry of Health and Family Welfare, with Union Minister for Health and Family Welfare as Chairman on 20th March, 2001. As 55 per cent of the increase in the population of India is anticipated in the states of Uttar Pradesh, Bihar, Madhya Pradesh, Rajasthan, Orissa, Chhattisgarh, Jharkhand and Uttaranchal, these states are perceived to be most deficient in critical socio-demographic indices. Through EAG, these states will get focused attention for different health and family welfare programmes. Thus, we can see that efforts for promotion of women's health are in right direction. If mass support is generated, obvious improvements can be seen. Also the slogan "Healthy Women, Healthy World" embodies the fact that as custodians of family's health, women play a critical role in maintaining the health and well-being of their communities. "A woman's health is her total well-being, not determined solely by biological factors and reproduction, but also by effects of workload, nutrition, stress, war and migration, among others" (Van der Kwaak, 1991). Women's health issues have attained higher international visibility and renewed political commitment in recent decades, hence due importance is well deserved.

References

AIDS Analysis, (1996). The Status and Trends of the Global HIV/AIDS Pandemic, Final Report, Satellite Symposium, *XI International Conference on AIDS*, Vancouver.

Chatterjee, M. (1990). "Indian Women: Their Health and Economic Productivity", *World Bank Discussion Papers*. 109, Washington, DC.

Desai, S. (1994). *Gender Inequalities and Demographic Behaviour*, India.

Park, K. (2007). *Preventive and Social Medicine*, Banarsi Das Publishers, 19th edition, Jabalpur.

Victoria, A.V. and Arjun A. (1998). "Women's of the World—Women's Health in India," *International Programmes Centre.*

3
Multimedia Prism in Primary Education: SVADES Experiment

Jagdish Solanki and *Sunita Nambiyar*

Human civilization has witnessed three major revolutions. These revolutions have been agriculture revolution, industrial revolution and information revolution. The present millennium of the information revolution has been witnessing widespread influence of information technology inclusive of media at global and local level impacting each walk and talk of life from cradle to grave. We are influenced by multimedia, multidimensionally in multiple sectors of society. Some of them are politics, religion, commerce, health, and education etc. Education is backbone and pivotal for the self and for the society. We in India, have been putting immense efforts to modify the content, quality, access and coverage of education through institutional and constitutional strategies, in which information technology and media have played very vital and crucial role. In the educational process, multimedia has occupied an indispensable tool to reach out to the people. The application of Multimedia in education has become an integral part of institutionalization of education starting from pre-primary to higher education in 21st century. The challenges of our increasing population call for an increased use of technology to reach out the millions. Further, there are many studies which authenticate the effective use of technology to improve learning and facilitate teaching-learning processes.

Media and Multimedia

Communication can take several forms from individual, group to mass. Mass communication media include radio, television newspaper, magazine and the internet which have an immense influence. Multimedia is the combined use of media such as movies, music, lighting, CD-ROM and the internet for education or entertainment. Media is used in multiple forms of information, content and information processing (e.g. text, audio, graphics, animation, and video, interactivity), to inform or entertain the (user) audience. Multimedia also refers to the use of (but not limited to) electronic media to store and experience multimedia contact.

Multimedia is more than one concurrent presentation medium (for example, on CD-ROM or a Website). Multimedia is typically used to mean the combination of text, sound, and/or motion video, graphics, audio, animations etc. based on the multi-sensory nature of humans and the evolving ability of computers to convey diverse types of information. Some people might say that the addition of animated images produces multimedia, but it has typically meant one of the following: Text, sound, and animated graphic images and video images, Video and sound, Multiple display areas, images, or presentations presented concurrently, in live situations, the use of a speaker or actors and "props" together with sound, images, and motion video etc.

The American Heritage Dictionary defines multimedia as "the combined use of several media, such as movies, slides, music, and lighting, especially for the purpose of education or entertainment." Some link multimedia as new application oriented computer technology, and is commonly defined as the combination of text, graphics, audio, video and animation on a computer and is referred as method of designing an integrating computer technology on a single platform that enables the end-user to input, create, manipulate and output text, graphics, audio and video, using a single user interface (Strothman, 1991). Multimedia is characterized by the presence of text, pictures, sound, animation and video; some or all of which are organized into some coherent programme. Multimedia is the exciting combination of computer hardware and software that allows us to integrate video, animation, audio, graphics, and test resources to develop effective presentations on an affordable desktop computer. Multimedia is the notion of using multiple channels of communication to present information. In computer-oriented terms, Multimedia can be defined as the combining of text, graphics, animation, pictures, videos and sound to present information (Bagui, 1998). Multimedia involves the simultaneous use of multiple media formats (Hede &

Hede, 2002). When one enables users to control the pace and direction of information, the programme becomes interactive multimedia. Multimedia activities encourage students to work in groups, express their knowledge in multiple ways, solve problems, revise their own work, and construct knowledge. The advantages of integrating multimedia in educational processes are many. Through participation in multimedia activities, students can learn:

- Real-world skills related to technology.
- The value of teamwork.
- Effective collaboration techniques.
- The impact and importance of different media.
- The challenges of communicating to different audiences.
- How to present information in compelling ways.
- Techniques for synthesizing and analyzing complex content.
- The importance of research, planning, and organization skills.
- The significance of presentation and speaking skills.
- How to accept and provide constructive feedback.
- How to express their ideas creatively.

However, some constraints in using multimedia are:

- Technological resources, both hardware and software.
- Technological skills, for both the students and teacher.
- Time required to plan, design, develop, and evaluate multimedia activity.

Multimedia learning integrates five types of media to provide flexibility in expressing the creativity of a student and in exchanging ideas through *Text, Sound, Video, Animation and Graphics.* In short, multimedia is media and content that uses a combination of different content forms. The term can be used as a noun (a medium with multiple content forms) or as an adjective describing a medium as having multiple content forms. The term is used in contrast to media which only use traditional forms of printed or hand-produced material. Multimedia includes a combination of text, audio, still images, animation, video, and interactivity content forms. Multimedia is usually recorded and played, displayed or accessed by information content processing devices, such as computerized and electronic devices, but can also be part of a live performance.

Major Characteristics of Multimedia

The use of multimedia technology has offered an alternative way of delivering instruction. Interactive multimedia learning is a process, rather than a technology, that places new learning potential into the hands of users. The National Council for Educational Technology (NCET) has identified potential outcomes, and states that the effective use of multimedia can:

- Provide the flexibility to meet the individual needs and abilities of each subject.
- Reduce the risk of failure of school.
- Provide student with immediate access to richer source materials.
- Present information in new relevant ways which helps students to understand, assimilate and use it more readily.
- Motivate and stimulate learning for students with special needs.
- Motivate student to try out new ideas and take risk.
- Encourage divergent thinking.
- Encourage teachers to take a fresh look at how they teach and ways in which students learn.

Multimedia is fast emerging as a basic skill that will be important to live in the twenty-first century. In the information age, Multimedia will be spread to millions of teachers/learners who have not yet used the computer. Multimedia educational computing is one of the fastest growing markets in the world today.

Advantages of Multimedia

1. Faster Learning Time

Multimedia components are an efficient way to deliver educational and training content. Course content equivalent to a two-day traditional lecture can be delivered in as little as two hours using multimedia.

2. Instructional Consistency

Multimedia programmes educate with the same content, presented in the same manner, from person to person. Each person will receive the same consistent, technically correct message. Educational and training content is delivered in a reliable, intuitive manner that does not change in quality from one learning environment to the next.

3. Flexible Delivery

Multimedia courseware makes it possible to present quality education and training across a variety of user levels. For example, in a complex training environment certain areas of the multimedia project may be locked/unlocked depending on the users' 'status'. Alternatively in an educational environment, tutors may undertake a 'tutor-only' learning component from the very same multimedia resource they will be instructing. Multimedia resources are available 24 hours a day, seven days a week, and can be accessed at a time that benefits both the learner and the instructor. Flexible delivery allows users, with a variety of expertise, to access resources at different points (levels) depending on their familiarity with the resource or personal experience.

4. Implicit Learning and Motivation

Multimedia education allows the learner to be actively involved in the learning process. This interactivity reinforces the educational component and helps the learner to retain the educational message. Rather than doing a course just once, new media resources allow the user to continually return to the resource and thus reinforce messages. Most new media projects can also be used as an ongoing reference tool, for example, all the content components may be accessed via a library. New media education provides a level of responsive feedback and individual involvement that has proven to be highly motivating.

5. Individual Learning Styles

Multimedia education allows learners, who typically have different abilities and knowledge levels, to control the pace and direction of the resource. As tasks are accomplished, users will seek out more knowledge, and go beyond the initial 'recipient of instruction' capacity. Traditional learning methods focus on one learning style at a time. By using graphics, audio, and interactive activities, new media education can fit a range of learning styles.

6. Testing of Learning Proficiency

Multimedia education programmes can incorporate pre- and post-tests as well as a variety of quizzes to demonstrate to the learner their level of proficiency with the content. Quizzes help users (and instructors) to know which areas they need to review. Tests can measure competency of the subject matter. Computer-based testing allows for instant results to the learner, and data can be statistically analyzed as needed.

7. Low Cost

Multimedia courseware has a low cost per learner with lower delivery costs because the initial costs are in the project design and production. The costs of replication, distribution, and course delivery, which are recurring costs in traditional education and training, are reduced or eliminated with multimedia courseware. The ongoing costs are substantially reduced, and the cost per learner goes down with each additional learner.

8. Safety and Health

Multimedia education allows learners to study potentially dangerous topics without risk. Interactive content allow learners to view the results of their actions and become skilled at proper methods and procedures while learning how to work safely.

9. Records

A benefit of multimedia courseware is its ability to test and track the progress of the learner. Data such as the user's progress, time spent in the programme, and test results can be tracked and monitored. Records can be used to support other documentation requirements and can also feed into on-line/off-line databases.

Practical Disadvantages of Multimedia

Multimedia requires high-end computer systems. Sound, images, animation, and especially video, constitute large amounts of data, which slow down, or may not even fit in a low-end computer. Unlike simple text files created in word processing, multimedia packages require good quality computers. A major disadvantage of multimedia is that it may not be accessible to a large section of its intended users if they do not have access to multimedia-capable machines. For this reason, courseware developers should think very carefully about the type of multimedia elements that need to be incorporated into applications and include only those that have significant value. Multimedia has other weaknesses too. While proponents of this new technology are very enthusiastic about its potential, they often leave the financial and technical issues unattended. Development in multimedia is very high and the process of developing effective multimedia takes time. Time spent on developing the multimedia package requires money so that the true cost of an interactive programme mounts with each delay. Further, if the prerequisites for using multimedia include to computers with related software, the user must possess a minimum level of computer literacy in order to exploit the capabilities of this medium for learning. And finally, of the educator who is unfamiliar with the production and design of multimedia or packages can be equally complicating. The critical question, then, is: How do we overcome some of the identified barriers and begin the process of multimedia implementation alongside the instructor, textbook, and blackboard? It is the barriers rather than the technologies which we must address before multimedia, or for that matter, any media technology becomes as accepted as the printed text or guidebook

It is here that the power of multimedia can be unleashed to provide long-term benefit to all. Multimedia enables learning through exploration, discovery, and experience. Multimedia enables learning to become fun and friendly, without fear of inadequacies or failure. The full potential of using multimedia technologies for learning in schools can only be realized after there has been some re-engineering of the way learning experiences are offered in the traditional schools. A critical element is for teachers to be familiar with multimedia technologies in order for them to know how to use them within their curriculum areas.

Harper & Hedberg, 1997; Sims, 1998; Shinde, 2003 have shown that an interactive learning environment can generate effective instruction and learning. There is empirical evidence that multimedia can enhance the learning of, at least, certain kinds of information. A review by various research of studies that have investigated the effectiveness of multimedia in learning information suggested that the people who used computer-based multimedia instruction performed better in terms of test scores, compared to those who received instruction through traditional classroom lectures.

SVADES (Society for Village Development in Petro Chemical Areas)

SVADES is a collective endeavour that binds the industry and rural community together towards effective socio-economic development in the rural areas surrounding industry. It is indeed a unique example of unified action in the corporate sector to contribute to the progress of rural community, their development and social upliftment.

SVADES is registered under the Societies Act, 1860, as a voluntary organization set-up by the giant public and private sector industries in the Nandesari Area of Vadodara Taluka, in the state of Gujarat, India.

Participating industries were:

— IPCL
— GE Plastics India Limited
— GAC
— Bayer ABS Limited
— IOCL
— GIPCL
— GSFC
— Deepak Nitrite Limited
— Ashok ABS Limited

SVADES works in 16 panchayats comprising of 40 villages, which covers a total population of around 1,80,000. It is backed by the financial assistance of its member industries, community contributions, national and state level funding agencies, and also district, State and Central Government grants.

Vision

To improve the quality of life of the villagers, through the active participation of the community and the industry.

Mission

- To reduce women's drudgery by ensuring water supply and constructing approach roads.

- To improve environmental and sanitary conditions by carrying out activities like forestation, wasteland development, construction of village drains and sanitary latrines.
- To give support to schools for overall development of the students.
- To provide training for rural youth and women in self-employing vocations.
- To develop a pragmatic model for village planning, taking into account the process of industrialization and development.
- To conduct research in areas of community relation, social changes, wasteland development, industrial pollution and water conservation.

Approach

- Need based, practical and collaborative.
- Involving the community at all stages of development, during the planning as well as execution, along with, NGOs, Government and participant industry.
- Ascertain and understand the needs of the villagers through meetings and personal interaction and conducting village surveys.
- Motivating the community to provide both monetary and human resources to execute the plans.
- Active involvement of the community during the implementation stage, integrating the programmes with the Governmental initiatives.

SVADES activities are guided and monitored by a Board of Governors, comprising of Chief Executive Officers and Managing Directors of member industries. A managing committee also meets every two months to evaluate and monitor the activities. The members of the committee are specialists in human resources, management and operations, including technical fields. Valuable inputs and support are also drawn from various academic institutions of Gujarat including Faculty of Social Work The Maharaja Sayajirao University of Baroda. The lead was taken by Indian Petrochemical Limited (Reliance) and Deepak Nitrite, which were instrumental in bringing together eight industrial houses and sensitizing them to the intense drudgery faced by women in the villages situated near the factories. The first slide show presented to the managing directors consisted of a series of pictures of a typical day in the life of a village woman. Unavailability of potable water near the house, lack of approach roads and drainage, poor sanitation and inaccessibility of fuel and fodder were some of the major problems highlighted.

The impact of the slide show was so great that it led to the birth of SVADES or the Society for Village Development in the Petrochemical Area. While most of the industries were individually carrying out rural development, SVADES provided a platform for an integrated approach. The industries promoting the activities of SVADES are IPCL (Reliance) Gujarat Refinery, Gujarat State Fertilizer and Chemicals Ltd., Gujarat Industries Power Company Ltd., GE Plastics, Deepak Nitrite Ltd., Ashok Organics Ltd., and Bayer ABS Ltd. Currently, the organization works in 40 villages with a total population of 1,40,000.

SVADES has now diversified into eco-restoration, wasteland development, a school support programme, and youth and community development programmes. SVADES is also tackling unemployment among youth and women in villages like Radhiyapura as a result of the closure of industries. SVADES has initiated vocational training for youth and women. Workers from SVADES are of view that none of these achievements would have been possible without the support of the community, University, and industries which forms a base for sustainable development.

SVADES and its Projects

1. Village Infrastructure Development

Major funds of SVADES are directed towards development of infrastructure in the villages, like water supply schemes, construction of roads, and low cost housing facilities. SVADES has laid 7.5 kms. of critical link roads interconnecting 10 villages. The roads are a boon to the villages, especially during monsoons. Most of the villages have none or inadequate sources of water. SVADES has initiated as well as commissioned village level water supply schemes. Apart from constructing underground water tanks and bore-wells, SVADES has laid some 8.7 kms. of pipelines in 8 villages, benefiting over 2200 families. Check dams and Recharging Dry Wells are the other schemes on the anvil. 108 houses have been constructed in 10 panchayat villages under the Sardar Awas Yojana, for families below the poverty line.

2. Eco-restoration and Sanitation

SVADES has adopted schools for the purposes of plantation of trees and over 12,000 saplings have been planted after fencing 10 schools. School children are imparted ecological environment training and they take up the responsibility of maintaining the plants. The success rate has been 70 to 80 per cent. Plans are on to carry out watershed management programmes in the kotar lands around the villages. Sanitation is another area where SVADES has many success stories. Sanitary latrines have been made for schools as well as households. 1250 household sanitary latrines and 38 school sanitary latrines have been constructed by SVADES, some of which have been funded by the government agencies. Training is imparted to the beneficiaries, for awareness as well as maintenance of different facilities.

3. Mahila Awareness

After providing indirect benefits to womenfolk in the village in the form of sanitary latrines, water and road, women's groups are formed. Talks supported by exhibitions on social and health related issues are held regularly. Competitions on low cost nutritional diet, housekeeping and healthy baby are conducted from time to time. A forum is also provided where Mahila Mandals of all villages get to interact with one another. "World Women's Day" is also celebrated.

4. Youth Support Activities

Capacity building through vocational activities is encouraged by SVADES. Youth development, self-confidence and master the skills through training and vocational programmes are undertaken. 126 youth so far have been trained and many of them earn a reasonable livelihood in various fields like wireman and motor rewinding, radio and TV repair, two-wheelers repairs and beauty parlours. Many youths have undergone through tailoring and laboratory assistance programme and some have steady job. SVADES also organizes functions like "Shramdan" and "First-Aid Programmes" where youth from different villages actively participate. Sports events like Marathon race, cycle rally, volleyball, and cricket matches are organized on regular basis to enhance team spirit and unity.

5. Health Awareness Programme

Under the head of partnership in "Sexual Health Project" granted by Gujarat State Aids Control Society, SVADES has participated in HIV AIDS AWARENESS CAMPAIGN. It has completed the need assessment programme along with the first partnership in Sexual Health Project in 2001-02, where the targets were both males and females of the surrounding nine villages. SVADES has now taken up a second project, which mainly concentrate on the industrial workers from the Three Industries, for health awareness under the head red ribbon club project.

School Support Programmes

SVADES has been carrying out the school support programme since last 10 years in 16 Gram panchayats and in 45 District primary education schools of 40 villages with the student's population of approximately 17,000 and 416 teachers. Activities like material support, school library, hobby centres, low cost playgrounds and awareness creation through street plays and puppet shows are undertaken for the students. "BAL-UTSAV" is held annually to provide the children an opportunity to interact with other schools, and also display their talents in sports, paintings, drama etc. Training and awareness programmes are arranged for the teachers with the cooperation from government educational authorities. The Annual Day is also held every year since 2001. "Teachers Magazine" in Guajarati language with inputs from the teachers is published half-yearly. Three low cost playgrounds have been constructed from used tractors, trucks and car tyres in three village schools.

Multimedia Project in Primary Schools

In August 2005, SVADES had started multimedia pilot project in Dasaratha, Koyali girl's primary school, with positive results and response, the project extended its coverage in few more schools viz. Kotana primary school, Nandesari primary school, and Sinhakuy primary school. The ultimate aim is to equip all the 45 schools under the purview of SVADES with the multimedia education. As a part of E-Governance in rural area initiated by the Govt. of India, SVADES has taken up a new initiative for the primary schools by launching multimedia computer training. SVADES has conducted training sessions for teachers to enhance their operating skills for the multimedia software and has conducted an impact study for testing the relevance of the project so that the findings may be utilized in extending this project in all the 45 schools. Further, a record book system in five schools has been introduced to facilitate the effective functioning of the multimedia project.

SVADES offers great opportunities to students of Faculty of Social Work, Faculty of Family and Community Sciences, Faculty of Law, Faculty of Journalism and Communication, and many more academic institutions of The Maharaja Sayaji Rao University of Baroda, Vadodara and other academic institutions of Gujarat and India. In these projects, students of Master of Human Resources Management, Master of Social Work and Diploma students of Social Development and Organizational Management Courses of Faculty of Social Work and National Service Scheme (NSS). The Maharaja Sayaji Rao University of Baroda are placed for their fieldwork training and students conduct fieldwork and undertakes small research projects and the Faculty members of different faculties also have academic linkages in the form of projects and research consultation.

One such research project was undertaken on "The study of use of multimedia in primary schools in 2010 with the objectives to study the applications of multimedia in primary schools and to find out views of students, teachers, and parents". Further the research project also aimed at finding out how the multimedia influences the educational life of students and also to find out teachers' and parents' opinion/view about importance of multimedia education programme.

This project was conducted in 6 primary schools of Dasharath, Asharath, Koyli, Nandesari, Sinhakuy, Kotana, and Undera villages of Vadodara Taluka, Vadodara. Thirty students of 5th, 6th and 7th standard, 30 teachers and 30 parents from these primary schools were selected by using purposive random method for collecting information and observations.

Students' Views

Some of the views of the students regarding the multimedia project are of tremendous importance in understanding the significance of prism of multimedia.

The subjects included for multimedia presentations were Social Studies, Science, Mathematics and Gujarati. 27 (90%) of the students did not find it difficult to operate through the multimedia. As 23 (76.67%) students reported that they had clarity regarding subject covered by multimedia and 20 (66.33%) students did not get bored while learning through multimedia whereas 25 (83.33%) students viewed multimedia in improving their results. Further 28 (93.33%) students also found that they had clear understanding of the subjects covered through multimedia and could get uniform and equal focus of the teachers. 30 (100%) of the students did not feel that it was waste of time. 29 per cent (96.37%) believed that they did not had to spend long hours to study various subjects due to multimedia.

Teachers' Views

The teachers are centrally significant in operating multimedia project and their views are of increasing significance for the effective implementations of the project. Some of the major views of teachers regarding the project are as under. 22 (73.33%) teachers could find the utility of using multimedia for various subjects and 25 (83.34%) teachers who had used the multimedia while teaching and regarded multimedia as useful and effective tool in educations. 23 (76.66%) of teachers were of the view that multimedia and software use in multimedia education takes care of individual differences. 27 (90.90%) of teachers expressed that the content of the subjects has been sufficiently covered through multimedia. 21 (70%) teachers regarded multimedia as systemic and scientific approach in learning and teaching. Majority of the teachers were of the view that the applications of multimedia has increased the strength of the students and decreased drop-out number in the school.

26 (86.67%) teachers were of the view that the teachers need to be trained properly before using multimedia further they were of the view that multimedia would increase the in-depth understating of the subject.

Table 3.1 depicts that 90 per cent teachers viewed that multimedia provide potential knowledge, 56.67 per cent teachers felt that multimedia makes education curriculum more interesting while 30 per cent teachers felt that the multimedia provide knowledge about new technology. Further 76.67 per cent teachers believed that students show interest in education through multimedia whereas only 26.67 per cent teachers felt that the multimedia helps students in getting good results.

Table 3.1: Teachers' Views Regarding Advantages of Using Multimedia

Sl. No	*Advantages*	*Frequency (f)*	*Percentage (%)*
1.	Provide potential knowledge	27	90
2.	Make education curriculum more interesting	17	56.67
3.	Provide knowledge about new technology	9	30
4.	Students show their interest in education	23	76.67
5.	Students get good result	8	26.67

It is remarkable to observe that 28 (93.34%) of the teachers did not view applications of multimedia in terms of increase in heavy workload but majority 27 (80%) of them expressed that the application of multimedia result into joyful learning. Further, it was also revealed that subject content covered in multimedia has been relevant. It was also found that 25 (90%) teachers reported as multimedia education has helped students to have change in learning style, and helped students to acquaint with electronic media. 26 (86.67%) teachers were of the view that the application of multimedia in teaching the subjects would also improve the performance of average and below average students. None of the teacher found multimedia as waste of time or time consuming. 26 (86.66%) teachers were of the view that it is fine to replace textbooks with multimedia.

Parents' Views

Parents play an important part in the education of their children and their views matter a lot. It is better that parents take interest in educational activities of their children which motivate children to perform better. Some of the views of parents regarding the use of multimedia in facilitating educational processes are as under: 24 (80%) parents were of the view that their children take interest in studying various subjects through multimedia and has helped in the increase in knowledge of their children. 26 (86.66%) of the parents were of the view that multimedia should be compulsorily used that would definitely improve the teaching pattern and quality of teaching in schools. 23 (76.67%) of the parents were of the view that multimedia has helped in understanding the new technology and have expressed the satisfaction about education given in the school and felt that multimedia education would help their children in future also. 29 (96.67%) parents were also of the opinion that multimedia would improve the performance of their children in future as it would enhance better understanding of the subjects. Majority of the parents were of the view that children have rightly taken the multimedia as their choice and they were happy about it.

Conclusion

Some of the conclusions are most revealing of the facts the use of multimedia can help students to understand the subjects with greater clarity without any pressure on teachers and students. Further, students have found animated form to learn as interesting and not boring resulting into decrease in drop-outs of student and increase in attendance of the students in the school. Further, students like to learn language and poetry through software because it's full of animation, storytelling with sweet voice and music.

Multimedia has also helped students to learn new technology. Since the method of communications through multimedia education is audio as well as visual, students understanding and retention of the subjects would be more.

Teachers are convinced of the usefulness and relevance of multimedia as tool for education and they need to receive scientific training to operate multimedia programme effectively. They were also of the opinion that some of the concepts which are difficult to teach are made easy because of multimedia thus teachers found multimedia very effective and result oriented.

There is a need for developing multimedia package for topics/ subjects other than English, Science, Gujarati and Maths. Multimedia should also cover current issues viz. population education, environment education, energy education, health education etc. Thus the views of children, parents and teachers make it amply clear and convincing that the use of multimedia in education has been a very workable result oriented and interesting innovations which would help all the stakeholders in being effective and meaningful in globalized India of 21st century.

References

Berger, A.A. (1991). *Media Research Technique*, Sage Publications, New Delhi.

Mistry, M. (2010). Unpublished Dissertation; The Study of Use of Multimedia in Primary School, Faculty of Social Work. The Maharaja Sayajirao University of Baroda, Vadodara, Gujarat.

Ragner, P. Wall and P. Kruger, S. (2009). *Media Study: The Essential Introduction*, London, Routledge.

Ravindran, Z.K. (2000). *Media and Method: Instructional Technology in Higher Education*, Indian Publication and Distribution, New Delhi.

Turow, J. (2009). *Media Today: An Instruction to Mass Communication*, London, Routledge.

Zahid, H. (2000). *Media and Communication*, Kanishka Publication and Distribution, New Delhi.

Webliography

Multimedia in Education—Introduction, The Elements of Educational Requirements, Classroom Architecture and Resources, Concerns

http://encyclopedia.jrank.org/articles/pages/6821/Multimedia-in-Education.html#ixzz0jHZHniGN

http://www.mgutheses.org/page/?q=T%201545&search=&page=&rad=#-Online thesis research Docs

http://www.wikieducator.org/images/5/5a/PID_598.pdf-enriching learning Exp of Rural Children

www.britannica.com/.../Multimedia—Primary-Kids—Highly-Educational-Fun

www.pjb.co.uk/mmeduc.htm

www.viktoria.se/nulden/Publ/PDF/Primary.pdf

www.encyclopedia.com/doc/1G1-91564850.html

www.ces.ed.ac.uk/PDF%20Files/Brief017.pdf

www.aare.edu.au/98pap/fer98083.htm

www.emeraldinsight.com/Insight/ViewContentServlet?Filename...

www.formatex.org/micte2006/pdf/801-805.pdf

www.infitt.org/ti2009/papers/singaravelu_final.pdf

4

Women and Education

Nirmala Kumari

Women constitute more or less half of the population in the world. No wonder then that women's education has been one of the key issues of concern of the government all-over the world and the society at large. It is so because of the fact that nowadays the educated women play a major role in overall development and progress of the households, family, society and the nation. They hold prominent positions in the society all-over the world. However, the male dominated ideology and thinking made them suffer a lot in the past as they were denied equal opportunities across the board. Against all odds, the rise of feminist ideas has led to the tremendous improvement in the situation in recent past throughout the world. Consequently, access to education has been one of the most pressing demands of the women's rights movements. In India too, women's education has been a major concern for both; the government as well as the civil society, as educated women can play a very significant role in the development of the country. The issue today is racing ahead at a far greater pace than in the last couple of decades in India. Statistics from various government sources show that the literacy rate of women is lower than men. Statistics also reveal that several girls drop-out prematurely from schools. Simultaneous efforts at the governmental level are on to improve the literacy rate through its various educational schemes.

Historical Perspective

In ancient India, women were denied opportunities and had to suffer for the male dominated ideology. As a consequence, girls and women received less education than men due to the set social norms. But it is noteworthy, interestingly, that in the Vedic period women were given great importance and they had access to education. In addition, Indian scriptures Rig Veda and Upanishads mention about several women sages and seers. Women enjoyed equal status and rights with respect to education during those times. But this status of women underwent decline gradually after 500 B.C. They had lost this right and were relegated to the oblivion and all the rights including the right of education were taken away. The Islamic invasions played a vital role in further restricting freedom and rights of the women. A drastic change descended and there was a tremendous constraint for women's education in India. Women's education further deteriorated in medieval India with the introduction of *purdah* system. This unjustifiable oppression all-over the world resulted into a movement that fought to achieve the equal status for women. However, in India there was revival of interest in women's education during the British period. During this period, various socio-religious movements led by eminent persons like Raja Ram Mohan Roy, Ishwar Chandra Vidyasagar laid emphasis on women's education. Mahatma Jyotiba Phule, Periyar and Babasaheb Ambedkar were leaders of the lower castes who took various initiatives to make education accessible to the women of India. In fact, in the year 1878, the Calcutta University became one of the first universities to admit female graduates to its academic degree programmes, before any of the British universities had done the same.

Women's education, however, got a real boost only after the country got independence in 1947. After independence, the government stepped up large scale measures to ensure that women were actually getting their rightful place in the field of education. It has adopted various measures to provide education to all its womenfolk. This has been so very successful that as a result women's literacy rate has grown over the last six decades and the growth of female literacy has in fact been higher than that of male literacy rate, as can be seen from Table 4.1. While in 1951 only about 9 per cent of Indian women were literate, 54.16 per cent female were literate by the end of 2001. Literacy rate for 15 to 24 years old, women as in 2007 was 77.1 per cent as per data available on the internet. The growth of female literacy rate is 14.87 per cent as compared to 11.72 per cent of that of male literacy rate. This is certainly an achievement.

Table 4.1: Literacy Rates in India (1951-2001)

Year	*Overall Literacy Rate (%)*			*Male Literacy Rate (%)*			*Female Literacy Rate (%)*		
	Rural	*Urban*	*Overall*	*Rural*	*Urban*	*Overall*	*Rural*	*Urban*	*Overall*
1951	12.10	34.59	18.33	19.02	45.60	27.16	4.87	22.33	8.86
1961	22.50	54.40	28.30	34.30	66.00	40.40	10.10	40.50	15.35
1971	27.90	60.20	34.45	48.60	69.80	45.96	15.50	48.80	21.97
1981	36.00	67.20	43.57	49.60	76.70	56.38	21.70	56.30	29.76
1991	44.70	73.10	52.21	57.90	81.10	64.13	30.60	64.00	39.29
2001	59.40	80.30	65.38	71.40	86.70	75.85	46.70	73.20	54.16

Source: Office of the Registrar General, India.

Note: Literacy rates for 1951, 1961 and 1971 Censuses relate to population aged five years and above. The rates for the 1981, 1991 and 2001 Censuses relate to the population aged seven years and above.

Contemporary Perspective

It has been well said that there cannot be an educated people without educated women in any society. Women have been fighting for equality for decades all-over the world. The struggle towards gender equity is one of the major hallmarks of the present times. For over a hundred years women have been striving for parity, and things really came ahead in the 1960s when the feminist movement started to take shape. Even after women could vote, there were heaps of disadvantages for women. They began realizing that gender equity is important not only for women, but for society as a whole.

Higher rates of high school and university education among women, particularly in developing countries have helped them make inroads into professional careers and better-paying salaries and wages. Education increases a woman's (and her partner and the family's) level of health and health awareness. Furthering women's levels of education and advanced training also tend to lead to late age of initiation of sexual activity, late age for marriage, and late age at first childbirth. For long, women have been denied education in order to keep them subjugated and financially dependent on the menfolk in their lives. However, access to large scale education programmes of Government has gone on to open up doors of immense opportunities and chances for them. This means that they are no longer in the secondary role but because of the education imparted to them they are able to come out of the home and hearth and take their rightful place in the society.

Since the 1980s, there has been a great amount of emphasis on equal opportunities for women in higher education, and more and more women are now realizing that they can have the opportunity to study science, mathematics and engineering, and be actually quite excellent at it. Even with all the equality movements which women have fought so hard for over the decades, cultural norms still dictate many education issues. Much of society still believes towards thinking that women should ultimately become mothers and therefore be responsible for looking after the children. Many women, therefore, pursue education which leads to an occupation allowing for long periods of absence, to give them the opportunity to stay at home and be full time mothers.

Women should share their life, thoughts and interests with men at par. They are suited to carry the same academic tasks as men, with no less thoroughness and excellence. The allocation of general ability among women is approximately the same as among men. Women have demonstrated their ability to think and work alongside of men. Women must, share the same programme as men or go without. There are ways in which many women's interests or appropriate fields of work diverge from those of men, and educational programmes should take this fact into account. There is a need to recognize the ways in which the education of women can well be differentiated from that of men. It is time to realize that the finest family relations result from the association of a man and a woman who have had much of their education in common—who have developed according to his or her own nature, and not in imitation of the other. Within the framework of a democratic polity, our laws, development policies, plan and programmes have aimed at women's advancement in different spheres. In India, from the Fifth Five Year Plan (1974-78) onwards there has been a marked shift in the approach to women's issues from welfare to development. In recent years, the empowerment of women has been recognized as the central issue in determining the status of women. The National Commission of Women (NCW) was set-up by an Act of Parliament in 1990 to safeguard the right and legal entitlements of women. The 73rd and 74th Amendments (1993) to the Constitution of India have provided for reservation of seats in the local bodies (Panchayats and Municipalities) for women, laying a strong foundation for their participation in decision making at the local level only. Towards this, schemes like Mahila Samakhya Scheme which has been introduced since 1989 especially in rural areas of Jharkhand, Andhra Pradesh, Assam, Bihar, Uttarakhand, Uttar Pradesh, Kerala, Gujarat and Karnataka is commendable step forward for women empowerment.

Importance of Women Education in India

Women's education plays a vital role in the overall development of the country. It not only helps in the development of almost half of the human resources, but also in improving the quality of life at home and outside. Educated women not only tend to promote education of their girl children, but also provide better supervision and guidance to all their children. In addition to this, educated women can also help in the reduction of infant mortality rate and growth of the population. Educated women are more vigilant towards the need of education for children and can take care of their children in an improved way. Thus, women education is the need of the hour if we want a better future of our children and better living standards for our countrymen.

Problems in Education of Women in India

Women still constitute a large body of underprivileged citizens despite certain outstanding examples of individual achievements by Indian women and explicit enhancement in their general condition over the last few decades. Women of course, do not form a homogenous group in class or caste terms. Nonetheless, they face typical problems that call for special attention. The Backward Classes Commission set-up by the Government of India in 1953 classified women of India as a backward group requiring special attention. The Ministry of Human Resource Development (HRD) had earlier clubbed girls with Scheduled Castes and Tribes as the three most backward groups in education. The social backwardness of Indian women points to the huge gap between their legal status which is more or less equal to that of men, and their actual position in society, which is still far from the ideal which exists only on paper.

The widespread education for girls and women and spreading awareness amongst men and women to accept new and scientific attitudes towards each other and to themselves is needed to convert the equality of women from *de jure* to *de facto* status. A changing society and a developing economy cannot make any headway if education, which is one of the vital means affecting the norms of morality and culture, remains in the hands of conservatives who subscribe to a fragmented view of the national heritage. The differences between the positions of men and women in society will not reduce; leave aside fading away, as long as there are differences between the education of men and women. Inadequate education or no education is the most important factor contributing to the backwardness of our masses, especially our womenfolk. It is the low literacy level among women which does not allow them to take informed decisions.

This gap which exists between the literacy rates of the two genders also exists between the enrolment of girls and boys at all levels of education. Right from the primary school to the university, we find that the number of girl students is significantly lower than the number of male students. According to Article 45 of the Constitution, universal compulsory and free education until the age of 14 was to be achieved by the year 1960. Looking at the present condition of primary education in villages, it seems doubtful that 100 per cent enrolment of girls can be achieved by the end of this decade. There is no doubt that we have made great headway in the education of women in the last few decades. But, it is unfortunately true of our society that children are sent to school not according to their intelligence or aptitude but according to their sex. Such attitudes need to be changed without any more delay if we want to achieve 100 per cent enrolment of the primary school-going children. Although the disparity between the enrolment of girls and boys has been shrinking in the urban areas, the gap between their enrolments is still very wide specially in rural areas.

The economic structure of rural areas is such that children, especially girls, are required to help in household work and perform their chores. Young girls have to look after their younger brothers and sisters, have to get water from the well, have to carry food to the parents in the field, etc. Since there is so much to be done at home, they may not be spared for the luxury of attending a school. The resources of the poor farmer are so limited that he does not have anything to spare for the education of his children. In case if there are resources available, then it is the boy who is sent to school first. Parents also do not see the value of educating their daughters who would get married after all and be only housewives. Since they cannot see any direct relationship between education and economic betterment, they have very little motivation to send their girl child to school.

It is still not being realized that there is definite connection between education, good motherhood and efficient house management. The management of millions of households and the upbringing of millions of children is thus in the hands of illiterate women. It is here that a change is required if our democratic and socialistic intensions are not to remain mere fictional or merely on papers. People can be motivated to have their daughters educated only if educational system is directly linked with economic and social development. As long as our education remains insensitive of the perceived needs of people to solve their immediate problems and on the contrary, actually alienates them from their natural, social and cultural environment, they will continue refusing to accept sending their daughters to school. It is the area of primary education, especially in rural areas, which needs maximum deliberation. Primary education for both girls and boys is what we should be concerned about while planning our policies and allocating funds.

In modern India, the status of women is a sort of a contradiction. If on the one hand, she is at the peak of ladder of success, on the other hand, she is suffering without a sound the violence afflicted on her by her own family members. Their path is full of roadblocks. But now some women have left the secured domain of their homes and are now in the arena of life, fully armed with their education and talent. The sex ratio in India shows that the Indian society is still biased and prejudiced against female. According to the census of 2001, there are 933 females (Rural-946, Urban-900) per thousand of males in India which is much below the world average of 990 females. Besides, there are many problems which women in India have to go through on a daily basis.

Leaving the past behind, the present state of affairs in India, particularly in urban areas has undergone a lot of change and women are opting for higher education. But majority of Indian population residing in villages still live in medieval age. Nevertheless, government schemes such as Sarva Shiksha Abhiyan (SSA) are praiseworthy and are way-ahead. The main obstacle thus remains the 'gender discrimination' which still persists in India and a lot more needs to be done and accomplished in the field of women's education in India. The gap in the male-female literacy rate is just a simple indicator. While the male literacy rate is more than 75 per cent according to the 2001 census, the female literacy rate is just 54.16 per cent. Prevailing prejudices and biases, low enrolment of girl child in the schools, indulgence of girl children in domestic works and high drop-out rate from schools are some other obstacles in the path of making all Indian women educated.

Literacy in India is the key to the socio-economic progress. The literacy rate in India grew to 68 per cent in 2007 and 72 per cent in 2008 from 12 per cent in 1947. According to the survey by the National Sample Survey Office (NSSO) released by the government on 19th May, 2010, the literacy rate among the population with age 7 and above was 71.7 per cent whereas the adult population (15+ years) had a literacy rate of 66 per cent. Although this was greater than fivefold improvement, the level is well below the world average literacy rate of 84 per cent. The 2001 census, however, indicated a 1991-2001 decadal literacy growth of 12.63 per cent, which is the fastest-ever on record. As per Government of India Press Release *ibid.*, in 2010 there was a wide gender disparity in the literacy rate in India: adult (15+ years) literacy rates were 76.9 per cent for men and 54.16 per cent for women. The low female literacy rate has had a considerable negative impact on family planning and population stabilization efforts in India. The census provided a positive indication that growth in female literacy rates (14.38%) was substantially faster than in male literacy rates (11.13%) in the 1991-2001 decadal period, which means the gender gap appears to be narrowing.

Women's Education, Development and Empowerment

Empowerment of women is a global issue and it is at the forefront of many formal as well as informal campaigns worldwide. The concept of women empowerment was introduced at the international women conference at Nairobi in 1985. It percolated thereupon that no nation can achieve success unless education is accorded to all its citizens. Education is a milestone for women empowerment because it enables them to respond to the challenges, to confront their traditional role and change their lives. Where India is poised to becoming a developed country by 2020, this can become reality only when the women of this nation get educated and empowered. India presently account for the largest number of illiterates in the world.

Women's development indicates the contribution of women's education in India to various dimensions of development. Women and men in India enjoy constitutional equality. Article 14 of the Constitution of India guarantees equal rights and opportunities to men and women in political, economic and social spheres, Article 42 of the Constitution of India directs the State to make provision for ensuring just and humane conditions for work and maternity and Article 51(A) imposes upon every citizen, a fundamental duty to renounce the practices derogatory to the dignity of women. Education as such, results in positive vibes. Not only does it have an inherent value in the sense of the joy of learning, reading etc., but it also has instrumental, social and process roles. Moreover, education may spread through interpersonal communication and motivation. When one individual sends his/her child to school, his/her neighbour is likely to do so as well. Women's education too, often spreads this way, more specifically, through same gender effects, i.e. an educated woman is far more likely to send her daughter to school than an uneducated woman. Also, she is likely to maintain better conditions of nutrition and hygiene in her household and thereby improve her family's health. The presence of a larger number of female teachers too may encourage parents to send their daughters to school. Thus, education is a fundamental tool for women's empowerment.

Efforts at the Government Level

However, this constitutional equality has not yet materialized into a *de facto* equality, despite the efforts made in the various Five Year Plans. The First Five Year Plan sought to "promote the welfare of women" by helping them to play their legitimate role in the family and the community but emphasized that the major burden of organizing activities for the benefit of the female population had to be borne by the private agencies. Five Year Plans continued to reflect the same welfare approach to women's interests though they accorded priority to education for both, men and women and launched measures to improve maternal and child health services and supplementary nutrition for children as well as expectant and nursing mothers. It was the Sixth Five Year Plan in which the focus on women's interests shifted from 'welfare' and 'development'. Planners and policy makers began to recognize women not only as partners but also as stakeholders in the development of the country. The Seventh Five Year Plan saw developmental programmes which aimed at raising the economic and social status of women and at ensuring that they get the benefits of national development. This is when beneficiary oriented programmes extending direct benefits to women in different developmental sectors began. There was a stress upon the generation of both skilled and unskilled employment through formal and non-formal education and vocational training. The Eighth Five Year Plan had a 'Human Development' focus. It tried to ensure that the benefits of development do not bypass women and it implemented special programmes for women to complement the general development programmes and to monitor the flow of benefits to women in education, health and employment.

The Ninth Five Year Plan was rather ambitious. It took up 'empowering women as agents of socio-economic change and development' as a major commitment. To begin with, it adopted the 'National Policy for Empowerment of Women', which among other objectives, sought to organize women into Self Help Groups to work for their own empowerment, accorded a high priority to schemes for maternal and child welfare. Most importantly, it made a bid at easy and equal access to education through the Special Action Plan of 1998, plans for the free education of girls up to the college level (inclusive of professional courses) and vocational training.

The United Progressive Alliance (UPA) Government when came to power in 2004, pledged in its Common Minimum Programme to empower women politically, educationally, economically and legally to ensure gender equality. The Tenth Five Year Plan had an overly ambitious target of reducing gender gaps in literacy by at least 50 per cent in 2007. Even the Mid Term Appraisal of the Plan conceded that the target was unrealistic. According to the 2006-07 Budget, Rs. 22,251 crore was to be spent exclusively for women. Schemes in which all the beneficiaries were women were to receive 100 per cent of their funding from this fund while those which benefited women indirectly were to get 30 per cent. However, even schemes like the Indira Awas Yojana in which only 77.17 per cent of the beneficiaries are women and the National Child Labour Project in which only 44 per cent of the expenditure is exclusively for girls were given 100 per cent of their funding from the fund that was to be used exclusively for women.

The Union Government's plan allocation for school education has increased by 16 per cent from Rs. 26,800 crore in 2009-10 to Rs. 31,036 crore in 2010-11. In addition, the states were to have access to Rs. 3,675 crore for elementary education under the Thirteenth Finance Commission grants for 2010-11. To further improve female literacy rate, the Government has recast the earlier National Literacy Mission as a new programme "Saakshar Bharat". It was launched in September 2009 with a target of 7 crore non-literate adults which included 6 crore women. In terms of percentage GDP expenditure, total allocation for education in 2010-11 stood at 0.71 per cent of the GDP, which is slightly better than the 0.64 per cent (of GDP) recorded for 2009-10 (RE). Such gradual and minuscule increases in the Union Budget outlays cannot result in any visible increase in overall public spending on education in the country leave aside achieving the target of six per cent of the GDP it ought to have done about 25 years ago. With just one more Union Budget (i.e., the Budget for 2011-12) left in the Eleventh Five Year Plan period, at least 80 per cent of the outlays recommended by the Planning Commission (for the five year period from 2007-08 to 2011-12) should have been made for the Plan schemes during 2007-08 to 2010-11. But, the total provision under

Plan schemes in the four Union Budgets from 2007-08 to 2010-11 has been only 12 per cent of the Planning Commission recommended outlay for Rashtriya Madhyamik Shiksha Abhiyan, 36 per cent for Teachers' Training and 46 per cent for UGC; although Sarva Shiksha Abhiyan (SSA) and Mid Day Meal Programme have fared better in terms of allocations with 76 per cent and 65 per cent respectively.

Access to Education and Educational Opportunities

Education is a basic human right and an essential tool for achieving the goals of equality, development and peace. Non-discriminatory education benefits both for girls and boys, thereby ultimately contributing to more equal relationships between women and men. Equality of access to and attainment of educational qualifications is necessary if more women are to become agents of change. Literacy of women is an important key to improving health, nutrition and education in the family, and to empowering women to participate in decision making in society. Investing in formal and non-formal education and training for girls and women, has proved to be one of the best means of achieving sustainable development and economic growth.

It can, therefore, be inferred that creation of a healthy educational and social environment would be extremely effective in the elimination of causes of discrimination against women and inequalities between men and women. Curricula and teaching materials remain gender biased to a large degree, and are rarely sensitive to the specific needs of girls and women. This reinforces traditional female and male roles that deny women opportunities for full and equal partnership in society. Lack of gender awareness by teachers/instructors at all levels, strengthens existing inequities between males and females by reinforcing discriminatory tendencies and undermining girls' self-esteem.

A substantial improvement in the situation of girls at all levels of education, including the higher level, is one of the factors contributing to their continued progress in professional activities. Nevertheless, girls and women are still concentrated in a limited number of branches. Even at a higher level of educational qualification, women encounter more prejudices than men in a number of sectors, which makes it difficult for them to maximize the use of their degrees. Hence, women's access to quality education and training for self-reliance at all levels and in all fields and sectors need to be ensured.

Problems and Remedial Recommendations

The United Nations Organization (UNO) is giving special attention to the development of women. Many worldwide conferences have been held under the aegis of UNO to consider the ways and means of empowerment of women. Main emphasis of all these conferences has been the rehabilitation of women, economically, politically and culturally, albeit women's educational development and economic security have been two main themes of such conferences. Problems in educating women in India include social taboos, dependency, parents' discriminatory attitudes, low social status, early marriage, heavy workload, lack of motivation, and family poverty. Changes in attitudes, laws, and funding are needed to expand opportunities. Majority of the problems confronting the educational development of women have been discussed one way or the other in the preceding paragraphs, while reviewing and analyzing the progress of education of women since independence. For the sake of consolidating, it would be better to consider these problems at one place from the point of view of suggesting corrective measures and special programmes required to address these problems. A brief description of these problems is given in succeeding paragraphs along with measures required for addressing these problems.

1. Quantitative Task

One of the major problems of girls' education is the quantitative task involved in bridging the gap between educational development of boys and girls. In spite of the astounding progress of women's education, the enrolment of girls' constitutes only 35 per cent of the total enrolment, as against their population proportion of 48 per cent, indicating the huge quantitative gap that is required to be bridged to achieve the desired goal of equality in educational development between boys and girls. While boys of the age-group of 6 to 11 have been covered under the programme of Universalisation of Elementary Education, girls with an enrolment ratio of 68 per cent have to still cover a gap of 32 per cent of this age-group. Educational programmes help girls enroll and stay in school and help women gain access to or create new educational, financial, and social resources in their communities. It helps girls and women improve their own lives, the lives of their families and the conditions in their communities. For parents and especially mothers this means creating conditions that ensure their daughters have equal access to basic education, are able to make informed decisions about their futures, and are able to protect themselves from trafficking, sexual exploitation, health consciousness etc. By improving educational opportunities for girls and women, women may develop skills that would allow them to make decisions and influence community change in key areas. In tûrn, these programmes have a positive impact on some of the most profound issues of our time: population growth, HIV and AIDS, peace and security, and the widening gap between the rich and the poor. All these will be successful only if the attendance of girls in schools at all levels is encouraging. Several reasons could be attributed for non-attendance of girls; some of which can be briefly put as:

1. From a very early age, girls begin to look after their younger brothers and sisters and do household work to relieve their parents to go out as labourers or to work in the farms. Some girls of the age-group of 6-14 are engaged in some sort of vocations. In such cases, the school hours of the formal system do not suit them.
2. In many communities, particularly in rural areas the idea of sending a girl of 7-8 years age to a school does not find favour. Even otherwise, apathy to co-education is found among illiterate parents.
3. Early marriage or betrothal, *purdah* system and segregation of girls from boys from early age affects adversely the enrolment rates of girls.
4. Cultural heritage and social constraints in many areas of the country hold back the girls at home.
5. Lack of qualified women teachers is another important factor which affects adversely the participation rates of girls in schools. Parents are not willing to send girls to schools where male teachers are teaching.
6. Parents prefer boys' education than to girls' education. The village community is not convinced of the usefulness of the educational programmes for the girls.
7. Lack of proper security measures for girl students and women teachers adversely affects the educational development of girls and women.
8. Inadequate means of communication in rural areas prevent girls from attending schools.

2. Other Problems and Constraints

Following are some of the other problems and constraints in connection with the development of girls' education in India:

Separate Institutions for Girls

Owing to cultural and social heritage, parents are reluctant to send girls to boys' schools particularly from middle level and above. Both the Secondary Education Commission (1953) and National Committee on Women's Education (1958) recommended the establishment of separate institutions for girls with a view to promoting education among them. But the percentage of girls' institutions to total number of major types of educational institutions still works out to be 10 to 15, as against their enrolment proportion of 35. In the case of middle and secondary schools, the proportions of girls' schools are in the range of 10 to 14 per cent as against their enrolment proportion of 34 and 35 per cent respectively. Similarly, only 15 per cent of colleges for general education are exclusively for girls as against their enrolment proportion of 30 per cent. Although the concept of co-education has gained ground and finds favour with the educational administrators and planners from the point of view of economy and standards of education, still it is felt that there is a definite need of establishing separate institutions for girls, because quite a large number of girls prefer to study in separate institutions, provided that facilities for all courses are available and same standards are maintained in girls' institutions as in boys' institutions.

Paucity of Women Teachers

One of the factors hindering the progress of women's education has been the inadequate strength of the women teachers in educational institutions. It has been one of the recommendations of almost all the committees and commissions set-up from time to time in the field of education, to appoint more women teachers in the institutions in order to attract more girls and to improve their enrolment ratios. It has been the acceptable view to appoint all women teachers in the mixed pre-primary and primary schools. The recommendations have still gone further in relaxing educational qualifications and training in case of women teachers and provision of special facilities like accommodation and special allowances to attract more women teachers to the profession, particularly in the rural areas.

Separate Curricula for Girls

Despite recommendations of the Hansa Mehta Committee appointed by the National Council for Women's Education regarding differentiation of curricula between boys and girls, and supported by the Education Commission and accepted by the Government of India, many of the states continue to prescribe different curricula for boys and girls at the school level. Girls' institutions often make provision for courses of Home Science, Needle Work and Fine Arts, but have no provision for Science and Mathematics. This has had an adverse effect, particularly on the teaching of Mathematics and Science for girls, consequently resulting in the inadequate supply of women teachers in these subjects and thus depriving the facilities of these courses to girls attending separate institutions for girls. In view of the socio-economic changes and the development of career consciousness and the economic liberty among women, the differentiation in curriculum and facilities available to them adversely affect their educational development and employment prospects.

Lack of Transport Facilities

Lack of transport facilities, particularly in rural areas for girls to attend middle and secondary schools, which are sufficiently far away from their homes and even their own villages, is one of the major causes of the large-scale drop-out of girls after completing lower primary education.

Inadequate Hostel Facilities

Many girls desirous of pursuing education above middle level where such facilities are available away from their homes, are unable to avail themselves of these facilities due to lack of hostel arrangements. Girls, particularly belonging to Scheduled Castes and Scheduled Tribes communities might continue their education at middle and above levels, provided they get free or cheaper residential facilities near the educational institution.

Insecurity

Parents often complain about existence of insecurity for girls to attend schools. Occurrence of cases of abduction, rape and molestation of girls often dampen the enthusiasm of girls in pursuing education beyond a certain age, when their parents bind them to homes.

Lack of Childcare Centres

As is known, girls are often required to look after their younger brothers and sisters at home, when their parents go out for their work. They may like to go to schools, if arrangements for keeping their brothers and sisters in an attached childcare centre are made. The non-existence or inadequate facilities for such arrangements, particularly in rural areas, have been one of the accepted reasons for non-enrolment of girls or a large-scale drop-out in schools.

Fixed Schooling Hours

Fixed schooling hours do not suit girls in rural areas, as they are required for domestic work at home or in farms and fields for collecting firewood, coal waste, cow dung and fetching water during these hours. This is one of the causes of lower participation rates of girls in school education. The enrolment rates of girls and their retention can be improved if educational facilities are made available to girls during the period suitable to them, that is, when they are free from domestic chores.

Unattractive School Environment

Most of the girls do not attend schools or drop-out after initial enrolment, because of lack of physical facilities and congenial environments in schools, particularly in case of co-educational schools. Lack of proper place for girl students' sitting in the classrooms, non-availability of separate toilets for girls, absence of separate arrangements for games and sports, existence of widespread rowdyism by boys, existence of unkindly and discriminating attitude of teachers and atmosphere in the institutions affect adversely the enrolment rates of girls in schools.

Illiteracy

Another problem regarding women's education in India today is provision of some basic education to the overwhelming majority of parents who have remained outside the reach of the formal system because of their age and social responsibilities as well as the literacy gap. A large majority of them are illiterate or semi-literate. The programme of adult literacy undertaken from time to time and introduction of 'Functional Literacy' programme from Fourth Plan that continued in the Fifth and Sixth Plan in the form of 'Rural Functional Literacy' has not created any visible impact on the problem of illiteracy. Although no formal evaluation of the programme has been made, the available reports show little progress in this regard. The adult education centres at present running in states have not attracted majority of the illiterate women and often the Adult Education Centres for Women are short of the requisite enrolment, whereas the stock of illiterate women is daily increasing with non-enrolled and dropped out adult women. Lack of proper physical facilities, unattractive environments, absence of advertisement, propaganda and persuasive drive, insecurity, unattractive contents of reading materials, lack of motivation among other factors are responsible for the sluggish progress of the adult educational programme for women.

Recommendations

A large number of recommendations have been made and measures suggested for bridging the wide gap between the educational development of boys and girls by various well-known Committees and Commissions set-up in the country from time to time. Notwithstanding, the wide gap between the educational development of boys and girls is likely to be narrowed by improving the rates of girls' enrolment and their retention by adopting the following measures in a big way as a package deal. Some of these measures are already in practice in some states in a partial way or on a pilot basis, but the adoption of these measures partially or on pilot basis has not made any visible impact on the issue. In general, the government should endeavour to attain the goals of equal access to education without distinction as to sex or sexual orientation at all appropriate levels for girls, adult women with little or no education and for women with disabilities to improve their work opportunities and ensure that procedures to address grievances are established.

Increase enrolment and retention rates of girls by allocating appropriate budgetary resources, and by enlisting the support of parents and the community, as well as through campaigns, flexible school schedules, incentives, scholarships and other means to minimize the costs of girls' education to their families.

Improve the parity in education to ensure that women of all ages are provided with the knowledge, reasoning ability, skills and ethical values required to develop their full capacities in health and dignity and to participate fully in the social, economic and political process of development.

Develop training programmes and materials for teachers and educators that raise awareness about the status, role and contribution of women in the family and society.

Mobilize additional funds whenever necessary, to meet the costs of education for all girls and women with a particular emphasis on underprivileged populations.

Remove all the barriers to schooling and eliminate all forms of discrimination against young mothers and provide child care and other support services to enable mothers to continue their schooling. In particular, ensure that the formal education of girls and young women is not permanently interrupted by early pregnancy and child rearing.

With the support of the parents and in cooperation with educational staff and institutions, encourage the collaboration of educational programmes for girls and the creation of integrated services related to youth sexuality, to raise awareness of their rights and responsibilities and to help them to assume those responsibilities, taking into account the importance of such education and services to personal development and self-esteem.

Monitor progress using educational indicators generated by national, regional and international organizations and make state governments accountable for implementing measures to close the gap between women and men in education and training opportunities, and in the levels of achievement in all fields, particularly primary education and literacy programmes.

In conclusion, the following imperative measures are suggested that may be adopted in totality and uniformly in a big way with larger scope.

Free Education

Free education should be introduced for girls up to higher secondary stage (up to 12th class) by all states as is done in Gujarat.

Separate Institutions

Wherever there is a demand for separate institutions for girls even at the elementary stage, these should be established, the need of co-educational schools notwithstanding.

Access to Education

Schooling facilities should be provided to the girls nearer to their place of residence (i.e. within easy walking distance). State level implementation of programme for providing bicycles to all school going girl students (as very successfully implemented in Bihar by Nitish Kumar government) can bring out a successful saga. Alternatively, mobile schools may be started for—girls of nomadic tribes, migrant labourers and construction workers.

Transport and Hostel Facilities

Adequate arrangements should be made for free transport of girls to school if it is situated more than one kilometre from their habitations. Free or cheap hostel facilities may be provided to girls.

Conclusion

India dreams of becoming a developed country in next 10-15 years or so, but quite ironical is the fact that the country whose population has crossed one billion mark, has literacy rates comparable with some of the underdeveloped countries. Various programmes initiated by the government like Total Literacy Campaign, the District Primary Education Programme and National Literacy Mission (NLM) set-up in 1988 are yet to reach a satisfactory level to attain the goal. Further, the gap between the rural and urban areas and that between female and their male counterpart is quite substantial. There are many education issues facing women, and although many of them are now recognized there's still a long way to go. The government should therefore continue massive publicity campaign extolling the virtues of educating a girl and the benefits of being educated. The publicity should also invite parents to form associations and register with the district authorities. They should be informed of the benefits of organizing themselves to protest against the low teaching standards and to ensure teacher regularity and service delivery. It is to be realized that education is not only a pillar of economic growth, but a prerequisite for long-term development by empowering individuals to become fully active citizens. Education also brings a reduction in inequalities and functions as a means of improving their status within the family. Education of women is the most powerful tool for change of position in society. To bring more girls, especially from marginalized families of Below Poverty Level (BPL), in mainstream education, the governments' efforts in providing a package of concessions in the form of providing free books, uniform, boarding and lodging, mid-day meals, scholarships and so on is praiseworthy and need to be pursued with vigour.

References

Eileen, M. Byrne, (1978). *Women and Education*, Tavistock Publications Limited, London, UK.

Ministry of HRD, Government of India (2004). *The Report of the Taskforce on Education for Women's Equality*.

National Sample Survey Office (NSSO), (2010). Government of India (Ministry of Statistics and Programme Implementation), Press Note on *Education in India, 2007-08: Participation and Expenditure*, Press Information Bureau, Government of India, New Delhi.

Patricia, S. (1976). *Women in Education*, Phi Delta Kappa Educational Foundation, Bloomington, Indiana, USA.

Sandler, B. Resnick, (1996). "The Chilly Classroom Climate: A Guide to Improve Education of Women", *National Association for Women in Education*, Washington DC, USA.

Shastri, S.R. (1959). *Women in the Sacred Laws*, Bhartiya Vidya Bhawan, Mumbai.

Website. *http://www. indiabudget.nic.in/es2006-07*

Websites. *http://www.nces.ed.gov* and *http://www.mchb.hrsa.gov//whusa_07*

5

Tribal Communities and Their Status in Valod (South Gujarat)

Rekha K. Talmaki

This chapter is devoted to the description of tribal life in the state of Gujarat in general and particularly in Surat district and Valod taluka, which comprises 28.19 per cent and 75 per cent of its population as tribal population respectively. A study was conducted in 11 villages in Valod to find out the important features and cultural background of the main communities as well as socio-economic status of women in Valod. The rapid reviews of the institutions, i.e. Vedchhi Pradesh Seva Samiti, Valod, Lijjat Papad Grihaudyog, Vedchhi Ashram have also been discussed. These institutions follow Gandhian ideology which has direct and indirect impact on life of tribal communities of Valod. Socio-economic profile, their consumption pattern, their habits, status of women etc. have been focused in this chapter. For this study, primary and secondary data is used, interview schedule was prepared to collect the information.

Tribes in Gujarat and their Distribution in General

In all, there are more than 30 tribes identified and scheduled in Gujarat. Some of them are very large in number and some are very small. The Bhils are the largest tribe of all. They are known by various names such as Bhil, Bhil Garasia, Dholi Bhil, Dungri Bhil, Dungri Garasia, Mewasi Bhil, Rawal Bhil, Tadvi Bhil, Bhanalia Bhilala, Pawra, Vasava, Vasave etc. Together they constitute more than 46 per cent of the total tribal population of the State. The second largest group is that of Halpatis including the Talaviya, who constitute eight per cent of the total population. They are concentrated in Valsad and Surat districts. They are settled in non-tribal villages. The other large groups are the Dhodias, Gamits, Chaudharis, Rathawas and Koknas. The Dhodias are mainly found in Valsad and Surat districts; whereas the Gamits are concentrated in Surat, Vadodara and Bharuch districts. The Chaudharis are largely found in Surat district. Since, the present study is based on sample survey, all tribes have not been covered in the sample.

Tribes in Gujarat

The population of Gujarat, in 2001, has been 5,06,71,017. Of this, 74,81,160 persons are the Scheduled Tribes (STs) constituting 14.8 per cent of the total population of the State. The State has registered 21.4 per cent decadal growth of the Scheduled Tribes population during 1991-2001. There are 29 notified Scheduled Tribes in the State. Rural, urban distribution of Scheduled Tribe Population of Gujarat State is given below.

The Scheduled Tribes population in Gujarat is predominantly rural with 91.8 per cent residing in rural and 8.2 per cent in urban areas.

Surat consists of 14,08,270 total tribal population. Out of it, 12,65,512 resides in rural areas (6,33,743 male and 6,31,769 female, respectively); and 1,42,758 reside in urban area (74,279 male and 68,479 female, respectively). Surat district consists of largest number of talukas (i.e. 15 talukas) with 1,280 villages which covers only 4,742 sq. kms. of area and according to 2001 census, its total population was 51,36,391.

Population, Size and Distribution of Scheduled Tribes

The Bhil with 34.4 lakh population represent majority of the total Scheduled Tribes population of the State (46%). Dubla or Halpati (8%), Dhodia (7.9%), Rathawa (7.2%) and Naika (5.3%) are the major Scheduled Tribes each having sizeable population. Along with the Bhils, they constitute about 74.3 per cent of the State's total Scheduled Tribes population. Gamit, Kokna, Chaudhari, Varli and Dhankar account for 3-4 per cent each of State's Scheduled Tribes population.

Table 5.1: Population of Major Scheduled Tribes (2001 Census)

Name of the Scheduled Tribes	*Total Population*	*Proportion to the Total Scheduled Tribes Population*
All Scheduled Tribes	74,81,160	100%
Bhil	34,41,945	46.0*
Dubla (Halpati)	5,96,865	8.0
Dhodia	5,89,108	7.9
Rathawa	5,35,284	7.2
Naikda	3,93,024	5.3
Gamit	3,54,362	4.7
Kokna	3,29,496	4.4
Chaudhari	2,82,392	3.8
Varli	2,55,271	3.4
Dhanka	2,52,637	3.4
Patelia	1,09,390	1.5
Koli	95,655	1.3

*Includes Generic population.

Source: Office of the Registrar General, India.

Varlis are concentrated in Valsad and Surat districts. They are settled in non-tribal villages. The Dhodias are mainly found in Valsad and Surat districts; whereas the Gamits are concentrated in Surat, Vadodara and Bharuch districts. The Chaudharis are largely found in Surat district. Thus, certain tribes are concentrated in certain areas and some are spread throughout the State.

Sex Ratio

As per 2001 census, sex ratio of the Scheduled Tribes population is 974, which is close to the national average for all the Scheduled Tribes (978). Individual Scheduled Tribe-wise, the Varli and Gamit have recorded sex ratio above 1000. The sex ratio among Chaudhari (996), Kokna (990), Dhodia (989), and Dubla (983) has been recorded above the State average for Scheduled Tribes. On the other hand, Koli have recorded a very low sex ratio of 921. It is comparatively lower among Dhanka (937) and Patelia (955).

The State has recorded child sex ratio (among 0-6 age group) of 966, which lower than the national average for the Scheduled Tribes (973). Among the individual Scheduled Tribes, Patelia have recorded low child sex ratio of 926. Literacy rate (7 years and above) among major Scheduled Tribes is given in the Table 5.2.

Table 5.2: Literacy Rate among Major Scheduled Tribes

Name of the Scheduled Tribe	*Literacy Rate*		
	Total	*Male*	*Female*
All Scheduled Tribes	47.7	59.2	36.0
Bhil	44.3	56.9	31.3
Chaudhari	62.4	71.3	53.4
Dhanka	52.9	66.7	38.1
Dhodia	75.9	85.3	66.5
Dubla	47.8	56.8	38.7
Gamit	52.9	61.7	44.2
Kokna	51.5	62.6	40.3
Koli	26.3	38.4	12.8
Naikda	35.6	45.6	25.2
Patelia	62.5	78.5	45.9
Rathawa	36.8	50.2	22.8
Varli	32.1	42.1	22.2

Source: Office of the Registrar General, India.

The Scheduled Tribes population of Gujarat has recorded 47.7 per cent literacy rate, which is at par with the national average for Scheduled Tribes (47.1%). The male and female literacy rate at 59.2 per cent and 36 per cent respectively indicates that, women are lagging behind male counterparts by 23.2 per cent points. Of the twelve major Scheduled Tribes, Dhodia with 75.9 per cent literary are ahead of others. Their female literacy rate is 66.5 per cent and male 85.3 per cent. Literacy position is dismal among Koli as only 26.3 per cent of their population has been literate, the picture is more depressing for female (12.8%) among them.

In the age group of 5-14 years, total of 56.9 per cent of the Scheduled Tribes population is attending schools or other educational institutions. Of the twelve major Scheduled Tribes, Dhodia has recorded the highest, i.e. 84.5 per cent. Other Scheduled Tribes, who have recorded above State average are Chaudhari (80.7%), Patelia (74.9%), Kokna (66.5%), Dhanka (63.6%) and Dubla (60.9%). Koli has recorded the lowest at 33.4 per cent and Naikda 44.1 per cent and Varli 44.9 per cent have recorded less than half of their population in the age group of 5-14 to be attending schools or any other institution.

Merely 2.5 per cent of total literates in the Scheduled Tribes population have educational level, graduation and above. The Chaudhari and Dhodia are well ahead, among the twelve major Scheduled Tribes, to register high of 5.3 per cent of their literates as graduate or above. On the contrary, Koli, Varli, Dubla and Naikda are at the bottom, each having less than one per cent.

Surat District

The present study refers to a Taluka named Valod in Surat district of Gujarat State. Surat district consists of large number of tribal people which is 28.2 per cent of Scheduled Tribes to total population of the district.

Population (General, Scheduled Castes/Scheduled Tribes)

Total population of the district according to 2001 census is 49,95,174 persons comprising of 27,22,539 males and 22,72,635 females. Rural population of the district is 19,99,357 (10,26,584 males and 9,72,773 females) and urban population is 29,95,817 persons (16,95,955 males and 12,99,862 females). Scheduled Tribes population of the district as per 2001 census is 12,65,512 persons, comprising of 6,33,743 males and 6,31,769 females. Rural Scheduled Tribes population of the district is 14,08,270 persons, comprising of 7,08,022 males and 7,00,248 females and urban-Scheduled Tribes population is 1,42,758 persons comprising of 74,279 males and 68,479 females. Surat consists of 15 talukas; of the 15 talukas Valod is 100 per cent rural taluka. Total population of Valod is 87,127, out of which 953 is Scheduled Castes and 64,112 is Scheduled Tribes population. Taluka-wise male-female ratio is given in Table 5.3.

Table 5.3 reveals that, the sex-ratio of Surat district, compared to 1991 census, has been declined in 2001. Sex-ratio of Nizer and Uchhal is favourable to female. Sex-ratio of Valod taluka has improved. Valod is a smallest taluka of Surat district. Earlier, it had the status of a mahal, a sub-division of the Bardoli taluka. It acquired the status of a taluka in 1972. Valod taluka consists of 40 villages shown in Table 5.3A. 11 villages and 498 women respondents were selected for the study to find out the socio-economic status of tribal women in Valod.

Population of Valod

Total population is 87,127 consisting of 44,133 males and 42,994 females. As elsewhere in the country, the sex ratio in the taluka is in favour of males. But the proportion of women to men is not as low as one finds in non-tribal areas.

Table 5.3: Taluka-wise Male-Female Ratio

(Per 1000 Male—Sex-ratio)

Zilla/Taluka	*Census 1991*	*Census 2001*
Surat Zilla	901	835
Olpad	949	899
Mangrol	961	948
Umerpada	961	993
Nizer	1016	1025
Uchhal	995	1018
Songadh	980	985
Kamrej	947	929
Choryasi	839	722
Palsana	930	793
Bardoli	766	766
Vyara	986	998
Valod	967	976
Mahuva	974	966
Mandvi	971	979
Surat City	839	774

Table 5.3A: Villages of Valod

1.	Adyapor	11.	Dadariya	21.	Kaher	31.	Pelad Buhari
2.	Algat	12.	Degama	22.	Kalamkui	32.	Ranveri
3.	Ambach	13.	Delwada	23.	Kamalchhod	33.	Shahpor
4.	Andhatri	14.	Dhamodla	24.	Kanajod	34.	Shiker
5.	Bahej	15.	Dumkhal	25.	Khambhla	35.	Syadla
6.	Bedkuva	16.	Goddha	26.	Kosambiya	36.	Titva
7.	Beldha	17.	Golan	27.	Kumbhiya	37.	Tokarva
8.	Bhimpor	18.	Hathuka	28.	Mordevi	38.	Valod
9.	Buhari	19.	Inama	29.	Nalotha	39.	Vedchhi
10.	Butwada	20.	Jamaniya	30.	Nansad	40.	Virpor

Before we proceed to the main communities in Valod, it is necessary to take rapid account of the three main institutions which are playing very important role in bringing the changes among the tribals particularly among women in Valod Taluka. These institutions are (1) Vedchhi Pradesh Seva Samiti-Udyogwadi, Valod (2) Lijjat Papad Grihaudyog (3) Vedchhi Ashram, Vedchhi.

Vedchhi Pradesh Seva Samiti (Udyogwadi)

Women's Section of Vedchhi Pradesh Seva Samiti (VPSS) was started in 1986. Late Shri Babubhai Shah was director and founder member of Vedchhi Pradesh Seva Samiti. Vedchhi Pradesh Seva Samiti's

Table 5.4: Population Data of Valod Block According to 2001 Census

Sl. No.	*Name of Village*	*Total Population*	*Male*	*Female*
	Valod Taluka	**87127**	**44133**	**42994**
1.	Bedkuva	3248	1620	1628
2.	Dhamodia	2136	1089	1047
3.	Kalamkui	2415	1234	1181
4.	Kaher	2134	1073	1061
5.	Beldha	273	135	138
6.	Syadla	1945	966	979
7.	Titava	961	497	464
8.	Kamalchhod	6013	3077	2936
9.	Tokarva	163	79	84
10.	Khambhala	359	182	177
11.	Shiker	2646	1343	1303
12.	Shahpor	954	483	471
13.	Nansad	505	262	243
14.	Inma	803	402	401
15.	Butvada	1457	743	714
16.	**Degama**	**5955**	**2985**	**2970**
17.	**Ambach**	**2925**	**1401**	**1524**
18.	**Vedchhi**	**2928**	**1552**	**1376**
19.	**Valod**	**14594**	**7388**	**7206**
20.	Delvada	1646	855	791
21.	Mordevi	1898	929	969
22.	Bahej	270	131	139
23.	**Kosambiya**	**8893**	**458**	**435**
24.	**Nalotha**	**1073**	**526**	**547**
25.	**Ranveri**	**2030**	**1018**	**1012**
26.	Kumbhiya	1002	517	485
27.	**Kanjod**	**881**	**424**	**457**
28.	**Bhimpor**	**1353**	693	660
29.	**Golan**	**2289**	**1136**	**1153**
30.	Dadaria	1837	927	910
31.	Hathuka	2043	998	1045
32.	**Dumkhal**	**1057**	**533**	**524**
33.	Adyapor	961	494	467
34.	Jamniya	1099	551	548
35.	Alghat	1513	781	732
36.	Godtha	1101	571	530
37.	Anthatri	3315	1711	1604
38.	Buhari	5273	2720	2553
39.	Pelad Buhari	1584	819	765
40.	Virpor	1595	830	765

Source: Unpublished document of VPSS.

(11 villages, which have been covered in the survey, are shown in bold letters).

Women's Section (Mahila Vibhag) is organizing various economic, social, educational programmes for the upliftment of tribal women in Valod, Vyara, Songadh, Mandavi, Mahua and Bardoli talukas from Surat district. Under this programme, VPSS's Mahila Section conducts various awareness programmes, educational and health awareness programmes, Self-Help Groups, training to women for Panchayat, knowledge of milk co-operatives, legal provisions, youth development, educational tours etc. It also celebrates International Women's Day. The very important part of these programmes is to give training to tribal women in the respective areas and to make them empowered. Today, women involved in these programmes have become aware of their rights. They raise their voice against injustice and hence their self-confidence and leadership qualities have increased.

Objectives of the Women's Section: (VPSS)

1. Active participation of women in village programmes.
2. Providing education to the women and helping them to become self-sufficient.
3. To make them aware of their rights and giving them equal status.
4. To make them aware of the environmental problems.
5. To make them aware of the family's health.
6. To make them understand their role in the Panchayati Raj, and the importance of Panchayati Raj.
7. To set-up their own organization and encourage their leadership qualities.

Today, numbers of small Mahila Mandals are emerging from the women's section of VPSS in Valod. These same Mahila Mandals are then transformed into Self-Help Groups. The Mahila Mandals get benefits from the women's section. Today, because of Mahila Mandals and Self-Help Groups, women are gaining more confidence and their status has also improved. Due to the activities of Self-Help Groups, their economic status has improved. Today, tribal women are seen doing bank transactions and maintaining their accounts on their own. Several Self-Help Groups have emerged because of the help given by Anganwadi workers. Even the women from small villages are getting developed because of micro-finance facilities. This matches with the dream of Gandhiji. One educated woman educates her whole family, several women are contributing in the developmental activities of their whole village.

Lijjat Papad Grihaudyog

Lijjat means an institution that is taking care of honour and self-respect of women. This institution was started on 15th March, 1959 to make the women self-sufficient. Two persons influenced the shaping of institution, they are respected, Acharya Vinoba Bhave and Shri Chaganbappa Karamshi Parekh. Lijjat was founded on the principle of Sarvodaya and it was started by Shri P. D. Dattani. In order to get different kinds of reputation and recognition Lijjat Papad was renamed as Shri Mahila Griha Udyog Lijjat Papad. In 1966 institution was registered and Pune (1968), Wadala and Valod branches were also started. Today every woman working in the institution is owner of the institution and has the right to understand the functioning of the institution.

Vedchhi Ashram, Vedchhi

Vedchhi is the name of a village in the Valod Mahal of Surat district. It is also known for the Swaraj Ashram, which was working under the guidance of Shri Jugatram Dave. Shri Jugatram Dave had observed the condition of Adivasis during the course of his work and had decided that, if educational work was to be done in Surat district, it had to be done keeping the Adivasis in the centre. The Adivasi children were to be given training in Khadi work, and to be trained into the discipline of Ashram life which was based on self-reliance and self-restraint. With these ends in view the educational work began at Vedchhi.

Vedchhi Ashram: Today

Swaraj Ashram Vedcchi was established by late Shri Jugatram Dave in 1930 and its influence was spread all-over the South Gujarat, especially Surat district. This process is named as 'Vedchhi No Vadlo' (Banyan Tree of Vedchhi). Swaraj Ashram, Vedchhi is an educational institution. It has Balwadi, secondary and higher secondary (10+2) school, residential school and primary teachers' training school (after 12th standard). Shri Narayan Desai was ex-President of Swaraj Ashram, Vedchhi. At present, Shri Bhikubhai Vyas is the President and Shri Madhubhai Chaudhari is Secretary and is looking after day-to-day affairs of the Trust as a Trustee and Secretary.

Sampurna Kranti Vidyalaya and Gandhi Vidyapeeth, Vedchhi

Dr. Sanghamitra Gadekar (Dr. Uma Desai, Daughter of Mr. Narayan Desai) stays at Sampurna Kranti Vidyalaya, Vedcchi. It is situated 1.5 kilometres away from Valod. (Vedchhi is 3 kilometres away from Valod). There is one more institution—Gandhi Vidyapeeth, Vedchhi, which was also started by Shri Jugatram Dave. This institution has all graduation courses. Late Shri Jhinabhai Darji, another eminent leader and follower of late Shri Jugatram Dave, also, had great respect for Mr. Narayan Desai. He wanted Mr. Narayan Desai to stay permanently in Vedchhi. Late Shri Jhinabhai requested him and they started Sampurna Kranti Vidyalaya, near Gandhi Vidyapeeth. The concept of Sampurna Kranti Vidyalaya is based on Late Shri Jayprakash Narayan's thought of total revolution. Dr. Sanghamitra Gadekar also decided to stay with her father. She is also a follower of Gandhiji. At present, she is involved in two prime activities—(i) Clothing—Natural tie and dye. She supports to Kutch artisans, who were victimized in Kutch earthquake, (ii) Anti-Nuclear activities, with her husband Dr. Surendra Gadekar. She is also actively involved in various activities of Sampurna Kranti Vidyalaya, Gandhi Kathas and publications related activities of Narayanbhai.

Important Features and Occupational Structure of the Tribal Communities

Over 60 to 65 per cent of the population in India still resides in rural areas. Some factors have contributed to changes in tribal communities during the last few decades. Most tribals are illiterate, even among the small percentage of literate tribals the level of education attained by them is very low. The picture of literacy and levels of education attained by tribal women is very dismal. It is very interesting to get some idea about the important features of the tribal people in Valod taluka, specifically, and their culture and kinship. It is also interesting to see what changes have been brought in the status of women in the particular community today.

1. **Chaudharis or Chaudhras**: The people of this community are found mainly in Surat district. They are also found in Bharuch and Valsad districts. They are concentrated in Mandvi, Vyara, Valod, Bardoli and Mangrol talukas of Surat district and Valia taluka of Bharuch district. In terms of

population, they rank second among the tribals in Surat district. Chaudharis are generally good agriculturists and some of them work as agricultural tenants. However, because of small landholdings, poor quality of land and some other factors, farming had become uneconomic for many Chaudharis and hence some of them had taken up other occupations such as carpentry, tailoring and shop-keeping on a smaller scale. As compared to other tribal groups, Chaudharis are a little more advanced educationally as well as culturally. Chaudharis have fair complexion and they have clean habits. They are very much conscious about the importance of education and are concerned about giving education to their children and introducing reforms generally through their caste Panchayats in their traditional customs. They follow many Hindu ways of life and practices. Their women participate in social ritual and religious activities and contribute to the family income. Today, many Chaudhari women in Valod taluka of Surat district are educated and along with agricultural activities they work in Panchayats, they keep animals for dairy product and actively work in Self-Help Groups.

2. **Halpatis or Dublas:** The tribal group of Dublas includes Takvias, Halis or Halpatis in the past, they used to work as helpers to Hindus who owned big land. They worked as bonded labourers known as Halis. Some of them were treated as domestic servants for the whole life. Dubla, working as Halis and their families, were asked to work as forced labourers in order to repay loans borrowed from their landlords. In 1948, the settlement between landlords and the Halis took place with the intervention of the then Home Minister, Shri Morarji Desai and the then Labour Minister, Shri Gulzarilal Nanda. The Hali system was abolished by an agreement which came into force on June 17, 1948. After this agreement, the condition of Halpatis has slowly began to change. Dublas or Halpatis are second largest group of tribals in Gujarat. They are located mainly in Surat and Valsad districts, but they are also found in a sizeable number in Bharuch district. They reside in villages situated on plains. They live in houses built of a variety of materials. Most of them live in Kachcha houses having mud and straw walls

and roof thatched with straw, leaves or country tiles. Very few Halpatis own land, most of them are agricultural labourers. Some of them work as domestic servants also. Being in close contact with non-tribals, mostly the Hindus, there is a considerable influence of the Hindu culture on their language, dress and customs but they have their own dialect. With the formal abolition of Hali system and a considerable influence of Gandhian ideology, a slow but growing trend towards obtaining education and job oriented training especially among the young boys and girls is growing. The Halpati were mobilized under the Halpati movement to remove the bonded labour system. Though they are basically agricultural labourers, in some instances they receive loans from banks for dairy farming. Today their women are members of Self-Help Groups and they are engaged in dairy production and papad making in Valod taluka (Surat district) even with low literacy level.

3. **Dhodias:** Dhodias are mostly concentrated in Valsad and Surat districts. Their number is the largest in Valsad district. In Surat district, their concentration is in Mahua taluka with Dhodia language as their mother tongue. Dhodhias live on the plains, their main occupation is farming and they are good agriculturists. In Surat district, more than 50 per cent of them cultivate their own land and others are tenants. In addition, they are also engaged in fishing. Compared to other tribes, the percentage of agricultural labourers among Dhodias male-female are very low. Dhodias are educationally the most advanced group amongst tribals in Gujarat as they are found in various other occupations. Some are working as clerks either for forest contractors or in different shops. Many are in teaching profession in schools and even some are peons in the different government offices. Quite a number of Dhodias women are primary school teachers. They play important role in Panchayat as well. Changes in the economic system brought considerable changes in their life in Valod.
4. **Gamit:** This group of tribals is composed of Gamit or Gamta or Gavit including Maveli, Padvi, Valvi tribes. The Gamit are migrated from their original home in Goa to Maharashtra and Gujarat. They are mainly concentrated in Surat district. A small percentage of Gamits is also found in Bharuch and

Vadodara districts. Gamits are mainly agriculturists. In the past, many Gamits, who held small piece of land, lost it due to indebtedness. Some of them regained their land after land reforms. They have small piece of land, yield is also small because the land is infertile and method is obsolete. They are progressive but not as good as Choudhari and Dhodia. Today many women are members of Self-Help Group in Valod. Mostly they are found in Kosambia and Bhimpor. Though literacy level of women is very low, they send their sons and daughters to school.

5. **Kuknas:** Koknas including Koknis, Kuknas are concentrated in Valsad and Surat districts. Koknas are relatively backward. Generally, they work in labour force. Most of them are agriculturists and remaining (25 per cent) are agriculture labourers. Some are collectors of forest products and some are forest labourers. Though they are agriculturists, they do not reap enough grain from the harvest. They live on a subsistence level of economy. Many a times they consume wild fruits, bitter roots, plants from the forests. The women participate in social, ritual and economic activities along with the men. They also work as daily wage or agricultural labourers and contribute towards the family income. Some of the women are working in the Lijjat Papad Unit and/or keep animals for dairy purpose.
6. **Kotwalia:** Historically, this community does not have any productive asset. This primitive landless community is found in the south parts of Gujarat, i.e. Surat. They are also found in Bharuch, Narmada, Surat, Navsari, Valsad and Dangs. Seventy per cent of Kotwalia community people reside in Surat. In Surat, they are basically located in Umarpada, Mandvi, Bardoli, Valod, Vyara, Songadh, Mahua, Nizar and Ucchal talukas. In Gujarat, the Kotwalia are also known as Vitolia. According to a story prevalent among them, a bamboo worker from the community made a coat of bamboo strips, which he presented to an officer, who in turn named Kotwalia. They are nomadic in nature and wander about in bamboo forests. They are distributed in the plains and hills of districts in Gujarat and Maharashtra. Separate population figures for the Kotwalia are not available, as they are grouped with the Vitolia and Barodia.

Basketry (Boorudkam) is the traditional as well as present day primary occupation of the Kotwalia. Today, the community is facing problem in accessing the raw material due to depletion of forest reserve and prohibition on cutting bamboo. With the changes in the lifestyle of people and introduction of new products, the demand of traditional items has decreased. In Valod taluka this community was located in Ambach village and the literary rate is very very low. Since 1982-83, the government has started providing foodgrains to some primitive communities including Kotwalia, so that they can send their children to schools. Today, men and women from Kotwalia community have started keeping livestock for milk production and earn money in the village Ambach (Valod). Women are members of Self-Help Groups but dairy activities are done collectively by men and women.

Culture and Kinship

1. **Chodhras (Chaudharis):** The Choudhras are divided into endogamous divisions which are sub-divided into smaller exogamous divisions called Kuls. There are not totemistic in origin. Generally, marriages do not take place between the members so long as a formal relationship can be traced between them. They may marry among the same Kul, but not within six or seven degrees of relationship. They have come from the Northern Zone where the general rule is that a person should not marry in his paternal family and should avoid marriages with the children of his mother's sisters, with the children of his father's sisters and with the children of his father's female cousins, this rule follows the traditions from Northern India and they speak Gujarati at home. They are non-vegetarian and their staple food is wheat, rice, and millet (nagli).
2. **Dublas (Halpati):** The Dubla society is based on endogamous sub-divisions which do not intermarry. Marriages are prohibited when a relationship can be traced between the contracting parties. Marriage with a mother's sister's daughter, father's sister's daughter and maternal uncle's daughter is not allowed. The concept of a Gotra or Kul, which is responsible for the avoidance of local marriages

among some Hindus, is not observed rigidly by the Dublas. This supports the theory that the Dublas form a group with foreign origin and with certain concepts which are not accepted by Rajputs or other Hindus. The Dubla are non-vegetarian and rice is their staple cereal. They believe in supernatural powers. The socio-economic movement advocating Santan Dharam among them has inspired vegetarianism, and the abolition of the bride price. [*The People of India*, Singh, K.G. (1998)]

3. **Dhodias:** The Dhodia kinship terminology is a mixed one, based on the structural adaptations of north Indian and Dravidian elements. The Dhodias are at present matrilineal, mostly patrilocal and do not allow cross-cousin marriage of any kind. The kinship organisation of the Dhodias rests on the patrilineal exogamous clans which govern all their marriage rules. Some of the clan names show the survival of totemism among this tribe. For example, Bhurvlia (named after field sparrow), Bagadia (named after Vaghia-named after tiger), Untbedia (named after camel), Belad-Khaya (named after cat), Pipal codia (named after Pipal), Vadorgoria (named after Vad), Kodana (named after Kode grain) and Darvav (named after Darvai-named after Darva grass). The main rule of marriage is that a man has to marry a woman from a different class than his paternal clan. Within this rule are contained the roots of the system of cross-cousin marriages, but at present there is a prejudice against such marriages. Cross-cousin marriage of the first degree is prohibited, but cross-cousins removed in the second or third degree can marry. Some of the terms are common for the blood-relatives and the relatives by marriage. They indicate existence of cross-cousin marriages in the past. The kinship terms also show exchange of brides between two families. In-law group relations are preferred, the rules of avoidance and joking relationships persist, some of the terms being common for the blood-relations, while other terms indicate existence of cross-cousin marriages in the past. The kinship terms also show exchange of brides between two families: rules of avoidances exist, in-law groups relations are preferred. The Dhodia are non-vegetarian who eat rice, wheat and jowar as their staple cereals. They have established a registered

association, the Samastha Dhodia Samaj, which works for the welfare of the community. [*The People of India*, Singh, K.G. (1998)].

4. **Gamits:** The Gamit kinship terminology is classificatory. Same terms are used for blood relations and relations by marriage. The kinship system is based on system of cross-cousin marriage. The rules of avoidance and joking relationship prevail. In-law groups are preferred relations. The terms are also defined on the basis of age and equivalence of siblings. The kinship system is patrilineal, patriarchal and patrilocal and descent is traced through a male. They are non-vegetarian and their staple food is also rice and jowar.
5. **Kukanas:** The kinship system of Kukanas is of a classificatory type. It appears that, Kukana social custom has obviously had its influence on their terminology. Thus, the same kinship term Mama is used for a mother's brother, mother's sister's husband and father's sister's husband. In the case of a cross-cousin system of marriage, which is rare, these relations are combined in one and the same person. Different terms are often used for the same class of relatives according to their age. The cross-cousin marriage is permitted in one generation only and a strict code of avoidance is not observed. There are rules regarding the terms of reference. The mode of greeting and salutation is regulated by kinship. The kinship is patrilineal and patrilocal and descent is traced through the male. They are non-vegetarian and rice is their staple cereal. Their average household size is only five [*The People of India, Singh*, K.G. (1998)].
6. **Kotwalias:** Kotwalia speak Kotwalia language among themselves. They eat fish, meat and their staple cereals are Nagli and rice. The Kotwalia are divided into clans (kul). Marriage with one's mother's brother's daughter or father's sister's daughter is common. They follow monogamy as the form of marriage and the pride price is paid in cash. The pattern of residence after marriage is patrilocal and both extended and nuclear families are common among them. Parental property is inherited by the sons in equal share and the eldest son succeeds father's authority. They have community council to exercise social control. They believe in Kali, Ganesh, Shiva, Krishna and also Pirs. The Kotwalia

women participate in social and religious activities and also play an important economic role by contributing to their family income and they have a positive attitude towards family planning.

Today tribal women in Valod are doing progress in all spheres of life. The status of women has improved a lot. They are aware of their rights and they send their children to school, they have formed their own Self-Help Groups. They also take part in social as well as in political activities. Role of Vedchhi Pradesh Seva Samiti and Lijjat Papad Grihaudyog is very important in bringing the changes in the status of tribals and particularly tribal women in Valod.

References

Dalal, S. (2006). *Introductory Booklet* (48th edition), published by Parichay Trust, Mumbai.

Desai, I.P. (2000). *The Vedchhi Movement: Centre for Social Studies*, Surat reprinted from *History of Rural Development in Modern India*, Vol. 2.

Patel, T. (1984). *Development of Education Among Tribal Women, Scheduled Tribes in Gujarat*, Mittal Publications, Delhi.

Singh, K.G. (1998). "People of India", Vol. 4, Indian Communities A-G, *Anthropological Survey of India*, Oxford University Press.

Zilla Panchayat Surat: *Statistical Outline of Surat District* (Guj.), Published by Surat District Office, 2004-05.

www.vanabandhukalyanyojana.gujarat.gov.in

http//www.censusindia.gov.in

http//www.gujaratiindia.com

office of the registrar general, India

censusindia.gov.in

6

Use of Computer for Non-Formal Education: A Programme on Wise Buying

Neerja Jaiswal and *Ami Shah*

The need to globalize "education" in today's world cannot be overlooked or ignored. Appropriate modern technologies have assisted the educational institutions to meet their goal of globalizing formal and non-formal education at macro level. This is possible only if meaningful efforts are initiated at micro-level, to literate masses and create awareness to improve upon their quality of life in specific, benefiting their families in general.

In a vastly populated country like India, the apathy of the Indian consumer is reflected in the fact that for a population of one billion, there are just over 400 consumer organizations in the country (Sethi, 1994). The solution, therefore, lie in concerted action by consumers as a group, in which consumer education plays a vital role. The urgent necessity for consumer education in India is because of sharp diversity in attitudes, awareness and spending habits of Indian consumers in both urban and rural areas. The consumer does not get the best value for his money, because he lacks accurate information about the use, implications and benefits of the products, is illiterate and ignorant about his consumer rights and responsibilities.

Today the consumer is very much confused as what to buy? When to buy? How to buy? and How to make the best use of what he buys in order to get the optimum value of his money? In view of the above practical difficulties, an effort has been made in the present study to satisfy all the queries of the "confused" consumer by way of developing an educational programme on "Wise buying", selected on the basis of feedback received by the consumer organizations of Mumbai metropolitan city. The findings of the study will undoubtedly be useful for the selected homemakers of the present study, in specific but at large also be quite useful for consumers in general to develop and gain awareness and comprehension about "Wise buying" and become more informed, cognizant and skilful. At the same time, for the governmental, non-governmental consumer institutions, academicians, extension workers, social workers and students, it will prove to be a ready programme for disseminating consumer education on "wise buying" more effectively, efficiently and conveniently to the desired rural as well as urban consumers. Simultaneously, the findings of the present study will also enrich the database.

An exhaustive review of literature indicated that there are researches on consumer attitudes, values, satisfaction, behaviour, awareness, knowledge, responsibilities, brands and advertisements, but there is hardly any research found on the development of the consumer educational programme, which motivated the investigators to undertake the present study.

Statement of the Problem

To develop and assess the effectiveness of the consumer education programme on "wise buying" for the homemakers of Mumbai metropolitan city.

Objectives of the Study

1. To develop an educational programme based on the feedback given by the consumer organizations of Mumbai metropolitan city.
2. To assess the impact of consumer education programme developed for the study on selected group.

Limitation of the Study

The study was limited to assess the impact in terms of comprehension of the selected respondents soon after the administration of educational programme on "Wise buying".

Methodology

The present descriptive as well as experimental study was conducted at Mumbai metropolitan city, Maharashtra. The unit of enquiry constitutes the head of nine consumer organizations and 108 home-makers as members of Nagher Nari Niketan Mahila Mandal of Dombivali area of Mumbai. Pre-validated and pre-tested interview schedule (in English language), questionnaires and educational programme (in Gujarati language) as tools were utilized to collect the data of the study. Interview technique was utilized to get the feedback from the consumer organizations on the suggested topic and media most aptly required in the present time to impart consumer education. Questionnaire method was used to collect information from the selected respondents about their background characteristics, their exposure to varied sources and their awareness pattern on the selected topic of the educational programme. The educational programme included 26 computer slides covering four informal stories in multicoloured pictorial form, followed by the live commentary on the "wise buying principles" highlighting the good and bad purchase behaviour of the two females. It also included informal lecture on "wise buying".

Data was collected on the scheduled date of the annual Mahila Mandal meeting. The respondents were given the questionnaire to fill in. An informal lecture on "wise buying principles" was delivered immediately after collecting the awareness scale from them. After a break, the educational programme on "wise buying" through slides on computer was administered to all the respondents. Respondent's queries on the related topics were satisfied by the investigators. Viewing the practical difficulty in gathering the whole mass of respondents and in procuring other infrastructural facilities, the post awareness scale was administered immediately after the administration of the educational programme on "wise buying". The responses collected were further subjected to categorization, tabulation and analyzed by employing descriptive and relational statistics.

Major Findings of the Study

Keeping in view the objective of the present investigation, the feedback by the consumer organizations on the most needed educational topic was invited by the researchers. The consumer organizations were asked to suggest the most urgently needed topics for the homemakers in the present times based on their experiences, which can cater to the immediate needs of the masses. The responses of the consumer organizations were collected on an open ended questionnaire which was further subjected to broad categories.

Multiple Responses

The highlights of Table 6.1 revealed that majority of the consumer organizations (89%) suggested "Wise Buying" as the most needed topic of the present time for an educational programme. This could be reasoned that due to introduction and launching of new products each day in the market the confused consumer need to be oriented with the intelligent and right choices to get worth of their money by utilizing their minimum resources to achieve maximum psychic income. Two-third of the consumer organizations (66.66%) suggested "Consumer Rights and Responsibilities". This being the second most preferred topic by the consumer organizations also seems to be important in today's global marketing infrastructure as it makes the consumer more strong and intelligent giving a sound base for strong consumer movement.

The third topic in the priority list as suggested by the consumer organizations was "Redressal Methods". Suggestions for the topics like "After Sale Service", "Social Responsibilities", "Avoid Plastics", "Apathy and Fight", and "Food Adulteration", were also given by

Table 6.1: Distribution of Consumer Organizations on the Basis of Topics Suggested

N = 9

Sr. No.	*Suggested Topics*	*F*	*%*
1.	Consumer rights and responsibilities	6	66.66
2.	After sale services	2	22.22
3.	Social responsibilities	2	22.22
4.	Avoid plastics	1	11.11
5.	Wise buying	8	88.88
6.	Apathy and fight	1	11.11
7.	Misleading advertisement	3	33.33
8.	Pollution	1	11.11
9.	Food adulteration	3	33.33
10.	Redressal method	4	44.44
11.	Co-operative management	1	11.11

couple of consumer organizations. But not a single consumer organization undertook topics like "Buy-manship Principles" or "The Art of Wise Buying", which made the investigators interested to take the same for developing an educational programme.

Selection of the Media, Teaching Method and Aid to be Used for an Educational Programme

The consumer organizations were asked to suggest the most suitable and appropriate media and teaching method for the educational programme of the present times. Their responses as highlighted in Table 6.2 revealed very clearly that majority of them preferred computer as a media. This could be reasoned that since it is the latest technology, it is going to be popular very soon. Computer being the need of all the institutions for other work too, is much easier to use. Moreover, it is convenient to run and store the programme too. Since computer was being used by all the consumer organizations, they would have had anticipated it as the most convenient and appropriate media of the present time.

Majority of the consumer organizations (77.77%) suggested "electronic slides" as a teaching aid to be used for imparting education. These being more compact, less expensive and easy to handle was thus considered as an appropriate media for the development of an education programme. Lecture as teaching method was also suggested by majority (77.77%) of organizations. As it has been the most traditional but widely used method of teaching, it has a potential for achieving certain objectives. It is a most exploratory method and a wide range of topics can be covered easily describing the concept in a vernacular language.

Multiple Responses

Hence, the investigators thought of combining all the three suggestions given by the consumer organizations, i.e. computer and slides as media, and lecture as teaching method and slide as teaching aid for the development of educational programme. The investigators decided to develop the educational programme with the help of slides which can be projected through computers, and use of lecture method to make the topic of the subject more clear and understandable to the homemakers.

Table 6.2: Distribution of Consumer Organization on the Basis of Media and Teaching Methods Suggested

N = 9

Sr. No.	*Suggested Media and Teaching Methods*	*F*	*%*
A	*Media*		
1.	Cable TV	1	11.11
2.	Computer	8	88.88
3.	Films	3	33.33
4.	Radio	1	11.11
5.	Booklets	2	22.22
6.	Slides	7	77.77
7.	Posters	4	44.44
B	*Teaching Methods*		
1.	Lectures	7	77.77
2.	Discussions	5	55.55
3.	Street plays	3	33.33
4.	Seminars	2	22.22

Background Information: It dealt with the demographic and socio-economic characteristics of the respondents and their families like age, education, and occupation of the respondents and their total monthly family income.

Age of the Respondents: To find out the distribution of the respondents in various age groups, information on their age was analyzed. The analysis revealed that a comparatively greater percentage (42.6%) of the respondents were middle aged (26-35 years of age). The analysis also showed that their age ranged from 19 years to 47 years with the mean age of 31.9 years (Fig. 6.1).

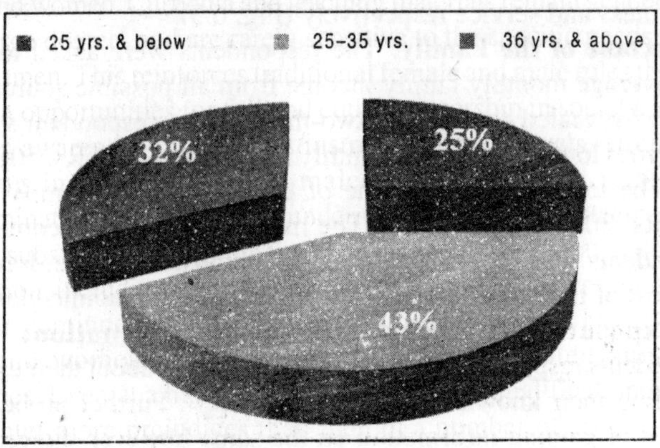

Fig. 6.1: Age of the Respondents.

Education of the Respondents: In order to study the effect of education on the awareness of the respondents regarding wise-buying, the data related to education of the respondents was analyzed. The data showed that slightly less than two-third (61.1%) of the respondents were educated from 8th to 10th standard concluding that the respondents' educational level was moderate (Fig. 6.2).

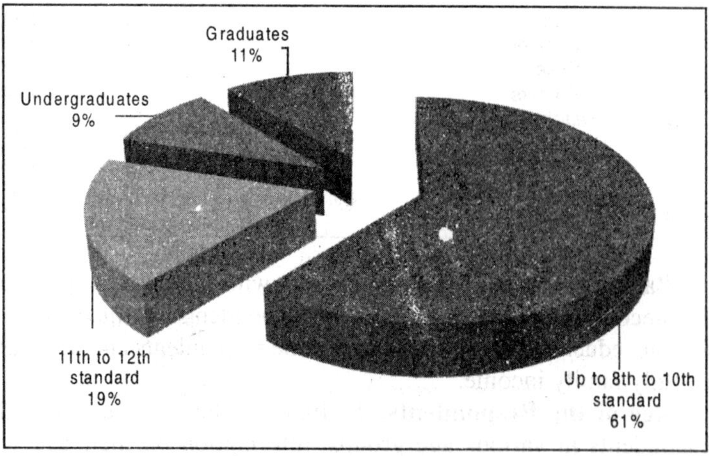

Fig. 6.2: Education of the Respondents.

Nature of Occupation: The analysis on nature of occupation depicted that majority of the respondents were housewives. A very small proportion (2.8%) and (1.9%) of the respondents were involved in business and service respectively (Fig. 6.3).

Income of the Family: The respondents were asked to report their average monthly family income from all possible sources. The findings revealed that nearly two-third of the respondent's family were from lower class with monthly income less than Rs. 5000 (Fig. 6.4). The total monthly income of the respondents' family ranged from Rs. 3000 to Rs. 15,000. The mean total family income of the respondents was Rs. 6127.7. Hence, conclusion can be drawn that the most of the respondents belonged to lower economic class.

Exposure to Different Sources of Information: All the respondents responded affirmatively when asked about their exposure regarding their knowledge on "wise-buying". Further probe on the sources of gaining information on the same however showed lot of diversity (Fig. 6.5). The most popular source of information was radio

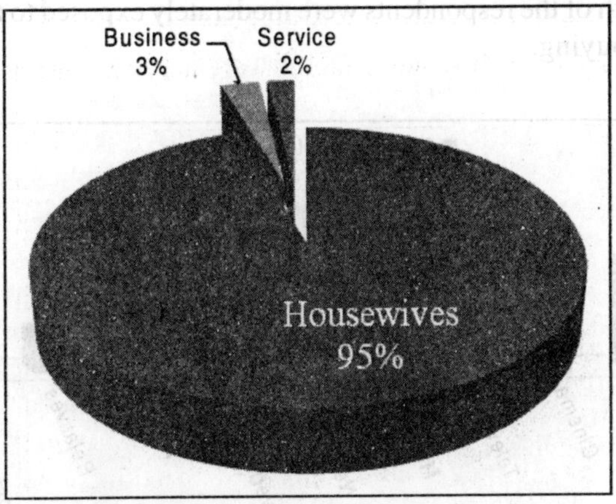

Fig. 6.3: Nature of Occupation.

among most of the respondents (61%). For slightly less than one-half of the respondents, television was the main source to gain information on wise buying, succeeded by social worker (39.8%) and friends (32.40%). A negligible group of respondents (2.7%) utilized cinema as a source of information.

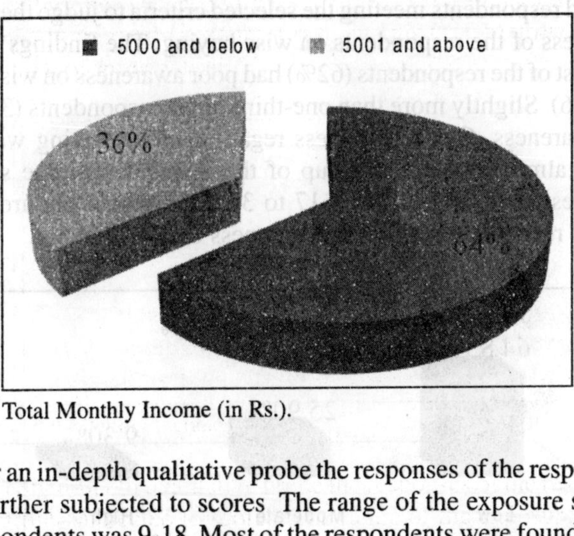

Fig. 6.4: Total Monthly Income (in Rs.).

For an in-depth qualitative probe the responses of the respondents were further subjected to scores The range of the exposure score of the respondents was 9-18. Most of the respondents were found having low exposure (64.8%). Only nearly one-tenth of the respondents were exposed to a high extent on the sources of information on wise buying.

One-fourth of the respondents were moderately exposed to the sources on wise-buying.

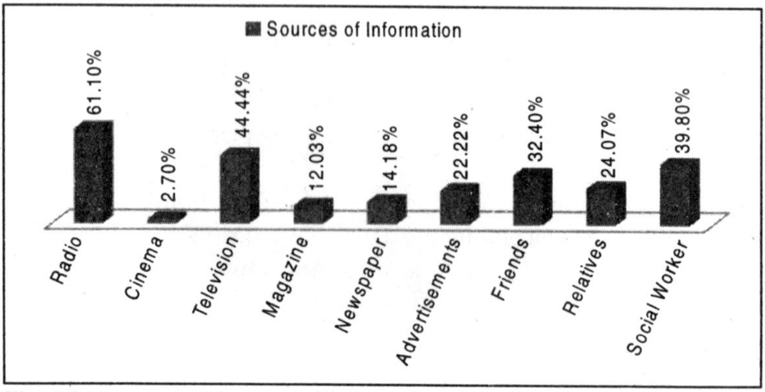

Fig. 6.5: Exposure to Sourcecs of Information of the Respondents.

Awareness regarding wise-buying before the administration of an educational programme: As one of the objectives of the study was to assess the impact of consumer educational programme developed for the study, awareness scale was administered on the selected respondents meeting the selected criteria to judge the existing awareness of the respondents on wise buying. The findings revealed that most of the respondents (62%) had poor awareness on wise buying (Fig. 6.6). Slightly more than one-third of the respondents (36%) had fair awareness. Good awareness regarding wise buying was found among almost negligible group of the respondents. The scores of awareness scale ranged from 17 to 34. The overall picture elicited that the respondents had poor awareness on wise buying.

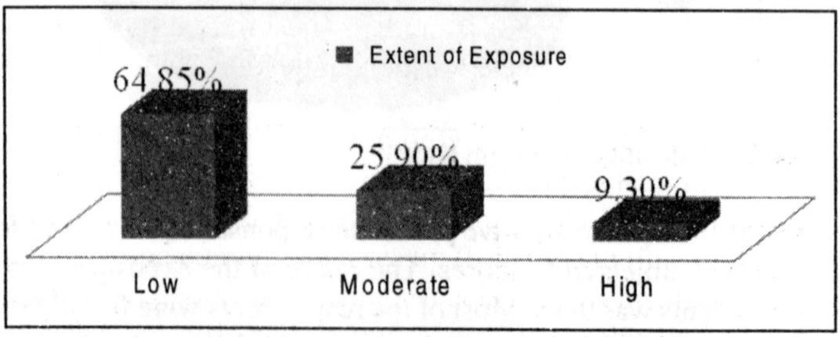

Fig. 6.6: Extent of Exposure to Different Sources of Information.

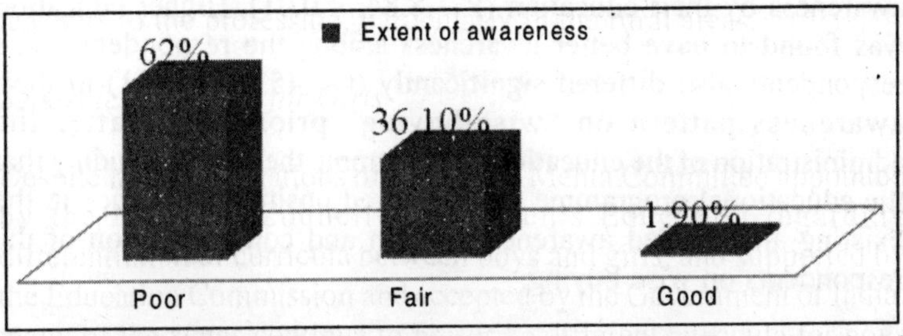

Fig. 6.7: Extent of Awareness Prior to the administration of educational programme on "wise buying".

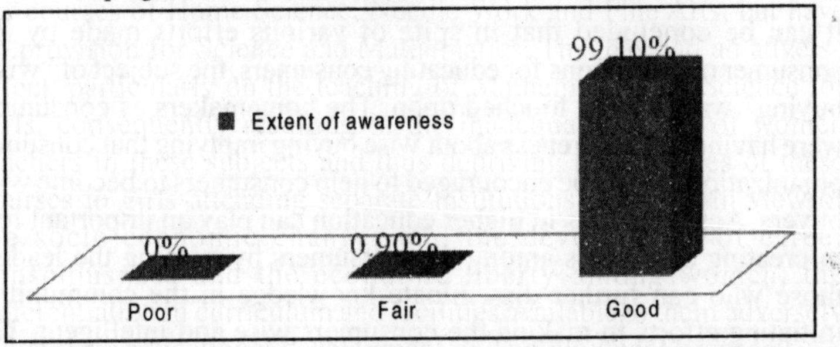

Fig. 6.8: Extent of Awareness after the administration of educational programme on "wise buying".

Awareness regarding wise buying after the administration of an educational programme: Comparisons on the extent of awareness of the respondents on wise buying prior to and after the administration of the educational programme showed a remarkable rise in the awareness pattern and comprehension of almost all the respondents. None of them had poor awareness pattern on wise buying (Fig. 6.7). Thus, it can be concluded that the administration of the developed educational programme on wise buying marked a major positive change and improvement in the awareness pattern and comprehension of the selected respondents.

Findings

The results of the hypothesis testing pointed that the respondents did not differ in their existing awareness pattern on wise buying by their age, income and their extent of exposure to varied sources of information on wise buying. However, the statistical findings depicted that the respondents differed significantly in their existing pattern of awareness by their education (F = 8.84, < 0.01). Higher education was found to have better awareness among the respondents. The respondents also differed significantly (t = 45.81, < 0.01) in their awareness pattern on "wise-buying" prior to and after the administration of the educational programme thereby concluding that the educational programme made marked positive difference in the existing and created awareness pattern and comprehension of the respondents on wise buying.

Conclusion

It can be concluded that in spite of various efforts made by the consumer organizations for educating consumers, the subject of "wise-buying" was still not touched upon. The homemakers as consumers were having low awareness about wise buying implying that consumer organization should be encouraged to help consumers to become wise buyers. Academicians in higher education can play an important role in creating awareness among the consumers by training the leaders those who can further disseminate knowledge in the communities initiating efforts in making the consumers wise and intelligent. The findings of the study will undoubtedly be useful for the selected homemakers of the present study, in specific but at large also be quite useful for consumers in general to develop and gain awareness and comprehension about "Wise-buying" and become more informed, cognizant and skilful consumers. At the same time, for the governmental, non-governmental consumer institutions, academicians, extension workers, social workers and students, it will prove to be a ready to use aid (tool) for disseminating consumer education more effectively, efficiently and conveniently to the desired rural as well as urban consumers. Simultaneously, the findings of the present study will also enrich the database.

References

Eleanora, A. (1987). *Consumers Education Knowledge, Attitude and Experiences of Selected Groups in Trinidad and Tobago*, Dissertation Abstract International. 42 (II).

Engel, J.F. and Black Well, R.D. (1990). *Consumer Behaviour*. 4th Edition. Holt Sanders. International E.

Gujarathi, R. (1995). "Consumer Protection by Mumbai Grahak Panchaya", *The Indian Journal of Commerce*.

Kapoor, S. (2002). *Understanding Buying Behaviour of Indian Families*. New Century Publications, New Delhi.

Kumar, N. (1999). *Consumer Protection in India*, Himalaya Publishing House, Mumbai.

London, D.L. and Bittla, A.J. (1990). *Consumer Behaviour*. McGraw Hill Series on Marketing, New York.

Mehta, D.S. (2002). *Handbook of Consumer Rights: Problems and Remedies*. Allied Publishing Ltd., New Delhi.

Mehta, P.S. and Sharma, A. (1989). *The Consumer, What to do? How to do?*, Published by Consumer Unity and Trust Society, Jaipur.

Seetharam, P. and Sethi, M. (2001). *Consumerism: Strategies and Tactics*. C.B.S. Publishers, New Delhi.

Sethi, M. and Seetharam, P. (1994). *Consumerism: A Growing Concept*, Phoenix Publishing House, New Delhi.

7

Health Education: A Success Story from Gujarat

Rameshwari Pandya and *Shridha Chokshi*

A healthy life always leads to happiness and prosperity. Health is not just about illness and treatment but is a state of well-being, free from physical, mental and social stress. It is recognized from the time immemorial that good health is a prerequisite to human productivity and development process; it is essential for economic and technological development. Healthy community is the infrastructure upon which an economically viable society is built. The progress of a society greatly depends on the quality of its people. Unhealthy people can hardly be expected to make any valid contribution towards development of the society. Health is man's greatest possession, where the solid foundation for his happiness lies. Health is not only to lead a happy life but also necessary for all the productive activities in society undoubtedly, health and development are interrelated. Health of all is important but health of adolescents is a very important issue.

Adolescence is a "Transition Period" between childhood to adulthood with specific physiological, psychological, social, emotional and cognitive changes which places additional requirements for nutrition. It is a phase during which many life patterns are learnt and established. The term youth encompasses ages 10 to 24 years, while the term adolescents as defined by WHO (1986) includes persons aged 10 to 19 years. Discouragingly, between the 1991 and 2001 census found that in the 0-14 age group there were an estimated 7.8 million fewer girls than boys and the 0-19 age group the number of "missing" girls was 13-34 million (CEDPA, 2011). Adolescent girls have their own development needs, which are peculiar to them and need to be addressed separately. In many countries, the concept of a transitional period between childhood and adulthood is relatively new. During this period, individual develops physical and psychological maturity and economic independence and acquire their adult identity.

As adolescence is a time of rapid growth and maturation in human development, this change leads to an increased need for micronutrients such as iron, calcium, iodine, Vitamin A, C etc. Nutritional requirements are significantly higher during this stage to meet the physiological demands of rapid growth and development. Many causative factors leading to serious diseases in adulthood have their roots in adolescence like micronutrient deficiencies, undernutrition, poor eating and exercise habits (WHO, 2009).

Mumbai, December 16, 2009: The National Family Health Survey (NFHS)-3, has reported that a large percentage of women and children in India are anemic. The report shows an alarming 5 per cent increase as compared to the earlier NFHS-2 (1998-99). In case of women, the anemia rate was found to be as high as 55 per cent, with 39 per cent mildly affected, 15 per cent moderately and 2 per cent severely affected. The most severely affected among women were those uneducated, poor or belonging to the Scheduled Tribes. The survey also found 25 per cent of men between 20-40 years to be anemic. Anemia is a major health concern among, especially women in India. Essentially referring to deficiency of iron, the cause for the prevalence of this condition is mainly the Indian diet that is predominantly cereal-based. It leads to an increase in a particular group of compounds, known as 'sulfate', which lowers the body's iron absorption capacity. Anemia, where the hemoglobin count is very low, increases the risk of infectious diseases, cognitive and motor development and mortality in children. In pregnant women, it leads to premature delivery and low birth weight. Anemia resulting from stress causes fatigue and decreased energy levels in working women. A balanced diet and consumption of iron rich foods such as fruits like kiwi, guavas and oranges, vegetables like spinach, capsicum, tomato and sprouts, soya and poultry products can help fight anemia. Iron supplements are available but should be used only under medical guidance. A major threat could be the escalating food prices that may make it difficult for women to ensure basic nutrition, thereby increasing the incidence of anemia in the country. In order to maintain a normal iron balance an adult women need absorbable iron ranges from 1.2 to 1.4 mg per ranges from 1.2 to 1.4 mg per day. However, despite such low requirements, iron deficiency anemia continues to be a major nutritional problem. These observations raise question as to:

Why is iron deficiency so widely prevalent in spite of near adequate dietary intake? In order to find answer to this question various factors have been shown to be associated with the prevalence of iron deficiency anemia namely, inadequate dietary intake of iron, low bioavailability of iron, increased physiological needs in certain stages in the lifecycle, blood losses, infections and infestations (Gillespie, 1998).

Types of Anemia

Iron Deficiency Anemia

Iron deficiency causes insufficient hemoglobin production which, in turn, causes anemia and anemia symptoms. The need for iron increases with rapid growth and expansion of blood volume and muscle mass. As boys gain lean body mass at a faster rate than girls, they require more iron than girls. The onset of menstruation imposes additional needs for girls. Adolescents should be encouraged to consume iron rich foods along with Vitamin C source to compensate for menstrual blood loss. Iron deficiency is the most prevalent micronutrient deficiency among adolescents. Iron deficiency and anemia are associated with impaired cognitive functioning, lower school achievement and most likely physical work capacity.

Sickle Cell Anemia

Sickle cell anemia, or sickle cell disease, is one of the hereditary causes of anemia. Most often seen in people of African descent, sickle cell anemia is characterized by the production of rigid, sickle-shaped red blood cells. These abnormal sickle cells break down faster than normal red blood cells, resulting in a chronic shortage of red blood cells and anemia symptoms. Sickle cell anemia is a form of hemolytic anemia, which describes types of anemia caused by the rapid destruction of red blood cells.

Pernicious Anemia

Certain types of anemia are referred to as megaloblastic, or vitamin deficiency anemia. Pernicious anemia is caused by an inability of the intestines to absorb sufficient amounts of Vitamin B12, which is required in the production of red blood cells. Pernicious anemia symptoms include vision problems, memory loss, difficulty in walking and numb hands and feet, as well as the more common anemia symptoms. Vitamin B12 injections and oral tablets are the standard pernicious anemia treatment.

Folic Acid Deficiency Anemia

Folic acid deficiency anemia, like pernicious anemia, is a megaloblastic anemia. Folic acid is essential for healthy blood and a healthy nervous system. A folic acid deficiency during pregnancy can cause birth defects. Folic acid supplements form the basis of folic acid anemia treatment. Anemia treatment also includes eating a diet high in folic acid, including such foods as: Beans and legumes, Citrus fruits juices, Wheat bran, Dark green leafy vegetables, Pork and Poultry.

Thalassemia

Thalassemia is one of the genetically inherited types of anemia. Thalassemia occurs when the body's genes, which are responsible for proper hemoglobin production, become damaged or mutated. Like sickle cell anemia, thalassemia is one of the hemolytic anemia types. Many possible gene variations can cause thalassemia, and the disease has both mild and severe varieties. The disease tends to be present at birth and its symptoms include: Dark coloured urine, Deformed facial bones, Fatigue, Swollen abdomen caused by enlarged spleen and liver weakness. Mild types of thalassemia may be treated with regular blood transfusions. Severe cases require multiple blood transfusions, iron chelation therapy to remove excess iron from the blood and bone marrow transplants.

Causes of Anemia

Broadly, causes of anemia may be classified as impaired Red Blood Cell (RBC) production, increased RBC destruction (hemolytic anemias), blood loss and fluid overload (hypervolemia). Several of these may interplay to eventually cause anemia. Indeed, the most common cause of anemia is blood loss, but this usually doesn't cause any lasting symptoms unless a relatively impaired RBC production develops, in turn most commonly by iron deficiency.

Treatments of Anemia

Treatments for anemia depend on severity and cause. Iron deficiency from nutritional causes is rare in non-menstruating adults (men and post-menopausal women). The diagnosis of iron deficiency mandates a search for potential sources of loss such as gastrointestinal bleeding from ulcers or colon cancer. Mild to moderate iron deficiency anemia is treated by oral iron supplementation with ferrous sulfate, ferrous fumarate, or ferrous gluconate. When taking iron supplements, it is very common to experience stomach upset and/or darkening of the feces. The stomach upset can be alleviated by taking the iron with food; however, this decreases the amount of iron absorbed. Vitamin C aids in the body's ability to absorb iron, so taking oral iron supplements with orange juice is of benefit. Vitamin supplements given orally (folic acid) or subcutaneously (Vitamin B-12) will replace specific deficiencies. In anemia of chronic disease, anemia associated with chemotherapy, or anemia associated with renal disease, some clinician prescribe recombinant erythropoietin, epoetin alfa, to stimulate red cell production.

In severe cases of anemia, or with ongoing blood loss, a blood transfusion may be necessary.

Strategies to Combat Anemia

1. Food Based approach
2. Control of infection
3. Supplementation with medicinal iron
4. Nutrition health education
5. Dietary intake

Broad Objectives

To spread awareness regarding Anemia, its signs, symptoms, causes and measures to prevent Anemia amongst the young girls and women of Sevasi Village, Vadodara.

Justification of the Study

Lack of knowledge and awareness of health and nutrition aspects, limited education, and deprived of adequate health care and good nutrition rural adolescents are a disadvantaged lot, as a result facing a slow pace of growth. They lag behind nutritionally and have higher morbidity rates especially due to various infections. Gujarat is one of India's most industrialized states in western India. Human development report states that "Objective of human development is not only simply to produce more goods and services for material enrichment, but to increase the capabilities of all people to lead full, healthy and satisfying lives". When the status of rural women of Gujarat is observed they continue to live in a state of deprivation. Ignorance accompanied by poor health status due to lack of exposure and knowledge as a result the majority of the women in Gujarat are anemic. We all will agree that women can play a significant role in contributing social, economical, cultural and political development of the country. In the family, women are the one who takes care of everyone. She is like a pilot in the family through which development can be attained. It is because when women get all the development inputs, it spontaneously gets passed on to the other members in the family. When needs exists one develops an urge to solve it but at the same time if there is lack of information regarding their needs it may lead to failure. So information about various health aspects is necessary for fulfilment of their health needs. As far as urban women are concerned many a times they get exposure and information from different sources which are available in urban areas. Whereas rural women are concerned they are still lagging behind in this field. It may be due to lack of information, awareness, and knowledge about various health practices because of which the rural women are left behind. So this study was conducted to increase the health awareness level of the women of Sevasi village of Vadodara.

Justification of the Study in the Department of Extension and Communication

The main objective of the Department of Extension and Communication is to help and promote national development and also to create awareness among students about different development issues. The department is preparing students since 1954 in formal teaching at school and college level and in imparting non-formal education to rural and urban communities. The department is constantly working with women as target group for many years in order to improve their condition. The department offers number of courses related to women at undergraduate and postgraduate levels. Moreover, researches are also conducted at postgraduate level and Ph.D. level which focuses on women issues.

The present study to raise the awareness on Anemia among the rural girls and women of Sevasi village will also contribute in terms of training related work in rural areas with women as the target group. It will also help the researchers and project workers of the department to carry on such studies in future keeping women's health in centre and contribute towards development of the society at large.

Justification of the Sample

Information is a key towards attainment of required things against need. As a result, realization as well as detailed information about one's need is very essential for accomplishment of desire or things which is lacking. As far as men are concerned in relation to women they have a better knowledge regarding information about their needs because men spend most of their time of the day outside the four walls of the house. Thus, men witness and become aware about the various changes around the world. Woman seldom gets chance to speak up her thoughts or ideas. In this way also, women lose the chance to discuss and update their information and different needs in their life. Thus, tend to remain in the same place with age-old information existing within the four walls of the house and deprived of being acquaint with the latest information. Also women are considered as followers rather than decision makers, therefore, many times information is not passed to them. Due to this, development and success remain out of sight. Information need is comparatively less amongst rural women in comparison to urban women. Thus, development of a country cannot be attained by keeping one section of the society behind inside the darker walls. Each and every section of the society should come forward to attain all-round development of the country. Moreover, Sathya Walter Rammohan (1992) states that "to awaken, once she is on the move, the family moves and then the nation". As a result, there is a great need for this study in order to give information related to anemia to the rural women of Sevasi village. Moreover, it will add a scope to Government and Non-Governmental Organizations, development workers and policy makers to design message keeping in mind the health requirements of rural women of Sevasi village. This will also help in easy assessment of information towards fulfilment of their needs which spontaneously tends to make their life more healthy and Anemia free.

Review of Literature

Adolescence is defined as a transient stage, between childhood and adulthood and a formative period during which many life patterns are learned and established, it is time of dramatic change in the life of every person. The relatively uniform growth of childhood is suddenly altered by an increase in the velocity of growth. This sudden spurt is also associated with hormonal, cognitive and emotional changes. All of these changes create special needs (Bonnie, 2002). The state of World Population 2003 report examines the challenges and risks faced by this generation that impact directly on their physical, emotional and mental well-being. The report stresses that increase in the knowledge, opportunities, choices and participation of young people will enable them to lead healthy and productive lives so that they can contribute fully to their communities and to a more stable and prosperous world. Now 6.3 billion, world population will grow to an estimated 8.9 billion people by 2050. Nearly all of the 2.6 billion increases will be in the developing countries of Africa, Asia and Latin America. There are 225 million adolescents comprising nearly one-fifth (22%) of the total population in India. Of the total adolescent population, 12 per cent belong to 10-14 age groups and nearly 10 per cent are in the 15-19 age groups. Female adolescents comprise almost 47 per cent and male adolescent 53 per cent of the total population (Census, 2001).

Growth and Development in Young Women

Young women are considered nutritionally vulnerable for several reasons. It is the phase for greater demand for nutrients because of the dramatic increase in the physical growth and development. Second, is the change of lifestyle and food habits of young women that affect both nutrient intake and the body needs (Bonnie, 2002). Variations in the onset puberty pose problems in determining nutritional status and nutritional requirements in adolescents (the well-being of tribal young women (Cordiero *et al.*, 2005-06). The main nutritional problems of adolescents are micronutrient deficiencies, iron deficiency Anemia in particular, and depending on the context, undernutrition and co-morbidity. Like in any other age group, poor nutrition is usually the result of dietary inadequacies, often combined with unhealthy lifestyle or infections, which further compromise nutritional status. Dietary inadequacies are more of a threat among adolescent because of erratic eating pattern and specific psycho-social factors underlying these, combined with the particularly high nutritional requirements for rapid growth. Studies conducted in different countries in the South-East Asia Region, reveal that nutritional status affects almost all growth parameters and final adult body size resulting in thinness and stunting. However, nutritional status of both boys and young women improves with age, showing that the effect of malnutrition is more pronounced at the time of peak growth. A large percentage of adolescents in South-East Asia Region suffer from nutritional deficiencies. Dietary intake with respect to adequate availability of food in terms of quantity and quality (Particularly, the mean caloric intake), ability to digest, absorb and Nutritional Anemia is one of India's major public health problems. India is one of the countries in the world that had highest prevalence of Anemia (WHO, 2007).

A latest study conducted in 16 districts of India among pregnant and young women showed that 84.9 per cent of pregnant women (n = 6,923) were Anemic (Hemoglobin < 110 g/L); 13.1 per cent had severe Anemia (Hemoglobin < 70 g/L), and 60.1 per cent had moderate Anemia. Among young women (n = 4,337) from 16 districts, the overall prevalence of Anemia (Defined as Hemoglobin < 120 g/L) was 90.1 per cent with 7.1 per cent having severe Anemia (Hemoglobin < 70 g/L) (Toteja, G.S. *et al.*, 2006).

The prevalence of Anemia was found to be 35.1 per cent among adolescent female in the urban area of Nagpur. A significant association of Anemia was found with socio-economic status and literacy status of parents. Mean height and weight of subjects with Anemia was significantly less than subjects without Anemia (Sanjeev M. Chaudhry *et al.*, 2008).

S. Goel carried out a study in Shimla on young boys and girls, which revealed that out of 840 subjects, Anemia diagnosed clinically was 13.1 per cent, mean age of adolescent girls was 15.1 years and the prevalence of Anemia in both males and females was highest in

10-13 years age group and it decreased with increase in age (S. Goel *et al.*, 2007). Overall prevalence of Anemia in Chandigarh calculated as per WHO guidelines was significantly higher among the girls (23.9%) as compared to boys. Anemia was observed more in rural (25.4%) as compared to urban (14.2%) adolescents. Iron stores estimated by serum feritin in 183 subjects were deficient in 81.7 per cent and 41.6 per cent of the adolescent girls and boys, respectively (Sabita Basu *et al.*, 2005).

A cross-sectional study in adolescent girls of rural Wardha showed that the prevalence of Anemia was 59.8 per cent and in unvaried analysis, low socio-economic status, low iron intake, vegetarian diet, history of worm infestation and history of excessive menstrual bleeding showed significant association with anemia. However, age, education, socio-economic status, BMI and status of menarche had no significant association (S. Kaur *et al.*, 2006). Anemia was present in 51 per cent of young girls as compared to 38.5 per cent in older girls in rural north India (Anand *et al.*, 1999).

A study carried out by the National Nutrition Monitoring Bureau in rural areas of India on Hemoglobin status indicated that over-all prevalence of Anemia among the rural adolescent girls was about 70 per cent (NNMB, 2003). The same result was found in one of the districts of Gujarat state, India where the prevalence was more than 70 per cent in adolescent girls (Kotecha *et al.*, 2000). Around 60 per cent of the adolescent girls in rural areas in Gujarat have been found to be anemic. NFHS-II reported Anemia prevalence of 46 per cent among women (age 15-49 years) in Gujarat, 74.7 per cent of the schoolgirls of Vadodara district studying from 8th to 12th standard were Anemic (Karkar, P.D., Kotecha, P.V., Nov. 2004).

Methodology

To make any programme effective and successful, the very first step is the drawing up of a plan of action, without a proper plan you cannot conduct programme successfully. So for conducting any programme planning is the most crucial and important stage as the rest of the programme depends on planning. A systematic planning can provide guideline to implement the programme successfully. The plan of action includes the list of activities to be conducted for a particular period of time. Plan of action answers the major questions like Where, When, Who, and How the activities will be implemented. Planning is required to carry out the work successfully and smoothly. To start the project, systematic planning of steps was done as follows:

Identifying the Place for Conducting the Project

To begin with the selection of the place, the project worker visited Sevasi village of Vadodara district. The project worker had a formal meeting with the sarpanch of the village for the permission to conduct the project. The sarpanch was very kind and wanted the young women of the village to get awareness about Anemia as he himself wasn't aware about it and found it a very important and serious topic to be taught. Thus, sarpanch showed keen interest and gave the permission to the project worker to conduct the Anemia project in Sevasi village, Vadodara.

Selecting the Target Group for the Project

A survey was conducted by the project worker in the village. The project worker made door to door home visits where she noted down the names of the women who were interested in attending the programme. The women who took keen interest in this project were from Patel fadiyu thus women of Patel fadiyu were finalized for the Anemia project.

Deciding the Venue and Time for the Project

A meeting was held with the target group in which all the interested women gathered at one common place, to decide the time and place for the Anemia project. As the success of the programme depends on the satisfaction of the beneficiaries, the project worker wanted the beneficiaries to decide the time and venue according to their convenience and personal choice and satisfaction. The women discussed internally and were comfortable with the afternoon 1:00 to 3:00 p.m. time as they get free from all their household work at 1:00 p.m. The place for conducting the programme was decided by the beneficiaries, it was the village Dairy which is situated at the entrance of Patel fadiyu, Sevasi village. It was a good place in terms of air ventilation, had a black-board and was also near to their residences.

Selecting the Content

The selection of the content for the activities on Anemia project was finalized after referring different books and magazines on Anemia available in the library. The project worker also referred Anemia related journals and booklets. The main content which was covered for the Anemia awareness was:

- What is Anemia?
- Importance of knowing about Anemia
- Causes of Anemia
- Symptoms of Anemia
- Types of Anemia
- Home and External remedies for curing Anemia
- Reasons for development of Anemia in young women.

Preparing the Teaching Aids

Teaching aids helps the learner to understand the concept easily, as the women were not highly qualified it was necessary to develop good teaching aids to support every point so that they could easily understand. Several experiments have shown that teaching aids can be helpful in making any programme successful. Project worker prepared teaching aids for using it according to the need of the particular activity under the health education.

Charts and Posters	:	Illustrative talk on what is Anemia? Illustrative talk on Importance of knowing Anemia.
Slide Show	:	Causes of Anemia, Symptoms of Anemia, Types of Anemia.
Rod Puppets	:	Home remedies to cure Anemia.
Samples	:	External Remedies to cure Anemia.

Schedule of Activities

To impart knowledge regarding Anemia and to create awareness about different activities were planned along with dates.

Illustrative Talk

Illustrated talks may be done individually or in a team, usually with two persons in the same age division. A team illustrated talk might be desirable when more than two hands are needed to illustrate the idea, friends or first-time presenters can work together talking and illustrating are difficult to do at the same time. Team illustrated talks require teamwork and cooperation, they also require practice to do well. Some topics are natural for a team illustrated talk, whereas other topics are difficult for a team to do well. If that's the case, it may be better to present the illustrated talk as an individual. When giving a team illustrated talk, it is important that both individuals talk frequently in a balanced approach. One person should not talk and illustrate for long periods while the other person stands and listens. There should be a smooth flow of talking and illustrating between team members. The presentation should seem natural, like a conversation between two friends. If questions are asked at the end, presenters should alternate in answering them. The other presenter may add more information at the conclusion of the answer. The most successful presentations reflect your own ideas and are expressed in your own words. The following items should be considered when planning and presenting an illustrative talk:

1. Select a subject or topic.
2. Gather information.
3. Choose a title.
4. Develop an outline.
5. Choose appropriate visuals.
6. Practice of delivery.

Details of activities conducted under the illustrative talks were as follows:

Orientation

Objective: To orient the beneficiaries regarding the project.

Activity: The project worker oriented the beneficiaries about health and different activities that are to be conducted under Anemia Awareness project.

Illustrative Talk: What is Anemia?

Objective: To create awareness regarding Anemia amongst the young girls and women of Sevasi village.

Activity: First the project worker explained about what is Anemia to the young girls and women. The project worker used charts and posters for the better explanation.

Gain: Through this activity the young girls and women got awareness about Anemia.

Illustrative Talk: Reasons of Developing Anemia in Young Girls and Women

Objective: To create awareness regarding the reasons of Anemia which is found in majority of the women.

Activity: The project worker explained the various reasons and facts about women health and menstrual changes which many a times develops Anemia in women.

Gain: Women became aware about body facts and changes that may cause Anemia in them.

Slide Show Presentation

A slide show is a display of a series of chosen pictures, which is done for artistic or instructional purposes. Slide shows are conducted by a presenter using an apparatus, such as a carousel slide projector, an overhead projector or in more recent years, a computer running presentation software. The term "slide" originates from the use of slides which have been around for many years. Slides originally were projected on a screen, for example in a theatre by magic lanterns, a practice that later evolved into moving picture shows. Even after the advent of motion pictures, slides continued to be employed for a time between showings of the films, especially to teach young adults so that it does not get boring for them and it can grab attention for a longer period of time. Trying to teach rural women can be quite a challenge, whether it is inside of the classroom or in their homes. With the help of modern technology, there are many things that you can do to improve the way that you teach. A great way to help rural adults learn with interest is to use slides as a teaching aid. If you have a computer; it is very easy to create a slide show that you can use on any other computer. There are many ways to present information, but slideshows are among the most valuable. They are an easy-to-use multimedia platform that will make any presentation more organized and effective.

Advantage of Slideshow Presentation

- **Slideshows are easy to create:** There are many presentations and slideshow software packages in the market and they are all generally easy to use, even for beginners. With just a few simple steps, you can make interesting and attractive slideshows that everyone in the audience will love.
- **Slideshows are attention-getters:** A well-designed slideshow is great for gaining the attention of your audience, which makes it a good choice for sales presentations, training sessions and other times when audience participation is important. When designing a slideshow you can incorporate transition animation, clip art, sound and other unexpected elements to get the attention of the audience.
- **Slideshows can go anywhere:** One of the biggest advantages of a slideshow is that it can be put on a flash drive and taken anywhere. Most modern projectors have slots for thumb drives, and it is easier to insert that drive into a projector and press "Start" than it is to carry a laptop and projector or portfolio of visual aids.

Objective: To make the project more interesting for the young girls and women, the project worker prepared a slideshow presentation on Anemia.

Activity: The slideshow presentation included three topics which were:

- Causes of Anemia
- Symptoms of Anemia
- Types of Anemia

The slides were made attractive and interesting by the project worker by adding music and various background pictures which could hold the attention of the young girls and women for longer period of time and also created a curiosity to see something new.

Gain: Through this activity the young girls and women got to see the slide presentation which was new to them and also they learnt about the signs, symptoms, causes and various types of Anemia.

Rod Puppet Show

Rod puppet is a puppet that is constructed around a central rod secured to the head. A large glove covers the rod and is attached to the neck of the puppet. A rod puppet is controlled by the puppeteer moving the metal rods attached to the hands of the puppet and by turning the central rod secured to the head. Puppetry has played an important role in disseminating knowledge in most parts of the world. Puppetry imbibes elements of all art forms such as literature, painting, sculpture, music, dance, drama, and enables learners to develop their creative abilities. Puppetry has been used traditionally in India as a popular and an inexpensive medium to transmit knowledge about Indian myths and legends. Since Puppetry is a dynamic art form that appeals to all age groups, this medium of communication has been selected to serve as an aid for imparting non-formal education in rural areas.

Objective: To make learning fun and innovative for the young girls and women puppet show was presented.

Activity: The project worker had prepared a rod puppet show which was conducted to show various food groups.

Gain: Through this activity the beneficiaries knew about different food groups and products to be consumed to prevent Anemia.

Educational Game

Educational games are games that have been specifically designed to teach people about a certain subject, expand concepts, reinforce development, understand an historical event or culture, or assist them in learning a skill as they play. They include board, card, and video games. Parents and preschool teachers use games to teach colours, numbers, names, and shapes; the process is drill and practice. Games engage us, capturing our attention. We willingly spend time on task. Although students in high school and college continue to play games, games rarely continue as part of the educational system past the early grades. Educational game utilizes both the efficiency of the learner—physical and mental. It is a fun with learning game where learners do not feel boredom, they learn and play at the same time. Sometimes, only theory gets difficult to understand for the learners, thus through educational game a fun and healthy environment can be created which helps the teacher to know that whether the learners have developed understanding or not.

Objective: To encourage the young girls and women to take active part in educational game and to learn with fun.

Activity: The educational game prepared by the project worker was "The Balloon game". There were balloons filled with air and chit containing questions were inserted inside the balloons. The project worker made the participants sit in a round arrangement so that the balloon could be passed easily. Then after music was played by the project worker and meanwhile the balloon was passed amongst them and when the music stopped the project worker asked the women who had the balloon in her hand to burst the balloon so that the question inside it came out. Then the project worker asked the question written on the chit and if the answer given by the women was correct she was rated accordingly and at the end the women who answered the maximum questions correctly was declared winner and was rewarded with a small gift by the project worker.

Gain: Through this activity the young girls and women gained self-confidence in giving answers and the project worker also came to know about their understanding level.

Evaluation of the Project

Success of any programme depends on the effective participation of the beneficiaries. Evaluation of any programme is equally important component to measure the success of the programme. Evaluation goes beyond measurement or answering the questions is the obtained measurement, desirable or undesirable. Evaluation is useful in revealing the stage at which the target group has arrived at a learning process. Thus, a written test was conducted by the project worker in which questions were prepared and were given to the women and they had to answer in a time limit of one hour. Then the project worker evaluated the answer sheets to know whether they have understood or not and marks were given accordingly. The woman scoring the highest marks was applauded. Through this activity, the women's gained self-confidence in writing their answers in a proper manner on their own.

Table 7.1: Percentage Distribution of the young Girls and Women according to their age

N = 15

S. No.	Age in years	Frequency (f)	Percentage (%)
1.	20-25	5	33.33
2.	26-30	7	46.66
3.	31-35	2	13.33
4.	36-40	1	6.66

Table 7.1 indicates that (46.66%) of the young girls and women were aged between 26-30 years while (33.33%) were between 20-25 years of age and rest (13.33%) were between 31-35 years and only (6.66%) were between 36-40 years respectively.

Table 7.2: Percentage Distribution of young Girls and Women according to the number of Family Members in the House

N = 15

S. No.	Number of family members (f)	Percentage (%)
1.	2-4	13.33
2.	5-6	20
3.	6-7	26.66
4.	More than 7	40

Table 7.2 indicates that majority (40%) of the young girls and women had more than 7 members in the family, (26.66%) of the young girls and women had six or seven members in the family, (20%) had five or six members in the family and rest (13.33%) had two to four members in the family.

Table 7.3: Percentage Distribution of the young Girls and Women according to their Occupation

N = 15

S. No.	Occupation	Frequency (f)	Percentage (%)
1.	Service	2	13.33
2.	Housewife	13	86.66

Table 7.3 indicates that majority (86.66%) of the young girls and women were housewife and only (13.33%) of the women were working outside the house.

Table 7.4: Percentage Distribution of the young Girls and Women according to their Education Level

N = 15

S. No.	*Education*	*Frequency (f)*	*Percentage (%)*
1.	Primary	4	26.66
2.	Secondary	3	20
3.	Higher Secondary	5	33.33
4.	Graduate	3	20

Table 7.4 indicates that (33.33%) of young girls and women were educated till higher secondary, while (26.66%) of young girls and women had only primary level education, (20%) of young girls and women were educated till secondary education and rest (20%) were educated till graduation.

Table 7.5: Percentage Distribution of the young Girls and Women according to their attendance in the Project Activities

N = 15

S. No.	*Attendance*	*Yes (%)*	*No (%)*
1.	Attended all the activities	60%	40%

Table 7.5 indicates that (60%) of the young girls and women attended all the activities while (40%) of the young girls and women did not attend all the project activities.

Table 7.6: Percentage Distribution of the young Girls and Women according to the reasons for not attending all the Project Activities

N = 6

S. No.	*Reasons for not attending all the activities*	*Yes (%)*
1.	Had gone out of station	16.66
2.	Were not well	66.66
3.	Other reasons	16.66

Table 7.6 indicates that (66.66%) of the young girls and women who could not attend all the activities as they were not well as they had fallen sick, further (16.66%) of young girls and women could not attend all the activities because they had gone out of station and rest (16.66%) of young women had other reasons for not attending all the activities.

Table 7.7: Percentage Distribution of the young Girls and Women according to their interest in the activities of the Project

N = 15

S. No.	*Activities*	*Interesting (%)*	*Less Interesting (%)*	*Not Interesting (%)*
1.	Orientation	100	—	—
2.	Illustrative talk	66.66	26	6.66
3.	Slideshow	100		
4.	Puppet Show	100		
5.	Educational Game	86.66	—	13.33

Table 7.7 indicates that all the young girls and women of Sevasi village (100%) found the orientation, slideshow presentation and puppet show to be interesting. Very high majority of the young girls and women found the educational game as an interesting activity, while (66.66%) of the young girls and women found the illustrative talk to be interesting. Whereas only (26%) of the young girls and women found the illustrative talk less interesting while (6.66%) of the young girls and women found the illustrative talk not interesting at all and (13.33%) of the young girls and women reported that the educational game was not interesting.

Table 7.8: Percentage Distribution of young Girls and Women according to the appropriateness of the Timing of the Project

N = 15

S. No.	*Time*	*Yes (%)*	*No (%)*
1.	Appropriate timing of the project activities	100%	—

Table 7.8 indicates that all the young girls and women (100%) reported that the timing of the project activities was appropriate for them.

Table 7.9: Percentage Distribution of young Girls and Women according to the information given through the Project

N = 15

S. No.	*Information*	*Yes (%)*	*No (%)*
1.	Information	86.66	13.66

Table 7.9 indicates that majority (86.66%) of the young girls and women easily understood the information given to them whereas (13.66%) of the young girls and women could not understand the given information.

Table 7.10: Percentage Distribution of the young Girls and Women according to the language of the Project worker

N = 15

S. No.	Language	Yes (%)	No (%)
1.	Language of project worker	100%	—

Table 7.10 indicates that all the young girls and women of Sevasi village understood the language of the project worker.

Table 7.11: Percentage Distribution of the young Girls and Women in relation to taking part in such future Anemia Control Programme

N = 15

S. No.	Future Actions	Yes (%)	No (%)
1.	Ready to take part in Anemia control programme	100	
2.	Every village should be aware about Anemia	100	
3.	Should Anemia control programme continue in future	100	
4.	Satisfied with the project	80	20
5.	Satisfied with the project worker	93.33	6.66

Table 7.11 indicates that all the young girls and women of Sevasi village (100%) reported that they would take part in Anemia control programme and also agreed that all the villagers should be aware about Anemia and Anemia control programme and it should be continued in future also. Whereas (80%) of the young girls and women were satisfied with the programme and rest (20%) were not satisfied with the programme. High majority (93.33%) of the young girls and women who were satisfied with the project worker and rest (6.66%) were not satisfied with the project worker.

Table 7.12: Percentage Distribution of young Girls and Women according to their Opinion about Anemia Control Programme

N = 15

S. No.	Opinion	Good	Average	Poor
1.	Opinion about Anemia Control Programme	93.66	6.66	—

Table 7.12 indicates that very high majority (93.66%) of the beneficiaries found the Anemia control programme to be good and only few (6.66%) of the young girls and women found the programme to be average, and whereas none of them reported it to be of poor quality.

Conclusion and Suggestions

The Department of Extension and Communication is working for community development since past several years and has been focusing on health aspects of children and women. Students have developed communication skills and techniques of making suitable teaching aids, posters, films, booklets, flip-charts, and puppets etc., which are very effective means of communication and are also an excellent tool for passing developmental messages among the weaker sections of the society. The objective of this project was to spread awareness among the young girls and women of Sevasi village regarding Anemia and its causes and what are the cheap remedies that can be followed. As we strongly believe that the development of any nation depends upon the status of health in the country thus there was a need of such contextually relevant activity which would help in shaping the human development.

Problems Faced during the Project

1. The project worker faced problems in reaching Sevasi village as it was situated very far from the city.
2. Sometimes, the beneficiaries did not reach on time so the project worker had to go to their houses to call them for the sessions.

Recommendations

1. A similar type of project can be taken up with the rural school children.
2. A similar type of project can be taken up with the pregnant and lactating mothers of rural areas.
3. A similar type of project can be taken up with the adolescent girls who have recently entered the menstruation cycle.

References

Anand, K.K. and S. and Kapoor, S.K. (1999). "Nutritional Status of Adolescents in Rural North India", *Indian Pediatr*, Aug; 36 (8): 810-5.

Bill, S. (2008). *The Skill of Communicating*, Jaico Publishing House Pvt. Ltd., New Delhi.

Bonnie, A.S. (2002). "Adolescent Growth and Development", *J. Am. Dietetic Association*, March, Supplement; Vol. 102, No. 3.

Budhwarkar, S. (1996). Interventions to Control Iron Deficiency Anemia in Young Women: Effect of Food Based Approach and Intermittent Iron Supplementation on Hemoglobin and Serum Ferritin, Dissertation (M.Sc.), Department of Foods and Nutrition, Faculty of Home Science, The M.S. University, Baroda, Vadodara.

Cyril, B. (1957). *Health Education: A Guide to Principles and Practice*, William Heinemann Ltd., 99 Great Rusell Street, London.

F. Ahmed, M.R. Khan, M. Islam, I. Kabir and G. J. Fuchs (2000). "Anaemia and Iron Deficiency Among Adolescent School Girls in Peri-Urban Bangladesh", *European Journal of Clinical Nutrition* 54, 678-683.

Goel, S. and Gupta, B.P. (2007). "Low Anemia Prevalence Among Adolescents of An Urban Hilly Community." *Indian Journal of Community Medicine*, Vol. 32, No. 1.

Goswami, T.M. (2007). A study of Anemia During Pregnancy and Its Impact on Maternal and Prenatal Outcome. Dissertation (M. Sc.), Department of Foods and Nutrition, Faculty of Home Science, The M.S. University, Baroda, Vadodara.

Gupta, N. (2005). *Human Values and Education*. Deep and Deep Publication Pvt. Ltd., Delhi.

Hong Soon Myung, Hwang Hye Jin, Kim HyunHee (2004). "A study on Iron Nutritional Status and Anemia of Middle School Girls in Ulsan metropolitan city." *Journal of Community Nutrition*.

Jayatissa, R., Ranbanda R.M. (2006). "Prevalence of Challenging Nutritional Problems Among Adolescents in Sri Lanka", *Foods and Nutr Bull*; Jun; 27(2:153-60).

Jill, S. Halterman, Jeffrey, M. Kaczorowski, C., Andrew A., Peggy A. and Peter G. Szilagyi (2001). "Iron Deficiency and Cognitive Achievement Among School-Aged Children and Adolescents in the United States", *Pediatrics*, Vol. 107, No. 6, June 2001, pp. 1381-1386.

Kurz, K.M. (1996). "Adolescent Nutritional Status in Developing Countries", *Proceedings of the Nutrition Society*, 55:32-33.

Mustaph, P. (1991). Situational Analysis of the Nutritional Anemia Control Programme and Assessment of its Impact on Pregnant and Lactating Women Beneficiaries of ICDS in Urban Slums of Baroda. Dissertation

(M. Sc.), Department of Foods and Nutrition, Faculty of Home Science, The M.S. University Baroda, Vadodara.

Nair, L. (1979). A Study of Existing Food practices of Sonarkui Village Women of Baroda district. Dissertation (M. Sc.), Department of Foods and Nutrition, Faculty of Home Science, The M.S. University, Baroda, Vadodara.

P. Deshmukh, B.S. Garg, N. Garg, N.C. Prajapati and M.S. Bharamb (2006). "Prevalence of Sickle cell Disorders in Rural Wardha", *Indian J. Community Med.* 2006; 31:26-7.

Pandya, R. and Matthu, A. (2000). *A Guide to Action Projects in Home Science Extension*, University Publication Sales Unit, Vadodara.

Reddy, M. and M.S. (2000). *Curriculum Development and Educational Technology*, Sterling Publishers Pvt. Ltd., Delhi.

Senger V. (2000). Effect of Ber (Zizyphus Jujube) Fruit Supplementation on Hemoglobin levels of Anemic Young Women: Implications for a Food Based Approach to Control Anemia. Dissertation (M. Sc.), Department of Foods and Nutrition, Faculty of Home Science, The M.S. University, Baroda, Vadodara.

Sethi, R. (2000). *Effective Communication on Rural Areas*, Infinity Books Publication, Michigan.

Thakkar, J. (1994). An Action Project on Anemia in Pregnant Women—does Vitamin A Supplementation Add to the Effects of IRON and Does Dietary Counselling make an Impact. Dissertation (M. Sc.), Department of Foods and Nutrition, Faculty of Home Science, The M.S. University, Baroda, Vadodara.

UNFPA State of World Population (2005). *The Promise of Equality: Gender Equity*, Reproductive Health and the MDGs.

Verma, Y. (2007). *Education in Human Values for Human Excellence.* Kaniksha Publishers, Distributors, Delhi.

White, S. *The Art of Facilitations Participation, releasing the power of grass roots communication*, Sage Publications Pvt. Ltd., Delhi.

WHO, (2007). Micro Nutrient Deficiencies www.who.int/nutrition/topics/ida/en/

8

Consumer Education

Santosh Tikoo and *Jagdish Gupta*

A consumer is anyone who buys or uses any kind of product for the satisfaction of his material needs. Every person is a consumer as everyone has certain needs and wants that must be fulfilled. The individuals work to earn an income with which to buy economic goods and services. Consumer may not necessarily be a purchaser but every purchaser is a consumer. The consumer is an integral and important part of a mixed economic system. Homemakers are consumers in an economic and marketing system. They create a demand for a variety of materials needed at home such as food products, furniture etc. Resources available in the market are directed towards satisfying human requirements. Purchasing is often a daily routine for homemakers depending mostly on commonsense and experience. However, some basic knowledge of economic principles, guidelines for selection of the products and awareness of consumer rights is both useful and necessary for homemakers. This will help her to play her role more satisfactorily and responsibly.

Consumer Activities

The consumer performs four basic activities as consumer:

Spending

In one's role as consumer or user of income, individual makes decisions to spend part or all of their income. They do so to satisfy their wants by acquiring goods and services. The real or opportunity cost of buying a particular item is to forgo the opportunity of purchasing a different item or keeping the income as savings.

Borrowing

When individuals decide to borrow money, they do so to consume more at the present time. The real or opportunity cost is to consume less later, since some future income must be used to pay back the money borrowed.

Saving

When individuals decide to save, they give up the pleasure of immediate consumption in order to consume more later or to have greater financial security.

Investing

When individuals decide to invest, they sacrifice the present use of income or saving in order to increase further income.

Why Study Consumer Behaviour

Consumer behaviour has two sides. On the one side, is the consumer and on the other, is marketing manager. We are all consumers but the art of consuming is an inexact activity. Some of us may become marketing manager and consumer orientation is essential to marketing strategy. The direct benefit from a clear understanding of consumer behaviour is that it can make us all better and more wise consumer. The improvement can result from—

1. A greater appreciation of the complexities of decisions facing consumers.
2. A better understanding of our own motives and decision processes as consumers.
3. A sounder choice of products, services, brands and stores.

All individuals should be interested in consumer behaviour because at some point almost everyone becomes involved in buying a product or service. As a buyer, an individual makes up one half of the marketing process. In its fundamental form, marketing consists of an interaction between a buyer and seller for the purchase of exchanging something of value for mutual benefits of both parties to the transaction. From the marketing manager's standpoint, knowledge about consumer provides one of the sound basis of consumer wants as well as their location, number, characteristics and expenditure patterns. The basis for all sales appeal comes from information about the consumer and it ignores the consumers which can lead to disaster in a modern economy.

Consumption Process

Table 8.1: The Consumption Process involves three interrelated activities

S. No.	*Terms for those engaged in consumption*	*Consumption process*
1.	Demander	Determines want
2.	Purchaser	Purchases products
3.	User	Consumes products

Demander: is one who has personal or group wants.
Purchaser: is one who is actively engaged in buying.
User: is a person who derives satisfaction or benefit from product sought.

Consumption process may involve any combination of these persons. So consumer refers to several persons, each performing part of the consumption process or one person who engages in all three activities of consumption. Consumer behaviour is a sub-division of human behaviour. It concerns specific types of human behaviour that are market related. Consumer behaviour includes both mental decisions and physical actions that result from consumer decisions. There are two broad types of consumer behaviour variables that directly affect how persons make purchase decisions. These variables are:

1. **Internal to the Individual:** These variables are needs, motives, personality, perception, learning and attitudes of the consumer. The object of consumer behaviour is to make decisions to satisfy the consumer's needs and wants. A need

is defined as any physical or emotional body requirement. A motive is an impulse or feeling that causes one to do something and makes us aware of our needs. Personality is defined as the human characteristics or traits built into a person that make each person different from every other person. Perception is the particular interpretation one gives to objects or ideas observed or otherwise brought to consumer's attention through the senses. Learning means any change in the consumer's thoughts, response or behaviour as a result of practice, experience or inhibition. In a sense it is known today what was unknown before. Attitude is used to mean a broad group of learned predispositions to behave in a certain way. There is a simultaneous interaction between these basic determinants.

2. **External to the Individual:** Consumers do not function in a vacuum; the individual is continually influenced by the environment. There are five broad environmental determinants of consumer behaviour, i.e. family influences, social influences (Work place, neighbourhood), business influence (Contact with person selling), cultural influence (Innate beliefs and sanctions) and economic influence (Constraints placed on the consumer by money).

The Societal Trends that Affect Consumers

Our economy has changed from one that was predominantly agricultural, to an industrial economy. With that change came dramatic changes in consumer values and the ways we interact in the market place. Changes of a similar magnitude will occur as we enter the post- industrial area in which our society shifts from a goods producing to a service economic. The post-industrial society will continue to maintain its agriculture and industrial sectors but the central economic focus will be different and will thereby require further changes in both the values and the behaviours of all its citizens. On the basis of this industrialization consumers can be divided into three types:

1. **Industrial Age Consumers**: These consumers typically reached adulthood between 1920 and 1960. As such they were socialized into seeking stressed ownership of material

possession, private dwellings, and private means of transportation, conveyance and relatively small nuclear families. "More is better" characterized the philosophy of the nation because resources of all kinds were thought to be unlimited. Many individuals still function primarily as industrial age consumers, they think little of the impact of their own consumption on society or the environment and they are oriented towards solving consumer problems by earning more money so that they will be able to spend more.

2. **Transitional Consumers**: Reached adulthood between 1960 and perhaps 1990. Socialized in their early years by parents and teachers holding industrial age consumption values. Transitional consumers made most of their early adulthood consumption decisions in an era characterized by inflation, shortages of materials, pollution problems, energy crisis and unprecedented government regulation of the market place. Transitional consumers find old values in conflict with societal imperatives and may have ambivalent feelings regarding the proper cause of action in consumption decisions. These consumers are torn between the wants stimulated by industrial age marketing mechanisms and the thoughts supportive of societal/environmental concerns.
3. **Post-Industrial Age Consumers**: These reached adulthood sometimes after the year 1990. They are being taught primarily by adults who are transitional consumers. The post-industrial consumer's primary concern will be with efficient and responsible consumption. Post-industrial consumers will realize that saving a marginal money through efficient consumption is superior to earning more money or income and will insist upon buying only those products supportive of the ecosystem in which they live.

Value Orientations of Industrial and Post-Industrial Age Consumers: Although consumers will continue to have serious problems in specific product and service categories. Analysis of these values is a starting point for confronting this most fundamental of all consumer problems:

1. **Consumption Level**: Industrial age consumers yearn to buy the extremes whereas the post-industrial age consumers will

think it best to consume only as much as they need and will purchase for typical rather than extremes situations.

2. **Ownership vs. Usage**: Industrial age consumers want to own as many of culture's artifacts as possible. But a value change on the forefront with leasing, rental and shared facilities becoming increasingly common.
3. **Disposability vs. Recycling**: Industrial age consumers use no returnable containers, disposable diapers, throw away cans and plastics and paper packaging. The post-industrial age consumer on the other hand will regard recycling as normal behaviour and waste creation as abnormal.
4. **Convenience vs. Cost**: Convenience in packaging and purchasing is a cornerstone of an industrial age marketplace. Consumers in the future will still value convenience but they will want to know its cost.
5. **Functional vs. Non-functional Change**: Industrial age consumers wanted things which have remained almost the same for so long. But in post-industrial age consumers will be demanding higher quality and longer product lifecycles with emphasis upon functionalism and durability.

Concern for External Costs: Industrial age consumers had little concern for the social and environmental cost of production, these costs were thought acceptable in the name of industrial growth and employment stability. Post-industrial consumers will be fully aware of the social and environmental costs of production and consumption.

Quantity in Life vs. Quality of Life: Higher gross national product, higher employment and more number of things per capita are accepted indicators of the industrial age consumer's state of well-being. The post-industrial consumer will place great value on stable monetary values, job security and the ability to maintain an acceptable standard of living.

Consumerism: Whereas industrial age consumers hold implementation of their rights as consumers as only a fringe value, post-industrial consumers will see consumerism as a central value and means of maintaining their level of living amid natural pressures to reduce it. Persons living in the post-industrial age will begin to see themselves as citizens who produce economic value part of each day and reduce economic value (through consumption the remainder of the day).

The Process of Buying

We live in a country that has the greatest abundance any people has ever known, and it is up to us, the consumers to make the best use of this abundance. Presumably the whole economic machine is operating just to increase our satisfactions. But developments have come so fast that the world has literally changed under our feet. We have not yet learned to live in this new world. It is advantageous to the consumer that goods and services are numerous, highly developed and better packaged goods and services have grown harder to judge. Virtually, every consumer need has been anticipated by some business. This means that it is profitable to learn more about what is available and about how to pick accurately the best from the many.

Development have Changed the Nature of Buying Process

1. The producer and the consumer of an article are generally so apart that there is little personal contact between them.
2. Productive capacity has run so far ahead of effective demand that there is sharp competition for the purchaser's money.

The opportunities open to the consumer and the problems that come with them are largely an outgrowth of the new kind of world we live in. One can take advantage of some of the opportunities and solve some of the problems by training themselves as a competent individual and by working intelligently and unselfishly as a citizen. Everytime consumers make purchase in the market they are making choices that together add up to a way of living. With each purchase they have opportunities to move their present level of consumption towards what is desired. Many purchases in addition may contribute towards attainment of values sought. For this to be possible, consumer buyers may increase their knowledge by keeping informed about changes in production of things they buy and the potential contribution new products make to the way people can live.

Buying is always a matter of making choices. Choices must be made: (a) between wants and needs, (b) between one product and another of the same kind, (c) between two entirely different kinds of products, and (d) between spending your money now and saving it.

Buying wisely is important to the economic well-being of the individual and the family. Earning money is important but how one spends it can be more important. In order to make wise buying decisions, consumer needs information and knowledge. The following specific buying guides will help one to make wise consumer decisions:

1. What does the product contain and how is it made?
2. Is the product beneficial?
3. How economical is the product?
4. How long will the product last?
5. How does its price compare with the prices of similar products?
6. Does the item carry any seals identifying its quality or any evidence of authoritative scientific tests?
7. What proof is used to back up the statements?
8. Are there any service or maintenance problems?
9. Are any of the advertising statements evasive or misleading?
10. Does the advertisement make you feel confident that if you buy you will be satisfied customers?

How to Complain Successfully?

To speed up complaint, processing and to achieve satisfactory solutions require especially courtesy and knowledge and sometimes courage and patience. Reporting unsatisfactory service and poor merchandise not only helps the consumer but assists the company to identify and correct mistakes. Here are few helpful hints:

1. Read and follow instructions carefully as to using, washing, saving oiling and general care which may eliminate the need for a product return.
2. Obtain a receipt for items left for repair or for a refund later by mail.
3. Return merchandise to the store and department where purchased if at all possible.
4. Assemble receipts, copy of cancelled checks used in payment, hang tags, warranty and care labels before returning everything purchased in original packing if available.
5. Make store returns not at rush hours, closing or lunch times and when you don't get to see the person who could be able to do the most for you, speak to a person higher in authority.

6. Think thoroughly why you are dissatisfied so you can present clearly and mention your reason for complaint or return.
7. Find the proper company name, department involved, address and code number before writing to the company or returning by mail.
8. Save time by writing a legible business like letters, keeping your own carbon copy.
9. Provide brand name, model number, size and colour which will help to identify the problem product.
10. Try to explain specifically what went wrong, send your letter with the package if small and insure it, with certified mail you can obtain a return receipt.
11. Send a second letter if you do not hear from the company. Most firms try to acknowledge customer service correspondence within two to three weeks. If there is not a word from them, refer the matter to the consumer court.

Consumer Power

We have monuments to the Unknown Soldier, statues of martyrs and tables for freedom fighters. But, so far as we know, there is no memorial for the forgotten man and the victim of our society—the poor consumer. And yet modern industrial society was hailed as one in which the consumer is the king, if so, he is a prince without a privy purse and is often indistinguishable from a pauper. Though in a free economy, a consumer is the king, the consumer in India has been neglected over the years. Slogans such as "Consumers sovereignty" are meaningless as in actual reality the consumer is reduced to the status of a prisoner with no hope of early release from the clutches of the exploiting forces.

In concrete terms, consumer exploitation takes place through underweight, adulteration and a number of other substandard deals. In a competitive market, consumers are victimized by certain unfair practices such as inferior workmanship, deceptive hire-purchase arrangements at concealed and exorbitant rates of interest, deceptive advertising and packaging, aggressive salesmanship and monopoly and restricted trade practices. Moreover, consumers are subjected to the sale of hazardous toys, foods, drugs and appliances without due regard for their safety. Consumer is the principal sufferer of inflation, controlled or otherwise. He pays more and earns less in real terms. He is the one to suffer from shortages of essential commodities.

Consumer Exploitation

There cannot be second thought about the fact that a consumer is being exploited to a great extent. In the course of his day long encounter in the marketplace, a consumer gets somehow cheated without his knowledge but cheating with his knowledge for which he is helpless is something miserable and unbearable and this kind of deliberate cheating is going on unchecked.

Consumer exploitation in simple terms means that a consumer is taken for granted—he has no choice of goods, has no voice for selection, he cannot address for redressal. In India, where illiteracy, poverty and ignorance exist, people cannot be expected to put their heads together to fight effectively against exploitation. The consumer is an integral and important part of a mixed economic system. An ideal economy operates solely for the welfare of the consumers and is therefore consumer oriented. It is assumed that the exploitation will occur between consumer and producer and that the consumer controls the nature and extent of production by means of his purchase decisions. It is also assumed that consumer decisions are rational and are made on the basis of full knowledge.

In the earlier days life was very simple and the goods were very few. It was very easy to appraise the consumers of the merits of goods of local markets. But due to expansion in the number and nature of products that are available now and which are generally entering into the daily life of consumers, the shares of the consumers have weakened. Modern business methods attract the consumers through misleading and deceptive practices and false representation. Substandard and spurious products, adulteration of foods and drugs, short weights and measures and misleading advertisements are the areas in which the consumer becomes a victim of the trade and industry.

No manufacturer has ever asked consumers what level of safety the actual users wanted in their product in relation to performance, durable style, convenience and cost. Almost universally, the manufacturer makes these decisions in terms of his interest namely a continuing and increasing profitability. To achieve his objective, the manufacturer overlook vital fact like faulty design, lack of standard to control quality, untested or unsafe ingredients, misuse or abuse of the products and contamination. These factors contribute to the hazardous and unsafe features of a product. If consumer pick up the courage to complain to the manufacturer either the complaint is totally ignored or gets a personal letter with stereo-typed contents. The manufacturer invariably thanks the consumer for being the first to point out the mistake and promises to look into the process of manufacture and the shop floor level. He offers to give a free replacement and perhaps sends a few free samples of his other products. Most consumers tend to believe that unsafe products are by mistake. If an occasional unit of a product proves faulty or unsafe, it may be a mistake. But if most units are hazardous, it is likely that quality and safety have not been designed into the product. The manufacturer has allowed short term cost and performance advantages to outweigh long term safety issues.

Consumers Need Education for Living

Most consumers do not perhaps even know that they are being deceived in a number of ways by the producers, businessmen and traders. The obvious and underlying reason for this is ignorance. But why are they ignorant? Why do they do not know what type of goods and services are good for them? Why they are susceptible to such influences? If living is important thing, why are they not trained in the area of living? Why is there hardly any consumer education programme in a country so devoted to the principles of mass education? Neither family nor school nor government has undertaken genuine education of consumers for living. One significant educational agency is business which through advertisement has undertaken a tremendous campaign to educate consumers. Its main objective is that of profit making rather than that of promoting the welfare of the community. It is assumed that consumers can learn by experience alone and the idea is to promote consumer welfare by attempting to increase individual income.

Prospects for Consumer Education

Consumer education is a valuable thing which helps in making wise choices especially in developing countries where scores of articles come into the market every other day and where standards are found to be rather loose. The possibilities of consumer education virtually are unlimited. On paper one can solve all consumer problems of building up a programme of education. If consumers are really educated, they would know what goods they want, would like to judge quality and price and consequently guide the entire economic system so as to yield maximum consumer welfare. If consumers are educated, much of modern advertising would be ineffective and would be revamped so as to become a helpful guide for wise buyers. Through consumer education individuals become conscious about the world around and of their responsibilities as members of the society. It will make them intelligent, informed and constructive consumers. This will influence their attitudes, beliefs, goals, customs and perceptions. It will bring about co-ordination and equilibrium between people in their different capacities as the government, manufacturers, sellers and consumers. In this age of awareness, to improve one's standard of living, we cannot deny that importance of education is gaining priority, either among the elite or the upper class and middle income groups or even among the weaker sections of our society. Consumer education not only enlightens the illiterate but also the literate ones who are also ignorant of the consumers' movement.

Need for Consumer Resistance

An effective and constructive opposition is essential if a government in a democracy has to function efficiently and progressively. Absence of such an opposition may tend to make the government unilateral and dictatorial in its policies and actions. Similarly, only an effective and constructive consumer reaction can provide basis for practical and realistic fiscal, industrial, social, educational and other policies of the government involving the public. Right from the President of India to the workers, everyone is a consumer irrespective of caste, creed, race, religion class, community, social position, sex and other difference. Everyone who uses anything either for his sustenance, movements, personal convenience and other purposes can be defined as a consumer, though some are in a privileged category, the bulk of the consumers have not much of a say in the various schemes and measures that concern them. While it is true that all citizens are consumers, it does not necessarily follow that all consumers represent the consumer interest. The consumer interest is often difficult to identify because consumers tend to be more involved in their roles as earners than in their roles as consumers. If consumers had realized their important role, then they would not be so passive, inactive and helpless in the present situation of rising criminal adulteration, diminishing quality, rampant corruption, unchecked black marketing and shameless exploitation. It is ironical that those responsible for all these maladies are also consumers but on a different footing. They are the privileged class. They can get what they want by the authority, by hook or crook and they do not have the troubles and worries like that of the average consumer who forms the bulk without any recognition or identity. What can this large mass of consumers do? Should they suffer and perish or fight for their rights and existence?

If consumers do not complain for malpractices in the market, then undoubtedly, manufacturers try to supply what the public wants and they make corrections if enough consumers make their objections or wants known to them. A manufacturer naturally assumes that his products are acceptable if he sells plenty of them. If consumers continue to buy his products and he receives no complaints about them, he has a right to believe that they are quite satisfactory. An apathetic public will not get the best value for its money and it should be remembered that merchants who cater to a discriminating clientele will supply the best goods in an acceptable manner. If the public do their part, it will not be necessary for government to interfere as much as it is an occasion urged to do. This desirable objective is of course, dependent on fair and reasonable criticism demands from well informed public.

Solution for Consumer Problems

Under the prevailing circumstances what the Indian consumers can do? A powerful consumer movement is the consumer salvation. For example, when a baby gets hungry, it cries to attract attention. Unless asked no one responds and comes to help. India is well endowed with takers but very few doers. Unless the consumers assert themselves and makes noise like the hungry baby, no one would care for them.

The vast category of consumers is very much a mixed group of different types. Individually no consumer can cause any ripple but united they become a group to be reckoned with. The working class and service personnel takes up their causes through organized trade unions and associations and achieve what they want at least in part. The consumers must organize themselves under established consumer societies or councils for effective action. It is high time that the consumers in the cities should strengthen the consumer organizations already functioning and assist themselves in a unified manner to create a strong public opinion for effectively controlling the rising trend in prices and bring them down to ground level.

The different consumer organizations in the city may also consider forming a federation, so that the consumer's interest can be protected and their rights assisted effectively and purposefully under one organization. The Consumer Guidance Society of India and All India Consumer Council should take up programme of continuous consumer education and create consumer awareness.

References

Anand, N.B. (1986). "Role of Women in Consumerism", *Social Welfare*, Vol. 37, No. 7.

Neelkanta, C. (1989). "Consumer Exploitation—How and Why", *Social Welfare*, Vol. 33, No. 12.

Rao, A.R. (1981). *Need for Consumer Resistance*, Keemat Publications, Delhi.

Walter, C.G. and Bergret, B.J. (1989). *Consumer Behaviour*, Chicago, South Western Publisher.

9

Information Communication Technology for Adult Education

Arpita Sharma and *Surya Rathore*

> "Information and communication technology has become within short period of time one of the basic building blocks of the society. Many countries now regard understanding ICT and mastering the basic skills and concepts of ICT as the part of core education, alongside reading, writing and numeracy."—*UNESCO*

In this era of Information and Communication Technology (ICT), there is unprecedented explosion of knowledge among different groups of people, whether children or adults. Adults are matured and responsible persons of our society and majority of the adult population of India resides in villages. Adult education is a lifelong educational process rather than being a single affair. Adult education is an important activity in all areas of development. It is an integral part of all educational programmes.

Among all the groups, adults suffer a lot of problems due to lack of education and knowledge. Due to gender bias, this problem is more intense in case of women as compared to their male counterparts. The most glaring evidence of gender bias is low sex ratio that is 937 females per 1000 males in our country. For the development of the whole country, the development of women is necessary because women perform a multiplicity of roles and makes critical contribution to the family and in the development of the country. Information and

Communication Technology (ICT) is a 'power resource' in terms of exciting influence on empowerment of women in the society. There are different forms of media in the field of Information and Communication Technology (ICT) as electronic, print, traditional and modern media. For effective communication, a communicator must select most appropriate media that will help the women to learn more, learn faster and remember longer.

Information and Communication Technology (ICT) is an umbrella term that covers all advanced technologies in manipulating and communicating information. The term is sometimes used in reference to Information Technology (IT), particularly in these two communities: education and government. The common usage Information and Communication Technology (ICT) is synonymous assumed the fact that IT or ICT encompasses all media, to record information (magnetic disk/tape, optical disks (CD/DVD, flash memory etc. and arguably also paper records); technology for broadcasting information—radio, television; and technology for communicating through voice and sound or images—microphone, camera, loudspeaker, telephone to cellular phones. It includes the wide varieties of computing hardware (PCs, servers, mainframes, networked storage). It has rapidly developed a personal hardware market that comprises mobile phones, personal devices (MP3, MP4, MP5 and MP6) players, laptops, palmtops etc. "ICT" makes more explicit technologies such as broadcasting and wireless mobile telecommunications. (Wikipedia, http://en.wikipedia.org/wiki/ICT)

However, the women in rural area have less access to media through which they get information on health. Even they possess media but they have less awareness about services provided by modern media. Government has initiated various programmes and also established Information Communication Technology (ICT) centres but their reach is limited to only some villages and there too, women are the neglected lot when it comes to harness the benefit of Information and Communication Technology (ICT). The development of any country can only be possible if the vast accumulated modern scientific knowledge and technology is disseminated to the women, especially the rural women. Different media are differing in their effectiveness so there is a need to assess the effectiveness of media. There are different media; traditional as well as modern media used to disseminate information in the field of family planning, care of child, sanitation and environment. It is difficult to say which type of media is effective among the women to impart nutritional education because there are few researches or database which talks about effectiveness of media in the field of nutrition. So, there is an urgent need to study the communication characteristics of rural women and on the basis of this, some media mixes can be developed. But the problem arises as to which type of communication media to select from the many that are available. Will these media be effective for nutritional education or not? The media selection should be based on their existing knowledge level and information need and further need to be presented in effective way, which is easily understood by them to the desired effect. There is also a need to analyze whether media discovered till now are sufficient in carrying out the effective communication or they need to be modified and these media are accessible even to those who live in remote areas and in the format that will suit their needs and means, taking into consideration their education and economic status. Keeping all these things in mind, a research study was fabricated with the objective to determine the relative effectiveness of Information and Communication Technology (ICT) tools in imparting Nutritional Education.

Research Methodology

Present investigation was carried out in the Rudrapur block of district Udham Singh Nagar of Uttarakhand. 75 married rural women in the reproductive age group of 15 to 45 years of age were selected from villages Raghavnagar (37) and Gukulnagar (38) through Simple Random Sampling using Chit method. The ICT tools which were developed for educating women on nutrition education were—

T_1 = Booklet plus Slide presentation
T_2 = Puppet show plus Recorded message through Mobile phone.

Interview schedule and knowledge test was used to collect data. Knowledge test was developed on the topic of "Balanced Diet for Pregnant Women". The sub-topics were Micronutrient deficiencies and Importance of Nutrients. Pre- and post-tests were conducted using the knowledge test prepared by the investigator.

Hypotheses of the Present Investigation

H_0 = Respondents do not have higher post-knowledge scores than pre-knowledge scores.

$H_0: X_1 = X_2$

Where,

X_1 = Pre-knowledge scores

X_2 = Post-knowledge scores

H_1 = Respondents have higher post-knowledge scores than pre-knowledge scores.

$H_1: X_1 > X_2$

Selection of ICT Tools

There were 75 respondents who have to be given the knowledge on Balanced Diet for pregnant women. Media mix is decided on the basis of what may be most appropriate and effective for the content of particular material to be produced. The following points were kept in mind:

- Literacy level of respondents
- Media availability, accessibility, purpose of utilizing media
- Production cost
- Time
- Objectives of the study

In this study, it was found that literacy level of respondents was average. Majority of the respondents possessed various media such as television, print media (magazines, newspapers) and modern media as mobile phones, internet *etcetera*. Respondents liked mostly to watch serials on television and used media more for entertainment purpose. There were different types of media that could be effectively used in this case. Previous researches have proved that health and nutrition information can be effectively transmitted through audio and visual combination. Leagans (1963) also observed that a combination of hearing and seeing was more effective in making the impact on people and was usually necessary to promote action.

Thus, considering these points one combination was selected Booklet plus Slide presentation. Print material was more effective channel of mass communication. The message was same for both the booklet and for the slide presentation.

Winterfeld (1974) studied the difference between (a) recorded message, (b) recorded messages with realistic pictures. He had found out that the group who had audio-visual treatment scored significantly higher than the group who had only audio treatment.

Phair (1975) observed that media having combination of audio and visual resulted in more effective learning than audio and visual alone. The film and film strip which involved pictorial images and sound track were more effective than either the printed material or sound track only on comprehension and retention of message. Print was found to be more effective than the audio presentation.

Malra (1998) compared the effectiveness of single media (only print media), two media combinations (print plus slideshow) and three media combinations (print plus slideshow plus group discussion). Researches reveal that selected communication media significantly differ in their effectiveness in terms of retention of message they propagate. Print plus slideshow plus group discussion was found to be more effective media combination with retention of message. It could, then be inferred that media when used in combination are more effective as compared to media when used individually.

Another combination used was Puppet show plus recorded message through mobile phone. The nutritional message was given to women through story as shown by the puppet show. Message was also recorded in cassette and this cassette was heard by the respondents through mobile phone. Personal touch was given before and after hearing the message.

The media mix which was selected for present investigation was given as follows:

T_1 = Booklet plus Slide presentation

T_2 = Puppet show plus Recorded message through Mobile phone.

Concept behind Selection of ICT Tools

A combination of extension methods or that of mass media and interpersonal sources is perhaps the most effective way of reaching people with new ideas and persuading them to utilize these innovations. The basic idea behind this is twofold: First, the more the senses of the learner are involved in the learning process, the greater the learning. Second, to ensure action on parts of learners, several exposures may be necessary in order to motivate, remind and persuade them. However, combination of methods will depend on each situation, objectives to be accomplished etc. Haas and Packer (1964),

(Sandu 1996) showed that learning takes places through various senses: Sight—87 per cent, Hearing—7 per cent, Smell—3.5 per cent, Touch—7.5 per cent, Taste—1.0 per cent

According to Ray (2001) while selecting media following steps should be followed:

Steps of Selection of ICT Tool

1. **Teaching objectives:** Whether to give information, to impart knowledge or to bring change in attitude *etcetera.*
2. **Nature of subject matter being taught:** Particular aspect of the technology and whether understanding depends on seeing or not.
3. **Nature of audience:** Their age, education, interest, experience, knowledge, intelligence *etcetera.*
4. **Size of Audience:** Small or Large.
5. Availability of equipments, materials and funds.
6. **Skill and experience of the adult educator in preparation and use of audio visual aids:** According to Ensminger (1957) before an extension worker can become efficient in use of methods, he must know what methods are available, when to use a given method and to be effective in using each method.

Designing of Message

The relevant information on the different aspects of balanced diet was collected from various sources like books, internet, journal, newspaper, magazines. After collecting all necessary informations on balanced diet, a complete and compact package of message was prepared, keeping all these points and the target audience in view. This message was then translated into local language. The message was validated with the help of experts in the area of Nutrition. Script was prepared in different formats: Booklet, Slideshow, Recorded message, Puppet show. These media mixes were also validated with the help of media experts.

Development of ICT Tools

Booklet: Booklet is a component of print media. A booklet is a small book or group of pages. A booklet is a printed and bound of less than

100 pages. A booklet is basically, something to be kept by individual and read at leisure whenever desired. The booklet contained information regarding Balanced Diet for Pregnant women. Under this the sub-topics which were covered were—for common understanding of Balanced diet, Importance of nutrients, Micronutrient deficiencies. The booklet aimed to give knowledge about balanced diet for the pregnant women. The message of booklet was written in Hindi language and visuals were also easy to understand. This booklet contained pictures with short printed message which could be easily understood even by the illiterates. It is believed that print media demands more active and creative participation and only literate have access to the print media but this belief is disapproved by the researches in communication. Hali (1980) pointed out that it is often our experience to see that during *Kisan Melas* and similar meetings of farmers, even illiterate farmers collect the publications if they find the subject interesting, they would get it read either by their literate children or school teachers, postman or village functionaries.

Slide presentation: Slide presentation is combination of audio plus visual medium for communicating message convincingly to the audience. The objective of slide presentation was to give knowledge to the rural women about Balanced diet for pregnant women. Total number of slides were 24. The language of slide presentation was easy to understand. There were clear visible pictures which represented the importance of balanced diet. Slides were prepared with animation effect with sound and music to make them more attractive and appealing.

Recorded message through Mobile Phone: Mobile phone is a system of equipment through which people can communicate both ways to distant places. A mobile phone (also known as a hand-phone, wireless phone, cell phone, cellular phone, cellular telephone or cell telephone) is a long-range, electronic device used for mobile voice or data communication over a network of specialized base stations known as cell sites. It provides interpersonal communication, in which the communicator and communicatee change their role while giving and getting information, though only two persons can communicate at a time through a mobile. Message was recorded in the cassette so that it is easy to understand and audible. It was communicated to rural women through mobile phone with a personal touch.

Puppet Show: Puppet show is a traditional medium. It is audio-visual aid that can be heard and seen (Haas and Packer, 1964). In a

Puppet show dolls are made to perform by controlled movement of the puppeteer from outside. Puppets may be of different types such as glove or hand puppets, string puppets, rod puppets and shadow puppets. Glove or hand puppets are simple to handle. This is like a three fingered glove which fits on the hand. The first finger is inserted inside the head and the middle finger and thumb fit in the hands. These are moved when the story is told. Proper dress and lightening is essential. While puppet show may be held in daylight or in night, this method had long been advocated as an effective method with rural masses for entertainment as well as non-formal education. Puppet play was written in Hindi language so that it is easy to understand by everyone. This Puppet show was held in the morning. Whether the community is illiterate or literate rich or poor this has been proved an attractive and most effective method of teaching to all social groups. Story was based on to create awareness among rural women about balanced diet. The Mac Bride Commission Report (1982) has very rightly said, "Even where modern media have penetrated to isolated areas, the older forms maintain their validity, particularly when used to influence attitude instigate action and promote changing". The great potential of puppetry a channel of socialization and education has been recognized by many Asian development and communication planners addressing the problem of literacy, 'Asian development, family planning and political movement' (Singh 1993).

Results and Discussion

Table 9.1: Paired 't' Test for Relative Effectiveness of Media Mix within the Group

Treatment group	*d*	*d²*	*-D*	*S (d)*	*'t' cal*
T_1	529	8684	13.84	0.98	14.08*
T_2	371	5685	10.02	1.47	6.81*

* Indicate that value is significant at 5 per cent level.

't' tab = at 5 per cent level of significance = 1.684.

$T_{1=}$ Booklet plus Slide presentation.

$T_{2=}$ Puppet show plus Recorded message through Mobile phone.

Thus, null hypothesis that the gain in knowledge of the respondents is not increased after applying treatment is rejected for both treatment groups and the hypothesis that the gain in knowledge score is more than the pre-knowledge score is accepted in both the groups. It can be concluded that the treatment had significant effect in terms of gain in knowledge.

Table 9.2: Mean Score of Pre-Test and Post-Test within the Group

Treatment group	*Pre-test score X_1*	*Post-test score X_2*	*Gain (X_2-X_1)*
T_1	18.5	32.73	14.23
T_2	19.94	29.29	9.35

There was significant difference in the pre-test and post-test scores of overall knowledge of the respondents as calculated 't' value was significant. Women had poor initial knowledge about balanced diet as indicated by low score that is T_1 18.5 and T_2 19.94 in pre-test. Tremendous improvement in the knowledge of the respondents was evident due to their participation as their post-test score increased from 18.5 to 32.73 in T_1 group and 19.94 to 29.29 in T_2 group. The gain was 14.23 in T_1 group and 9.35 in T_2 group. It can be concluded that respondents have gained a lot after exposure to Information and Communication Technology (ICT) tools.

Conclusion

This is the age of knowledge explosion and exploration. Rapid progress in Information and Communication Technology (ICT) has invaded the arena of education. Technology revolution has touched all facets of human life including learning. Worldover, women are struggling to break the shackles that bind them and challenging the unequal distribution of power in society. The condition of women in India may be improved if women are educated in all the different aspects of life. Information and Communication Technology (ICT) tools can be very effectively used to educate the rural women.

References

Ensminger, E. (1957). "Knowledge and Use of Extension Methods." In: *A Guide to Communication Development*. MacMillan Company, London.

Hali, R. (1980). *Are Farm Journals Effective?* Kerala Bureau sets an Experimental Communicator. Vol. 15, No. 4.

Hass, K.B. and Packer, H.Q. (1964). *Preparation and Use of Audio-Visual Aids*. Prentice-Hall of India (P) Ltd., New Delhi.

Leagans, J.P. (1963). *Adoption of New Ideas and Practices*, Iowa State University Press.

Malra, P.K. (1988). A Comparative Study of the Effectiveness of Communication Media on Retention of Message on Rice Production Technology. Unpublished M.Sc. Thesis. G.B.P.U.A. and T., Pantnagar.

Phair, A.J. (1975). Comparison of Cognitive Learning From a 16 mm Motion Picture, a 35 mm Filmstrip Sound Track and Printed Narration using Immediate and Delayed Retention Score Dissertation. Abstracts International.

Sandhu, A.S. (1996). *Textbook on Agricultural Communication*, Oxford and INH Publishing Co. Pvt. Ltd., Delhi.

10

Role of Family in Era of Globalization

Poonam Tewari and *Rameshwari Pandya*

Family plays a pivotal role in providing the most congenial atmosphere to an individual to form his style of life and the basic patterns of behaviour. The aspiration, values and goals of an individual are influenced by the family. Whether an individual develops into a well adjusted human being or maladjusted person depends on the family. Family in the Indian culture is the most significant group that influences the personality of the children. The basic relationship between mother and child builds bond and attachments and fosters other relationships with father and siblings. The attachments grow stronger throughout the person's life. The close family relationships exert a great influence over children's relationships with members of social groups. Parents are the chief architects in shaping the personality of an individual. The quality of relationship with parents is a key factor for the wholesome development of an individual. Secure bond between parents and their children allow them the freedom to grow, explore the world, gain experience and adopt positive things.

The process of globalization, industrialization and modernization is widely affecting our family life and society. Globalization is a term widely used to express the idea of making the whole world follow one culture, that is, the consumer culture. The nature of globalization is to incorporate the world into the capitalist market. In this process, the diverse local cultures are being replaced by the uniculture of the market. Globalization, industrialization are the basis of economic progress in the world. Production and sales are improved to the level of export oriented quality with the expectation that this is going to transform the life of the people. Trade along with migration, communication and dissemination of scientific and technical knowledge has helped to break the dominance of rampant poverty yet the life is still very nasty, short and brutish for most people.

The sphere of the family is a fundamental arena where globalizing processes have a lot of impact. For most individuals, family in whatever configuration still remains the primary arrangement that meets certain social, emotional, and economical needs. It is within families that decisions about work, care, movement, and identity are negotiated, contested, and resolved. Globalization has profound implications for how families assess the choices and challenges that accompany this process. Families are integrated into the global economy through formal and informal work, through production and consumption, and through their relationship with nation-states. Many times people have to migrate to other cities or countries. They have to work overtime to meet their job requirements. Moreover, ever growing communication and information technologies allow families and individuals to have access to others in an unprecedented manner. These relationships are accompanied by new conceptualizations of lifestyles, identities, and ideologies even among those who may never be able to access them.

A globalized society without borders has brought about different forms of insecurity: personal, financial, health, cultural, environmental and political. In this process women are suffering twofold. As women in developing countries move into the workforce, their domestic responsibilities are not alleviated. Women work two full time jobs. One in a factory, where they are paid next to nothing, the second is in the home. They are getting lesser time to look after their children as a result the development and personality of children are affecting. Children instead of playing indoor and outdoor games are engaged in television, internet and learning aggression, isolation, violence etc. The inappropriate use of new information and communication technology—television and internet have become potent socializing agents capable of endangering, individualism, materialism and self-centredness, which is weakening the foundation of family and society.

Husband and wife both are working, are overbusy, have less time for each other as a result the relationship between husband and wife are also deteriorating. It is leading to lack of time for each other, misunderstanding, maladjustment even violence or divorce. The mixture of corporate capitalism and western culture models are dissolving family life as witnessed by higher rates of family violence, rape, divorce, and family breakdown.

In earlier times families were usually very happy. They used to have a close interaction. The father used to work outside the home and the mother stayed at home. Mothers used to do household work and take care of the family members. Children used to play outside after school. They rode bicycles and climbed trees, played tag and made up games of their own. They did their homework on desks in bedrooms writing on paper with pens and pencils. Later, everyone would gather in the living room to share their experience, have fun with each other or watch T.V. But they were all together. Families were forced to be together because there was only one television, one telephone, one living room, one car just one of everything. Today our families and houses and lifestyles are very different bigger, blended, better, faster and yet we feel isolated and lonely and disconnected. We have so much, and yet we have so little.

The most intimate interactions were in person. With the advancement of science and technology it has converted to telephonic conversations, text messaging, instant-messaging, and finally e-mail. The most intimate time spent is the rarest, while the least intimate is the most common. Because of our busy schedules, it is difficult to find time to be together in person. It requires two people to be in the same place at the same time. With e-mail, we are communicating more but interacting less. We feel empty, isolated, alienated, ungrounded, and lonely.

The family politics, i.e. the leadership style, the decision-making policy, and the rules and methods of enforcement are powerful forces that manage all interactions of the family. The atmosphere of the family should be such that we feel stable, fair and free. The politics of the family that is freedom of speech, privileges, safety, and respect for leadership describes the parenting method in the family. The emotional atmosphere of the family whether it is warm and safe, or cold and dangerous temperature affects the mental and physical health of the family. The language of the house is the communication style of the family. Words, tone, and frequency of conversation express ideas, wants, needs, and desires. Kind and respectful or critical and judgmental language, does the language of the house make you feel understood and heard? Is there freedom of expression? or there is censorship, abusive language, silence, or freedom of speech, a shared language during frequent conversations?

The culture of the house is made up of the customs, religion, spiritual traditions, and ethnic rituals in the house as it is the soul of family life. Holiday celebrations, family values, culture and traditions. Culture of the house make you feel loved with a sense of belonging. Globalization though has many positive effects; it also has negative impacts on family life. It has made the dual personality. Children are confused what to follow family values or outside world which is following western culture and lifestyle resulting into the identity confusion. Some people are able to adopt part of their culture and part of western culture whereas others are not able to do so. This identity confusion among young generation may be reflected in problems as depression, suicide and substances abuse.

Globalization has also led to the growth of self-centred culture. The values of global culture which are based on individualism, free market economics, democracy and include freedom of choice, individual rights are part of global culture. People try to be with the like minded people. Positive parenting is the need of the hour. We should create nurturing environment for the members of the family. We should try to become responsible parents and respect the child's uniqueness and individuality. It is the parents who can make the home atmosphere congenial for the overall growth and personality development of its members so that can face the challenges of their life successfully.

Influential Factors to Make Family Atmosphere Congenial

- Love and affection
- Values
- Communication
- Socialization
- Etiquettes
- Morals
- Education
- Discipline
- Guidance
- Better upbringing of children
- Motivation
- Attitude towards healthy lifestyle

Love and Affection

God's love is unconditional, and that is what parents should strive for with their family. Although many parents know they love their children, sometimes the message is not clear to the children. Some may feel that they are loved, but only when they are behaving well or if they are getting good marks in school. Children need to know that they are loved even when they make a poor decision or fail to meet expectations. Unconditional love does not mean letting kids do whatever they want. Parents need to lead and guide their kids so that they can become independent and good human being. Being permissive in the name of love is a disservice to the children. They need structure to learn how to navigate in this world.

Discipline

It is important for parents to find a balance in how they raise their children. To create an atmosphere of respect in the home, parents need to be kind in their actions to steer away from being too controlling and authoritarian. They also need to be firm and consistent to ensure they don't become permissive in their parenting style. Positive discipline focuses on the future and what is needed to prevent problems. What skills and attitudes are needed? How can parents and kids work together towards problem solving and prevention?

All children need to have limits set for them. Children whose parents give firm but loving discipline are generally more skilled socially and do better in school than children whose parents set too few or too many limits. Here are some tips:

- Direct your child's activities, but don't make unnecessary restrictions or try to dominate.
- Offer reasons when asking your child to do something. For example, say, "Please move your things from the stairs so that no one trips over it", instead of, "Move it because I said so."
- Listen to your child to find out how he feels and whether he needs any special support.
- Show love and respect even when you are angry. Criticize your child's behaviour, not your child.
- Help your child make choices and work out problems.
- Be positive and encouraging. Praise your child for a job well done. Smiles and encouragement go much further to shape good behaviour than harsh punishment.

Guidance

Proper guidance is necessary for upbringing of children so that they become responsible citizen. Parents should aim for an environment of supporting their kids. Life is about making mistakes and learning from them. See mistakes as an opportunity for children to learn, not as a time to shame or blame them. The goal is not to punish kids or let them "suffer" the consequences of their actions. The goal is to let kids make choices and experience the consequences in an environment where they feel understood and supported. Allowing kids to learn lesson from mistakes is how parents can help them learn new skills and become more confident in themselves. Children might be responsible for the mistake and should take ownership to remedy the situation, but it is important for them to know that "Team Family" is on their side. Parents can talk with kids about what happened and guide the conversation to help kids see how they can remedy the situation. Parents can also do the same for themselves. Parenting is no easy job, and mistakes will be made. It is better to show self-love and look for solutions to make things better for the next time.

Faith

Parents must be dedicated in teaching their kids about having faith in God. It is also important for them to have faith in themselves and their children, especially when it seems most difficult. Parents need to believe in themselves, that they have the skills, intuition and support to help them be the best parents they can be. It is also important for parents to have faith in their children and let them try new things and face challenges that are within their reach.

Values

Show the values and behaviours which you want your child to imbibe through your actions and mould him to understand the family norms such as respecting elders. Avoid having heated exchange and arguments between the adults in the family, in your child's presence because it will threaten the child's sense of security and well-being; this may affect her inner world seriously. Children absorb the family values and try to fit within the pattern, or standard set by the parents. If parents are warm, friendly, and cooperative, the same relationship may possibly develop in the children. Most children, who have had a secure, healthy childhood, are unlikely to have many problems in adolescence, in comparison to those with traumatic childhood experiences like parental fights, divorce witness to any major event like accidents etc. Those who share a healthy relationship with their siblings have been found to have a better time getting through the phase of adolescence.

Education

Education is one of the cornerstones and effective elements in the solidification of personality. Development and improvement of human factor in every dimension of personality takes place during childhood. Educate your children in a way so that he or she gets prepared to distinguish between what is right and what is wrong for him. Build your child's self-confidence. Parent's influence can make the difference between the child who has enough self-confidence to reach out to others and one who is too uncomfortable to get to know someone new. Try to build-up your child's self-esteem so that he or she can enjoy the special feeling that friendship gives. Educate the family members with regards to their roles and responsibility. Educate the children to critically evaluate the information technology and mass media.

Morals and Etiquettes

One of the effective factors in the solidification of family is morals and etiquettes. Moral values form a trustable and valuable basis for starting and continuing of a healthy life. Moral values cover observance, patience, politeness, respect, loyalty, equity, orderliness, gratefulness. They help people to interact in a healthy way to cope with the outside world and be a good citizen. Moral values are the standards of good and evil, which govern an individual's behaviour and choices. Individual's morals may derive from society and government, religion, or self. At the end of the day truth and moral values prevail upon bad and unethical thing. As technology advanced, we were forced to drift away. Ironically, newer and modern transportation and communication systems saw to the dissipation of the physical human contact and hence even the moral code. Our own individual religious beliefs represented whatever minimum morals we needed to survive and get along with one another. The desire to maintain morals is deep-rooted within all of us. But, it is the technological developments which have eroded this and will continue to do so even more as we become more advanced. Why should one imitate western culture for bad things only and not take good things from western culture, their work culture, their dignity of labour, not pub culture and violence? We must preserve our culture and add on good things to our culture. Give good to the society, good will come back to you. For everything should be in limits, any thing which goes beyond limits is bad. The moral values become individualistic, and it becomes personal. Whatever moral values of one person may not be moral value to other person. The urge for money and materialistic things are eroding the value system. The "corruption" may not be moral value to someone but "not be corrupt" may be moral value to others. At some point of time, the immoral person may be caught and punished under land of law.

Communication

Effective communication among family members is the key for personality development. The atmosphere of the family should be such that the members feel free to express and share their feelings, emotions. They feel free to discuss their problems, ideas and information. They should feel free to come to their parents whenever they need their help, support or guidance. Encourage the children to share their daily routine and initiate the talks whenever you have free time.

Motivation

Every child is unique individual and two children can't be motivated in the same way. We need to know what motivates a child by observing and listening to them. Once we know we can always explore related ways to encourage them. All these methods need change as kids grow older. Motivation does not mean putting conditions in front of the children. Children gradually start applying the same technique on you and everybody. The means of motivation should never be tempting them with offers of their choice. Motivate them to first believe in themselves and assert the words "You can do it". Let them know for sure that they are trusted, loved and respected. Respect is one of the magic words.

Role Model

Try to be a role model of your children as the moment a child wakes up, he sees his parents. He notices their behaviour pattern towards each other; he notices how they handle tough, stressful situations. He is bound to acquire his parents' traits. Children are the mirror image of their parents mostly. So, parents must try to become role models so as to help their children grow up as responsible citizens. As parents, try to become role models throughout the child's life and your child will learn from the examples you set or display. When parents exercise and eat nourishing food, their children are more likely to do so. When parents treat others with respect, their children probably will too. If parents share things, their children will learn to be thoughtful of others' feelings. If a father consumes alcohol saying he can do so as he is a parent or that he is stressed from work, while trying to dissuading a teen from doing so, the teen will feel discriminated against, and will obviously borrow the father's reasons for drinking sooner or later.

Attitude Towards Healthy Life

Family atmosphere is the first and in many ways the most influential factor in determining your child's attitude towards life. From its very first day, an infant discovers sights and sounds and observes and experiences the effects of personal relationships. As they grow, children are constantly making decisions about how to choose friends based on the qualities that were encouraged within their own family unit. So if the atmosphere within a family encourages mutual affection and respect, children naturally find making friends an easy thing to do. Encourage your child to have positive attitude towards life and guide them what is right and wrong for them. They should be encouraged to adopt positive things of their surroundings. Children come into this world with a powerful need to discover and to explore. As parents, you need to encourage this curiosity if your child is going to keep it. Enthusiasm for what your child does help to make her proud of her achievements. Talk about exciting activities, such as going on field trips, and making fun art projects.

Conclusion

Globalization has emerged to be a significant force in social and psychological development of people. The process of globalization, industrialization and modernization is widely affecting our family life and the society. It has many positive and negative impacts on our family and social life. Family is a fundamental arena where globalizing processes is have a lot of impact. It has led to the development of bicultural identity, identity confusion, self-centred culture and emerging adulthood. Although family structures have changed due to urbanization and modernization, our family orientation still remains "joint". Psychologically and socially, Indian families present a more interdependent picture where family unity is of utmost importance. Newer forms of residence where older parents and/or siblings and their families stay close by are coming up; they may no more share a common kitchen and living space like before, but would meet on a regular basis or for rituals and celebrations of numerous festivals. Due to an interdependent mentality which still continues, family values like sacrifice, sensitivity to other members and their needs, sharing and unique forms of conflict resolution (some of which may depend on role hierarchy and responsibility) can be seen. This is particularly seen in child rearing practices which parents use with children of different ages. Even if the family size is small, interactions with extended family remain, like children's interactions and play behaviours with close cousins, neighbours etc. Individualism is creeping in slightly but surely into Indian families. This may be due to smaller family size, increase in levels of education, change of women's status in the family, especially in the urban, upper middle and middle classes. This is often seen as a threat to family unity and cohesion. Size of family or number of family members does not affect family unity that seriously as if often perceived. In fact, Indian families are known to accommodate the views of all members amicably, while resolving issues of importance. Examples could be education of children, marriage related matters, sharing of space and resources etc. A major change that has come about at least in urban families is the empowerment of women through education and income generation from various formal and non-formal sources. This has led to better child care and investment in children's education and future planning. This is one of the most important indicators of social change within the family. From a traditional/patriarchal point of view, women's work outside the house and increasing say in family matters may however be resented to a great extent but the different contextual factors like inflation need for economic mobility and materialistic aspirations of people regulate the process. Family hierarchy and more importantly, gender hierarchy are still guiding our roles and responsibilities. This has both positive and negative influences in our families. One major influence on congenial family atmosphere is the modelling behaviours used by adults in the family. The subtle family values, beliefs and ethos that they project are internalized by the younger members of the family (children and adolescents). This becomes the fulcrum of change in the family and reinforces the belief that "as you sow, so shall you reap" or "like parents, like children". When parents embody and display appropriate behaviours and family values like respect, loyalty, sacrifice, accommodation of others' views, children imitate and internalize them, when this does not happen, the ripple effect is unseen immediately but has long ranging effects on the way children will lead their lives in future, within and outside the family or in larger society. The family is being rapidly democratized. This could also have good effects on children and other vulnerable members of the family like women and elderly. However, it requires immense maturity from powerful members of the family like the men—head of the household (father) or older women (mothers-in-law) in the family to bring about this change. This can also ensure a congenial atmosphere in the family. Parenting skills are not necessarily inborn and it is important that they are learnt by reading books, discussing with experts like counsellors, teachers, and other sensible parents. It is imperative to calmly deal with the children individually and not compare them with other kids or your own childhood. Children who have an open, relaxed and strong rapport with their parents are likely to continue confiding their apprehensions, desires and adventures to the parents even during adolescence, automatically taking the worries out of this period.

References

Bhargava, B. (2005). *Family Resources Management and Interior Decoration*, M/s. University Book House (P) Ltd., Jaipur.

Chowdhury, A., Carson, C., Carson, D. (2006). *Family Life Education in India; Perspectives, Challenges and Applications*, Rawat Publications, Jaipur.

Deacon, R. and Firebaugh, F. (1975). *Family and Resource Management, Principles and Applications*, Allyn and Bacon INC. Boston.

Duncan, S. and Goddard, H. (2005). *Family Life Education, Principles and Practices for Effective Outreach*, Sage Publications, New Delhi.

Gandotra, V. and Jaiswal, N. (2008). *Management of Work in Home*, Dominant Publisher and Distributors, Delhi.

Gross, I.H., Crandall, E.W. and Knoll, M.M. (1980). *Management for Modern Families*, New Jersey, Prentice Hall Inc.

Moore, W. (1963). *Man, Time and Society*. New York. John Wiley and Sons Inc.

Nickell, P. and Dorsey, J. (1967). *Management in Family Living*, Wiley Eastern Limited, New Delhi.

Pandya, J. (2006). Financial Management Competencies of Head of the Family and Family's Financial Satisfaction. M.F.C.Sc. Dissertation, Department of Home Management, Faculty of Family and Community Sciences, The Maharaja Sayajirao University of Baroda, Vadodara.

Pandya, K. (2008). Saving and Investment of Two Generations: Their Plan and Extent of Satisfaction Experienced. M.F.C.Sc. Dissertation, Department of Home Management, Faculty of Family and Community Sciences, The Maharaja Sayajirao University of Baroda, Vadodara.

Ray, G.L. (2001). *Extension Communication and Management*, IV Edition, Naya Prakash Publication.

Singh, R. (1993). *Communication Technology for Rural Development*, B.R. Publishing Corporation.

Winterfeld, H.F. (1975). A Study of the Effect of Speech Slide Tape Programme in an Educational Setting. Dissertation Abstract International. Vol. 39, No. 9.

Webliography

http://www.encyclopedia.com/doc/1O88-familysociologyof.html
http://ehe.nmsu.edu/financial-management.html
http://www.nios.ac.in/srsec321newE/321-E-Lesson-10.pdf
http://en.wikipedia.org/wiki/Family
http://www.answers.com/topic/family#ixzz19TM5iuCM
(Wikipedia, http://en.wikipedia.org/wiki/ICT).

11

Family Resource Management: A Necessity

Rameshwari Pandya, Varsha Parikh and *Leena Chauhan*

Family is when two or more people share their goals and values, have long-term commitments to one another, and reside usually in the same dwelling place. Each family has their own needs and wants. They can be fulfilled by the use of family resources. The means used to meet the needs are called resources. There are many resources available to the people which can fulfil their needs and solve their problems as well. Resources help people and give them sense of satisfaction. Through optimum utilization of resources we can sustain them for long. Resources which are the part of an individual and can be used only by that person are called 'human resources' like time, energy, knowledge, skills and abilities. They can be increased by giving knowledge and experience in certain fields. The other resources which are available for everyone to use and can be more easily recognized than human resources. They are non-human resources like clothes, property, time saving equipment, money, public facilities like public transport, bus stop, park, hospitals etc. and time and energy too. All resources are interlinked and generation or utilization of one will surely affect another. Only optimum and correct utilization of resources will lead to successful and satisfactory accomplishment of goals. Change in family structure plays vital generation and utilization of resources. The 3-R's-(Reduce, Reuse, and Re-cycle) can be used to maximize satisfaction from their use.

The family is an intimate domestic group made up of people related to one another by bonds of blood, sexual mating, or legal ties. It is a semi-closed system whose members are integrated and interdependent.

Family is responsible for the physical maintenance of its members; fulfilling that function involves the production, distribution, and consumption of goods and services. According to Wikipedia (2009), "In human context, a family is a group of people affiliated by consanguinity, affinity, or co-residence. In society, it is the principal institution for the socialization of children. It is extended from the human "family unit" by affinity, economy, culture, tradition, honour, and friendship are concepts of family that grow increasingly inclusive extending to nationhood and humanism." Family is when two or more people share goals and values, have long-term commitments to one another, and reside usually in the same dwelling place. Dubey (1969) "In a family both man and woman are members and they have social approval for sexual relationship and have children to form a family." Maciver and Page "The family is a group defined by a sex relationship sufficiently precise and enduring to provide for the procreation and upbringing the children." Family is a group of biological relations and basic unit of society. In which adults take care of their younger ones. They fulfil each other's needs by performing various roles like mother, father, brother, sister, daughter, son etc. Each family has their own needs and wants. Wants forms the economic base for life. Family wants are related to each member of the family and they can be fulfilled by the use of the family resources.

According to Bhargava, B. (2005), there are *three* main elements of wants:

1. **Desire for Goods and Services**: There should be a desire to acquire goods and services then only it becomes a want.
2. **Sufficient amount of Resources**: Having desire for something cannot fulfil the wants. One will require sufficient resources to satisfy the wants. Desires and wants can be fulfilled by using various resources like money, knowledge etc.
3. **Willingness to use Resources**: If one has resources he should be willing to use it to satisfy his/her family wants and needs, otherwise the resources are of no use.

Thus, fulfilling family wants and needs require proper resources and their optimum utilization and this can only happen by proper Family Resource Management. Management is using what you have (resources) to achieve what you want (goals and objectives). Family resources are all the resources the individual or family has available to help them to reach their goals. These include human resources such as knowledge, skills, health, time and energy; material resources such as housing, money and investments; and community resources such as the library, cooperative extension service and various agencies. Through educational programmes, we can help individuals and families to recognize resources they may be unaware of, and increase their skills in properly managing all the resources available to them.

Family Resources

One will need land and money to build a house or even when we want to buy a simple footwear, we need money. Similarly, when we want to go to our friend's house, we will walk or use a vehicle to reach the destination. In the same way, we need other resources, like knowledge, material things, skills to perform all our day to day activities. We can say, we need a lot of things to perform our day to day tasks. These things can be called our resources. Therefore, we can say that the means used to meet our needs are called resources. Resources are the means for satisfying our needs and reaching our goals.

There are many resources available to the people which can fulfil their needs and solve their problems as well. Resources help people and give them the sense of satisfaction. According to Deccon, R. and Firebaugh, F. (1975), "Resources provide the means to satisfy the family systems purposes or demands; they are necessary in solving every management problem."

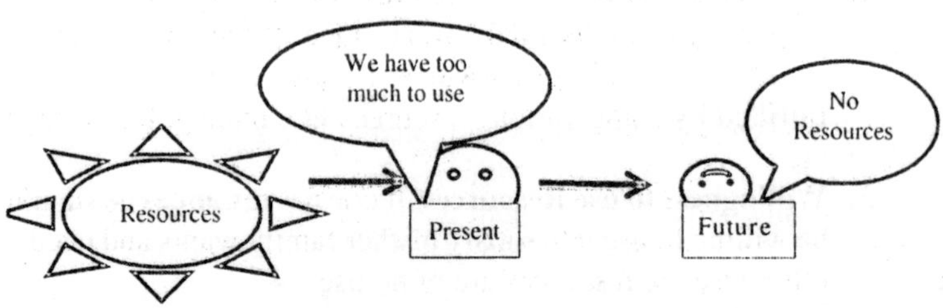

According to Bhargava, B., "Every human being recognizes the available resources and tries to utilize the same and goals can be achieved by the proper use of resources." Resources are essential to cater family needs and to accomplish family goals. Through optimum utilization of resources we can sustain them for long time. Today human beings are not recognizing the importance of limited resources and taking too much advantage out of it, fear is because of this pattern we will not be able to sustain for long and we will not be able to preserve them for next generation.

Types of Resources

There are different types of resources available to use. Some of them are:

- Money, salary, rent, interests from savings bank account etc.
- House for living and working.
- Time, like an hour a day, month etc.
- Energy to do work.
- Knowledge, skills and abilities for doing our work, like sewing, driving, swimming, etc.
- Material goods like household equipment, car etc.
- Community facilities like park, hospitals, roads, bus etc.

But, there is a difference between resources like money, house, equipments, etc., and resources like knowledge, time, skills and abilities.

A good equipment would have a same price for everyone, i.e., anybody can buy these things at the same price. However, knowledge or skill, attitude can be very valuable for an individual and his family whereas it may not be of the same utility to others.

One's energy is a resource for oneself and can be utilized by him or her for doing any work that one wants. It cannot be used by others to perform what they want to do.

There are varieties of resources available to use. We can categorize them in the following manner:

Human Resources

Resources which are the part of an individual and can be used only by that person, such resources are called 'human resources'. Examples of human resources are time, energy, knowledge, skills and abilities. The resources possessed and utilized by human beings. Human resources are used to meet demands of the people and they are internal in nature. Human resources can be increased by giving knowledge

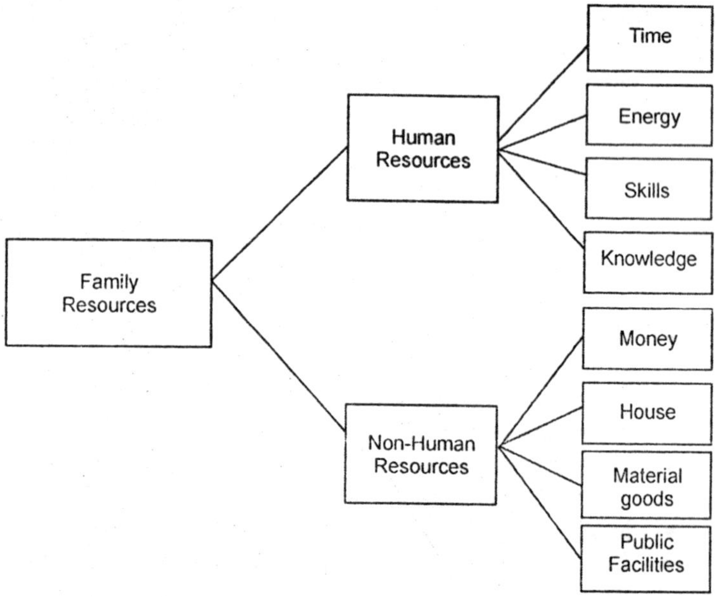

and experience in certain fields. They are characteristics of the people like—knowledge, energy, skills, attitude, time etc.

Knowledge: It is an important and essential resource for the mankind. It is an asset which is useful to solve the problems and bring solutions and alternatives. Lack of knowledge in a person can lead to wastage of resources.

Energy: It is another important resource, through which a person can accomplish his goals. Higher the energy, lesser the time will consume. If one is doing his work more energetically (speedily), he consumes lesser time. But energy is limited resource, so one has to plan his activity and time to prevent tiredness.

Skills and Attitude: Each human has different skills in him. Use of skills in performing and planning some activity may lead to successful attainment of goals. Skills can be learnt or taught. A positive attitude towards the work can lead to complete the work fast and in the best capacity. The amount of human resources available will vary from one person to another, therefore, they can be acquired and cultivated. At the same time, there are some other resources which are available for everyone to use. They are more easily recognized than human resources. They are non-human resources.

Non-Human Resources

Non-human resources can be acquired as Non-human resources are usually materialistic things like clothes, property, time saving equipment, money, public facilities like public transport, bus stop, park, hospitals etc. and time and energy too. Some of these resources like park, and community facilities are available to all of us. However, it is for us to make use of them properly and take advantage of their uses. Such resources are known as 'non-human resources'. Some examples of non-human resources are money, house, land, material goods and community facilities. Money can buy all kinds of facilities, equipments and material goods. It can provide a control over the accomplishment of goals. Time and energy are both human and non-human resources. Non-human resources are external to individuals, but they can be possessed and utilized by them.

Characteristics of Resources

Both human and non-human resources have some common characteristics. They are as follows:

1. **They are useful:** Resources can be used to fulfil our needs and wants. For example:
   — A house provides shelter.
   — A public transport helps to reach the office or school.
   — Mother's ability to cook food helps the family to get good food on time and save money.
2. **Resources are limited**: Every resource is limited in supply. We have only 24 hours in a day. Similarly, if one is doing job, his salary obtained in cash is also fixed. Human beings have limited supply of energy. In the same manner, resources like water, electricity, fuel, etc. are all limited in supply. To get maximum benefit, we must make efforts to conserve them.
3. **The Resources are interrelated**: When we work, we require resources like time, energy, skill, equipments etc. Without adequate supply of time and skill, one will not be able to use his energy to operate the equipment. Thus, one will realize that all these resources are used at the same time, because their uses are interrelated.

4. **Resources have alternate use**: Most resources have alternate uses. For example, a homemaker can use the same time for a number of activities like cooking, studying or watching television. Similarly, she can use her family savings for the purchase of a house, equipment or for higher studies of the children. Thus resources have alternate use.
5. **Resources can be substituted**: To achieve the same goal, we can use one resource or the other. For example, a new dress one can stitch it by using one's own skills or may use money for buying a readymade dress. Other example is the use of ready to eat or ready to cook food instead of preparing them at home. Therefore, one resource can be substituted for the use of another resource.

Therefore, we can say that all resources have similar characteristics. Thus, we should

- Generate and cultivate them to enhance their availability.
- Conserve and ensure proper utilization of them as they are limited in supply.

Generation and Utilization of Resources

Family resources may be used immediately or can be preserved for the future. The human resources are used rapidly to bring the satisfaction. They can be increased by usage for e.g. if we use our knowledge or skills planning and execution, we will surely gain experience and learn new things. Resources can be developed or gained as we can use the preserved or stored resources like materialistic things; property, share them; like using community library, park etc. We can buy resources with money. Money investment is a way to store the resources, it also contribute to the economic security. Resources can be generated by training, for e.g. if we give training to homemakers on 'Time Management' as a result of the training she will acquire new knowledge about it and utilize the same to fulfil the needs. As we have discussed earlier, all the resources are interlinked.

If a homemaker has a good health then only she is able to use her skills, knowledge to perform her task properly. Her skills depend on her knowledge e.g. knowledge of using time and energy saving equipment will lead to saving of time consumption in her domestic work. If she is working women then also her job is affected by her knowledge and skills. Job will provide earnings, which allow her to purchase new things and use facilities as they all are interlinked. Generation or utilization of one will surely affect another. Only optimum and correct utilization of resources will lead to successful and satisfactory accomplishment of goals.

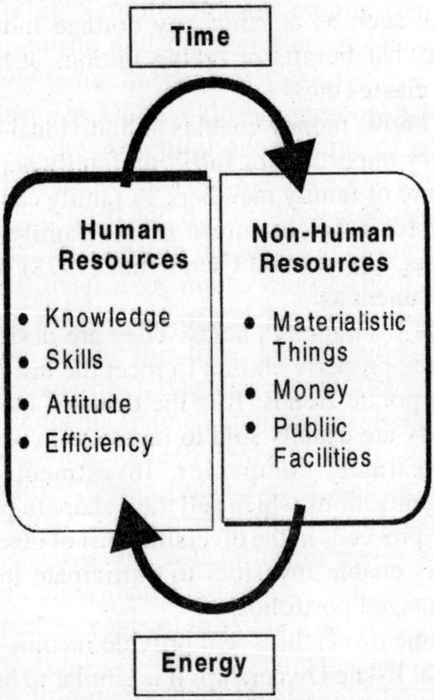

Determinants of Change in the Family Structure

Change in age at marriage and age at first birth, migration, women's economic participation, urbanization, changing demography of aging, globalisation etc. have played vital role in changing family structure and also its generation and utilization of the resources.

Resources can be Generated by the Following Ways—

1. Knowledge can be acquired by books, reading materials and by mass media. Good knowledge will help in creating awareness about the recent trends and technology.

2. Skills can be acquired. One can join any hobby classes, adult education centres or institute of interest for skill upgradation.
3. Energy and time can be saved by using energy and time saving equipments. They can also be stored by work division. If work is divided equally among all the members, it will surely consume less energy and time.
4. Money can be generated by doing some income generation activity such as starting any cottage industry, jewellery making, handicrafts or taking tuitions at home or starting hobby classes etc.
5. As we know, money enables an individual to buy facilities. It is very important for fulfilling family needs and securing the future of family members. A family can invest and save money for a bright future of the family and the family members. Chirsty and Clendemin (1978) described modes of investment as:
   (a) Life Insurance Policies: They are desirable investment when properly chosen to meet the insured's needs.
   (b) Corporate Bonds: It is the debts of business concerns. They are usually sold to investors in units.
   (c) Investment companies: Investment companies are organizations which sell their share to public and invest the proceeds in the diversified list of other security. They thus enable investors to participate in professionally managed portfolios.
   (d) Home ownerships will provide income from rent.
   (e) Real Estate Ownership: It is similar to home ownership. It allows profit from rental real estate.
   (f) Business Ownership: Ownership of one's own business firms is one of the great sources of psychic satisfaction in life.
   (g) Miscellaneous Tangibles: Now-a-days growing number of investors are placing part of their wealth in highly durable, easily saleable goods, such as gold, silver coins, jewellery, gems, paintings, antiques and rare books.
6. Having a kitchen garden can also work as helping hand in generating and saving resources as it will save energy, time and money.
7. Use of technology: Older technologies were time consuming and used to take more energy. If one has money he/she must

replace their equipments with newer ones so that it will aid them in storing resources.

8. One should invest money: As investments are always less liquid in nature and ensure security and fewer risks.
9. Planning is always essential before starting up. So, it is necessary to plan the work before finally executing it. It will save time and reduce wastage of resources and give sense of assurance for goal achievement too.
10. Recycle, Reuse and Reduce: Through this concept we can reduce the wastage of resources. One should recycle and reuse wherever it is possible and should reduce the overusage of resources.

Proper Ways of Utilizing Resources for Maximum Satisfaction

While using resources, we have to ensure that we utilize them in such a way that we get maximum benefits from their use. This way we will be able to get maximum satisfaction. The different ways by which we can achieve this are listed below:

- Identify all the available resources.
- Make use of only the right amount of resources.
- Substitute the less expensive resources for the more expensive ones.
- Develop the habit that can enhance the use of resources.
- Cultivate practices to increase the availability of resources.
- Learn to share resources so that you do not deprive others of their use.
- Do not waste resources.

Role of Extension and Communication in Generation and Utilization of Resources

Through extension education one extends knowledge to create awareness. It means reaching to the unreached people. Extension and Communication can play a pivotal role in generation and utilization of family resources.

- Extension workers generally reach to the grass roots and teach them some skills to improve their standard of living.

- They usually find out the wrong practices followed by the people and try to teach them correct practices.
- Extension workers can teach variety of income generation activities to the people, e.g. vermi-composting, jewellery making, hand bags making or other handicraft articles,
- Kitchen Gardening: This can help people to generate and conserve resources.
- Extension workers usually deal with rural, semi-rural, urban slum communities. Majority of these people do not know the importance of resources as a result they blindly consume and ruin them. Extension workers can create awareness among them regarding the generation and proper utilization of resources.
- In the Department of Extension and Communication there are *two* major elements :
  1. Extension
  2. Communication.

Students are trained in preparing good Teaching Aids like posters, charts, flash cards, educational games, specimen, documentaries, slides and films etc. and using different communication methods like demonstration, folk media, role play, play way methods, group discussions etc. in the field. They can be the best used to tell the communities regarding the proper utilization of the family resources.

References

Bhargava, B. (2005). *Family Resources Management and Interior Decoration*, M/s. University Book House (P) Ltd., Jaipur.

Chowdhury, A., Carson, C. and Carson, D. (2006). *Family Life Education in India: Perspectives, Challenges and Applications*, Rawat Publications, Jaipur.

Deacon, R. and Firebaugh, F. (1975), *Family and Resource Management: Principles and Applications*, Allyn and Bacon Inc, Boston.

Duncan, S. and Goddard, H. (2005). *Family Life Education: Principles and Practices for Effective Outreach*; Sage Publications, New Delhi.

Gandotra, V. and Jaiswal, N. (2008). *Management of Work in Home*, Dominant Publisher and Distributors, Delhi.

Gross, I.H., Crandall, E.W. and Knoll, M.M. (1980). *Management for Modern Families*, Prentice Hall Inc, New Jersey.

Moore, W. (1963). *Man, Time and Society*, John Wiley and Sons Inc, New York.

Nickell, P. and Dorsey, J. (1967). *Management in Family Living*, Wiley Eastern Limited, New Delhi.

Pandya, J. (2006). Financial Management Compentencies of Head of the Family and Family's Financial Satisfaction. M.F.C.Sc. Dissertation, Department of Home Management, Faculty of Family and Community Sciences, The Maharaja Sayajirao University of Baroda, Vadodara.

Pandya, K. (2008). Saving and Investment of Two Generations: Their Plan and Extent of Satisfaction Experienced. M.F.C.Sc. Dissertation, Department of Home Management, Faculty of Family and Community Sciences, The Maharaja Sayajirao University of Baroda, Vadodara.

Webliography

http://www.encyclopedia.com/doc/1O88-familysociologyof.html
http://ehe.nmsu.edu/financial-management.html
http://www.nios.ac.in/srsec321newE/321-E-Lesson-10.pdf
http://en.wikipedia.org/wiki/Family
http://www.answers.com/topic/family#ixzz19TM5iuCM

12

Corporate Social Responsibilities: Glimpses of Vadodara Corporates

Uma Joshi, Rameshwari Pandya, Dimple Saluja and *Jagrati Vadnerkar*

Business houses, right from the inception of human race, have been regarded as constructive partners in the communities in which they operate. Though they have been instrumental in creating employment, wealth, products and services, yet the pressure on business to play a role in social issues involving employees, stakeholders, society, environment, government etc. is continuously increasing. Corporate Social Responsibility (CSR) is the focused actions of a company/corporation that desires to do well while simultaneously doing good for the community, the society, the environment and/or all other aspects with respect to general human upliftment and well-being. Kotler and Lee (2005) define CSR as "a commitment to improve community well-being through discretionary business practices and contributions of corporate resources" whereas Baker refers to CSR as "a way companies manage the business processes to produce an overall positive impact on society."

The World Business Council for Sustainable Development in its publication "Making Good Business Sense" by Lord Holme and Richard Watts, used the following definition, "Corporate Social Responsibility is the continuing commitment by business to behave ethically and contribute to economic development while improving the quality of life of the workforce and their families as well as of the local community and society at large".

The same report gave some evidence of the different perceptions of what this should mean from a number of different societies across the world. Definitions as different as "CSR is about capacity building for sustainable livelihoods. It respects cultural differences and finds the business opportunities in building the skills of employees, the community and the government" from Ghana, through to "CSR is about business giving back to society" from the Phillippines. Traditionally in the United States, CSR has been defined much more in terms of a philanthropic model. Companies make profits, unhindered except by fulfilling their duty to pay taxes. Then they donate a certain share of the profits to charitable causes. It is seen as tainting the act for the company to receive any benefit from the giving.

Importance of CSR

Corporate Social Responsibility (CSR) is the responsibility recognized by the companies for acting in socially responsible manner. The ideal corporate citizenship has ethical and philosophical dimension, particularly in India, wide gap exists between people in terms of income and living standards as well as social status. There is no single universally accepted definition of corporate social responsibility, it has generally come to mean business decision making linked to ethical values, legal compliance, and respect for people, community, and environment. Corporate Social Responsibility (CSR) accepts a company to go further than required by law so as to:

- Treat employees fairly and with respect.
- Operate with integrity and in an ethical manner in all its business.
- Dealings with customer, suppliers, lenders, and others.
- Respect human rights.
- Sustain the environment for future generations.
- Be a responsible neighbour in the community and a good 'corporate citizen'.
- Enhanced 'brand image' with regards to trust and reputation.
- New customers and development of a strong relationship with consumers.
- Better ability to attract and motivate talented workforce.
- Availability of new resources by influencing key stakeholders —such as investors and policy makers.

On the other hand, these days, there are various negativities with companies that do not incorporate CSR:

- Unfavourable public opinion and increased reputation risk (which might lead to decreased shareholder value and diminished stock price).
- Increased litigation and related legal costs on various social and environmental issues.
- Decreased customer loyalty, loss of customers and/or stakeholder support due to the negative publicity garnered.

CSR in India

In India, most of the corporates do not have a clear policy on social responsibility. While developed countries like England have separate ministries to look after the issue of Corporate Social Responsibility. In India, the government does not have a clear policy on this issue. Out of the very few companies who contribute to the social development, the basic intention was not to ensure the good of the nation, rather a business policy to stay away from the tax net. The corporate and the government should try to build up a relationship between the business and the society. The concept of Corporate Social Responsibility (CSR) has so far failed to take deep roots in India because the nomenclature is not properly defined. The Corporate Social Responsibility (CSR) is in a nascent stage. Much needs to be done to bring changes in attitude towards Corporate Social Responsibility (CSR) and bring awareness among the corporate about their social responsibilities. The corporate should be made aware about the changing nature of business due to globalization, transformation of market environment and deepening of competition. The market economy has paved the way for enterprise-led development and a new cultural perspective is taking place in Indian business environment that has a strong bearing on social responsibilities.

Moving away from the traditional approach, corporate rather than following top to bottom mechanism are increasingly bearing stakeholders' perspectives in mind, thereby considering Corporate Social Responsibilities (CSR) as a comprehensive set of policies, practices and programmes that are integrated throughout the business operations. It can thus be deduced that radical transformation is happening with Corporate Social Responsibility (CSR) practices across India. The changes happened at conceptual level where charity oriented approach is now being seen as a stakeholder oriented approach and at implementation level where other important resources except finance are being dedicated.

Several innovative programmes in thematic areas of public health, education, environment, micro-finance and related areas are being developed. These programmes are developed bearing in mind the local cultural context and the needs of the people. Apart from devoting funds, expertise in terms of knowledge and human resource is also allocated for successful implementation of these programmes. In a growing number of companies, these processes are encouraged and rewarded by top management. The implementation of programmes through a trained resource makes a real difference in the community that has been chosen for implementation.

Social responsibility encompasses the different sectors like health, education, employment, income and quality of life. It should be binding on the corporate sectors to work on the above aspects, which are thought to be primary social indicators. They have enough money to serve the nation on the above segments of the society. They should not forget that if general health of the mass were good, they would also have better buying capacity.

Significance of CSR for India

India is a vast developing country. Development needs differ from region to region and are specific at local level. It has been proven that government-public partnership model in development show better outcomes for its sustainability. The corporate sectors contribute significantly to such partnerships. In India, small and medium size of Multi National Companies (MNCs) are comparatively a newer phenomenon than the other countries of Asia due to the Government's restrictive trade practice till 1991. In Gujarat, barring a very few big MNCs many small and medium sized MNCs are still in its transitory form in terms of collaboration and takeovers. This in itself may be limiting factor for creating a image of their business operations to the outers.

There is a need to develop a more coherent and ethically-driven discourse on corporate social responsibility. Because:

- Corporate Social Responsibility offers a two-way street to companies: on the one hand, stimulating innovative business and technological initiatives which would open up new avenues for company operations and focus on the prospect of touching new market zones.

- It would give a cleaner societal reputation and socially responsible identity to companies, involving the companies and their employees in the long-term process of positive social transition.
- All public institutions need to be accountable to the people at large, especially in the context of health hazards, radiation, genetically-modified food, the chemicalisation of the food processing industry and of agriculture.

Involvement of Education Department in CSR

The roles and responsibilities of college and university faculty members are closely tied to the central functions of higher education. One primary formal description of these functions was contained in the 1915 "Declaration of Principles" formulated by a representative committee of faculty members including members of the American Association of University Professors (AAUP). According to the Declaration, the functions of colleges and universities are "to promote inquiry and advance the sum of human knowledge, to provide general instruction to the students, and to develop experts for various branches of the public service" (Joughin, pp. 163-164). Correspondingly, college and university faculty members undertake research, teaching, and service roles to carry out the academic work of their respective institutions. Each of these roles enable faculty members to generate and disseminate knowledge to peers, students, and external audiences.

The Department of Extension and Communication, Faculty of Family and Community Sciences, Vadodara is actively engaged in planning and conducting various types of developmental projects like empowerment through self-employment, imparting health education, reproductive health education, functional literacy project etc. The department develops and employs a variety of teaching learning strategies for imparting knowledge. The main objective of our department is to bridge the gap that exists in the society through various intervention strategies so that we can change their position from dependence to independence and improve the quality of life.

Since CSR is emerging as a strong component of the business of the corporate houses, and the department has been collaborating with corporate houses in Vadodara for development work, it was of the interest to find out the Corporate Social Responsibility (CSR) trends in the corporate sectors of Vadodara. Thus, to generate an unbiased and authentic informal researcher considered it right to approach any group of stakeholders, i.e. employees of the respective companies to give information of their companies Corporate Social Responsibility (CSR) practice and their perception on Corporate Social Responsibility (CSR) undertaking by the companies. In light of this, it was felt important to know the Corporate Social Responsibility initiatives taken up by various industries of Vadodara city.

Objectives

1. To find out the different companies, which are participating in the Corporate Social Responsibilities.
2. To find out the types of activities carried out for Corporate Social Responsibilities.
3. To find out benefits of Corporate Social Responsibilities for the company and local communities.

Methodology

The required data was collected using a structured questionnaire. The survey was used to collect information regarding:

1. Social development activities and coverage of the Company.
2. Budget and fund allocation for social activities by the company.
3. Trained personnel for performing Corporate Social Responsibility activities.
4. Collaboration with other organizations.
5. Motivating factors for undertaking Corporate Social Responsibility.
6. Problems faced during implementation of CSR activities.
7. Future plans for Corporate Social Responsibility.

Sample Size and Sampling Plan

The survey was carried out across a sample of 11 corporate houses out of which 10 were from Vadodara, Gujarat. A purposive sampling procedure was employed. At the outset, about 15 corporate houses who are engaged in social development activities in and around Vadodara were identified and contacted. Informed consent was sought for participating in the survey over telephone. Next, the person In-charge of corporate social responsibility in the Company was handed over the survey tool to be filled up and returned in a given period of time. Out of these 15, only 11 corporate houses returned the questionnaire duly filled. The following corporate houses participated in the survey:

1. **GACL:** Gujarat Alkalis Chemical Limited, Vadodara
2. **ONGC:** Oil and Natural Gas Company, Vadodara
3. **ABG:** Aditya Birla Group (Cellulosic), Vadodara
4. **ABI:** Aditya Birla Insulators, Vadodara
5. **Danke Electrical Ltd.:** Danke Electrical Limited, Vadodara
6. **GLPP Ltd.:** Gujarat Liquid Pharmacaps Private Limited, Vadodara
7. **IPCL:** Indian Petro Chemical Corporate Limited, Vadodara
8. **Goel Pvt. Ltd.:** Goel Scientific Glass Works Limited, Vadodara
9. **CGPL:** Coastal Gujarat Power Limited, Vadodara
10. **HDFC Std. Life:** HDFC Standard Life Insurance Company, Vadodara
11. **Sarabhai:** Ambalal Sarabhai Enterprise Limited, Vadodara.

In order to fulfil the objective of the survey, 11 corporate houses were interviewed. The gathered data was analyzed using frequency and percentages. The corporate houses involved in the study and their area of work is shown in Table 12.1.

Table 12.1 shows the different products in which these corporate houses were involved. As it can be observed that, all the 11 companies were involved in very different and diverse fields such as oil and petroleum, pharmaceuticals, electric parts production and power generation, glass equipments production and life insurance, etc.

Table 12.2 shows more than fifty per cent (50%) of the companies did not have any fixed fund allocation for carrying out Corporate

Table 12.1: Corporate with respect to their nature of the product

N=11

S. No.	*Name of the Corporate*	*Nature of Product*
1.	GACL	Alkaline and chemicals
2.	ONGC	Oil
3.	ABG	Cellulose Production
4.	ABI	Ceramic insulator
5.	Danke Elec. Ltd.	Transformers production
6.	GLPP Ltd.	Pharmaceutical
7.	IPCL	Petroleum
8.	Goel Pvt. Ltd.	Glass equipments
9.	CGPL	Power generation
10.	HDFC Std. Life	Life insurance
11.	Ambalal Sarabhai Enterprise Limited	Pharmaceuticals

Table 12.2: Allocation of fund for the Corporate Social Responsibility

N=11

S. No.	*Name of the Corporate*	*Fund allocation for Corporate Social Responsibility*
1.	Sarabhai Chemicals	35%
2.	GACL	12 – 15%
3.	ONGC	10%
4.	ABI	2 lakhs
5.	IPCL	1%
6.	Danke Elec. Ltd.	Not fixed
7.	GLPP Ltd.	Not fixed
8.	Goel Pvt. Ltd.	Not fixed
9.	CGPL	Not fixed
10.	HDFC Std. Life	Not fixed
11.	ABG	Not fixed

Social Responsibility activities. Those companies who responded in affirmative revealed having allocating 10 to 15 per cent of the total profit whereas one of the company reported as low as 1 per cent and only one company was found to be allocating 35 per cent of their profit for Corporate Social Responsibility activities.

Table 12.3 shows that health and environment sector was taken up by 9 companies followed by 8 companies engaged in livelihood and income generation. Whereas 7 companies were engaged in education work and 6 companies were concentrating on disaster relief work. Only 5 companies were focused towards rainwater harvesting and four companies contributed in the area of disabled, women's empowerment, HIV/AIDS, and agriculture. Only 3 companies

Table 12.3: Areas of Social Development taken up by the companies

N=11

S. No.	Areas of social development	Frequency (f)
1.	Health	9
2.	Environment	9
3.	Livelihood and Income Generation	8
4.	Education	7
5.	Disaster relief	6
6.	Rainwater harvesting	5
7	HIV/AIDS	4
8.	Women empowerment	4
9.	Agriculture	4
10.	Disabled	4
11.	Child issues	3

reported that they were engaged in issues related to children. Similar trends were found in nearly all leading corporate houses in India who are involved in Corporate Social Responsibility programmes, they are also mainly working in the areas like education, health, livelihood creation, skill development, and empowerment of weaker sections of the society (CII Update, March 2010). The corporate sector is going green in a steady manner. With an eye on preserving energy, companies have started initiatives including application of renewable energy technologies, moving to paperless operations and recognition of environmental standards. In the present survey consciousness towards environment was revealed as high as 81 per cent of the companies were involved in projects concerned with the environmental issues.

Table 12.4: Beneficiaries of Corporate Social Responsibility of the selected companies

N=11

S. No.	Beneficiaries	Frequency (f)
1.	Children	8
2.	Women	7
3.	Adolescent	6
4.	Disabled/Handicapped	5
5.	Senior Citizens	4
6.	Marginal Farmers	3
7.	Tribal	2
8.	Any other (specify)	—

Table 12.4 shows that under the social development activities, the beneficiaries selected were largely children and only six companies were contributing for the development of women. Whereas, there were four companies which were having programmes for adolescents while five companies worked with disabled people. Similarly, four companies worked with senior citizens, three companies worked with marginal farmers and only two companies reported that they were working with the tribals.

Table 12.5: Staff Status of Corporate Social Responsibility

N = 11

S. No.	*Staff status*	*Frequency (f)*
1.	Had special staff/employee for Corporate Social Responsibility activities	5
2.	Trained in-service training	3
3.	Trained as part of their studies	3

Table 12.5 clearly reveals that five companies had special and trained staff as well as employees to perform work related to Corporate Social Responsibilities. As the table indicates that the staff of three companies had undergone 'in-service' training whereas the remaining three companies had staff who had undergone training as part of their studies before joining the job.

Table 12.6: Motivational Factors for Undertaking Corporate Social Responsibility

N = 11

S. No.	*Motivational factors*	*Frequency (f)*
1.	Building rapport	8
2.	Income-tax benefits	5
3.	Building clientele	3
4.	Others	3

Table 12.6 shows that there are several reasons or motivation that drives a company to get into philanthropy. When these reasons were explored in this survey, it came to the forefront that for eight companies, i.e. nearly seventy percentage (72%) felt that rapport building with the community was the foundation step to boost up the growth of the institution. Hence, they were engaged in social activities. Less than half of the companies (45%) informed that they had

embarked upon social initiatives for the income-tax benefits besides other reasons. Little more than one-fifth (27%) percentage of the companies had undertaken social responsibility for building up their clientele and similar per cent of companies revealed other reasons like increase in human development index of India and also mentioned that as their company was customer oriented and so they were concerned about their development too.

Table 12.7: Nature of Collaboration for Social Initiatives

N = 11

S. No.	Nature of collaboration	Frequency (f)
1.	Providing money	6
2.	Providing staff	4
3.	Providing assets or resources	4
4.	Providing place/space/room	4
5.	Any other	2

Table 12.7 shows that to perform social activities in the society different corporate have different kinds of collaboration with the people or with the society. As the table reveals that six companies (54%) provided money for the betterment of the society as their social initiatives, while a smaller number of companies (36% each) collaborated with the society in terms of providing staff to teach them about different topics, provided assets/resources and provided space to conduct these social activities. Whereas, only two companies (18%) were involved in welfare activities like providing shoes and clothes to the needy children of the nearby villages, etc.

Table 12.8: Problems Faced by the Corporate in CSR

N = 11

S. No.	Problems Faced	Frequency (f)
1.	Collaboration problem	4
2.	Any other problem	2
3.	Lack of money to perform social initiatives	2
4.	Lack of staff or person to perform social activities	2
5.	Problems regarding place to perform social initiatives	1
6.	Lack of coordination among beneficiaries	1
7.	Lack of Audio-Visual facilities	—
8.	Lack of coordination among staff	—

Table 12.8 shows the problems faced by the corporate houses while performing Corporate Social Responsibility activities. Only four (36%) corporate faced collaboration problems, whereas only two companies (18% each) faced the problems of trained staff, financial support and other problems like lack of concentration of beneficiaries or illiteracy problem, etc. for performing their social initiatives. Very few corporate, i.e. nine per cent (each) faced the problem of lack of coordination among the beneficiaries and location problems.

Conclusion

The above findings reveals that at one end of the spectrum, corporate social responsibility can be viewed simply as a collection of good citizenship activities carried out by various organizations. While at the other end, it can be a way of doing business that has a significant impact on society. The present Corporate Social Responsibility survey conducted with 11 companies functional in different sectors like oil and petroleum, pharmaceuticals, electric parts production and power generation, glass equipment production and life insurance revealed that these companies were mostly active in the field of health, education, livelihood and environment. It is more than likely that these priorities will continue. The beneficiaries of these activities were largely women and children while some also worked with adolescents, disabled people, senior citizens, marginal farmers and tribals.

Thus, the present survey of the 11 companies based in Vadodara reveals that the Corporate Social Responsibility initiative undertaken requires further strengthening. Companies here lack proper standards and policies that have a realistic agenda of grass roots development through alliances and partnerships with sustainable development approaches. The survey revealed several gaps in terms of partnerships and collaborations that are required for proper implementation of development activities at the field level. These gaps are required to be plugged. Although Corporate Social Responsibility activities are supposed to be voluntary, there should be specific guidelines for corporate governance.

Recommendations

The recommendations for companies to enhance Corporate Social

Responsibility performance and spread the movement of Corporate Social Responsibility:

1. Companies should be continuously motivated to work for the betterment of society by organizing seminars, conferences, consultations and workshops inviting diverse stakeholders on the subject of social concern and role of the corporate sector.
2. It is important to integrate and synergize the work done by various organizations, NGOs, Corporate sector, Governmental and International agencies.
3. There is a need for academies and research organizations in social work to participate in the developmental programmes by conceiving, implementing and monitoring various projects and programmes.
4. It is also important that the educational institutions particularly business schools, colleges, Department of social work should take a lead role in promoting Corporate Social Responsibilities practice. It is necessary to develop and document literature related to Corporate Social Responsibilities relative absence of curriculum and indigenous literature of Corporate Social Responsibilities. Thus, it is very important to impart knowledge, skill and methods to enhance the competence in Corporate Social Responsibilities. Conceptual and operational framework and prepare empathetic and sensitive managers of business to respond to the social issues through corporate sector initiatives.

References

ASOCIO Policy Paper, June 20, Source: Positive Outcomes website http://www.positiveoutcomes.com.au *04*

Nagolwala, A. (2006). "A Study on Impact Assessment of Corporate Social Responsibility with Respect to Community Development Programme of Industries of Gujarat", *Faculty of Social Work*, The Maharaja Sayajirao University of Baroda, Vadodara.

Peter, U. (2003). "Implications of Corporate Social Responsibility: Promoting Development through Corporate Social Responsibility—Does it Work?", *Global Future*, Third Quarter.

Richard, R. (2009). *Universities and Corporate Social Responsibility: A Competitive Advantage?*

13

Education: A Catalyst for Women's Development

Rameshwari Pandya and *Krutika Muley*

The women population in India, according to 2001 census is about 500 million, which is nearly 50 per cent of India's total population. Despite such a huge margin, the status of Indian women in society is not very pleasant. The question is why? Human beings are born equal but are never treated equally. Unequal treatment to women or the gender bias is not a new phenomenon. The hegemonic masculine ideology made them suffer a lot as they were denied equal opportunities in different parts of the world.

In India, since the 19th century, when the first voice was raised against the inferior status of women in society, social reformers gave high priority to women's education. With the establishment of the Bethune School in Calcutta in 1949, and a few indigenous efforts in Gujarat and Maharashtra establishing schools for girls during the same period, first steps towards acceptance of women's education were taken (Desai, Raj, 1987). Though the liberal reformers recognized the value of education for girls, its content and the levels to which girls were educated was very much determined by their limited notion of women's role in the family. They believed that, in the gigantic task of transformation of society in which educated middle-class men were involved, women, if given education, would not only appreciate the changes taking place in the society but would also collaborate in hastening the process of change. They never envisaged any change in the traditional wife/mother role of women. However, it goes to the credit of these social reformers that they were able to generate a climate of acceptance of the value of giving education to girls.

Equality for women is a far cry. Women have been under-represented in all spheres of social, economic, educational and political activities. Since women are considered as "secondary sex", so there is poor representation in all important areas of development. Due to "sex role ideology", women have acquired subordinate status in relation to men in almost all fields such as 'society, economy, politics, and education.' Till date, researches have shown that the girl child, who belongs to the weaker section of our society, are undernourished and only a few manage to complete eight years of satisfactory education.

Although literacy level is low in India, there has been progress in improving educational attainment for both the sexes in India, over the last several decades. In 1971, only 21.97 per cent of women and 45.86 per cent of men were literate. (Table 13.1) By 1991, 39.29 per cent of women and 64.13 per cent of men were literate. Thus, there has been a large increase in the proportion of women who are literate in just 20 years. Despite the improvements in the literacy rate, there continues to be a large gap between the literacy levels of men and women.

Table 13.1: Literacy Rates in India

(In per cent)

Census year	*Persons*	*Male*	*Female*	*Male-Female gap in Literacy*
1951	18.33	27.16	8.86	18.30
1961	28.30	40.40	15.35	25.05
1971	34.45	45.96	21.97	23.98
1981	43.57	56.38	29.76	26.62
1991	52.21	64.13	39.29	24.84
2001	65.38	75.85	54.16	21.70

Source: Census of India, 2001.

Women education in India plays a very important role in the overall development of the country. It not only helps in the development of half of the human resources, but in improving the quality of life at home and outside. In India, Jyotiba Phuley, a social reformer from Maharashtra started movement for the women's education. He decided to strive to educate the lower castes and women.

He taught his wife, Savitri to read and write and she became the first women teacher in the state of Maharashtra.

Importance of Education for Women

- Education enables women to effectively participate in the affairs of the country and indeed, in their own family.
- Educated women can be an effective voice for articulating women related issues. They can be the voices in the fight against social evils like female feticide, child marriage, dowry, and addiction as well as against the discrimination and biases that exist in society against women.
- They can be the advocates for improved working conditions for women, gender equality and welfare of women. Educated women can help other women to become self-reliant and self-confident.
- Education is a prerequisite for women's development because over the period, it acts as a catalyst to bring a distinct change in a person or within a situation. Hence, it has been perceived as a liberating instrument. The issue that holds prominence relates to the content of women's education. The general consensus among almost all societies is that women's education should be such that serves her dignity and role as women. Through education, women's suppression can be intellectually perceived and understood and gradually efforts can be directed towards removal of the subordination. Evidence indicates that education has helped women to fight for their autonomous status in society. Their achievement could be possible only with their intellectual perception and understanding of the total situation along contribution of education to women's liberation as autonomous individual outweighs its negative impact.
- Educated women not only tend to promote education of their girl children, but also can provide better guidance to all their children. Moreover, educated women can also help in the reduction of infant mortality rate and growth of the population.
- Education helps women to have more balanced and a regulated life.

- Education increases feeling of security among women by enhancing self-confidence.
- Education in women develops suitable habits of health care, application of time management and conservation of physical, mental and emotional energies.
- Education in women enhances the scientific thoughts for day to day activities. It improves quality of life by applying analytical approach.
- Educated women develop the ability to think critically by broadening their vision and horizon.
- Education makes facilities for effective decision making process which is a powerful tool of any managerial exercise.
- Education imparts in women the moral support and knowledge which can ensure dignity.
- Education helps in creating awareness on social issues in the community and the world. It becomes easier for educated women to develop social interaction.
- Women can develop leadership qualities through education, as it improves her position in family, community and society.
- Educated women develop independent attitude and confidence for meeting their ends and have more employment opportunities.
- Educated women become a part of community and political affairs by being aware of their rights and duties.

Hurdles in Women Education

Indian women are capable as any other women from any part of the world. Unlike women, in many western countries, Indian women are denied equal opportunities for working with men in different spheres of life. Constitutionally, Indian women have been granted equal rights with men, but practically speaking they are kept much behind men in various life activities. There are many problems in women education:

- Many people think that it is wastage of time and money to give education to their girls.
- Parents have negative attitude towards girl's education.
- They think that after marriage girl have to look after domestic work and so, educating them is a waste of time and money.
- Lack of girl's schools at all stages of education is another

factor which forces the parents not to send their girls to the school.

- Poverty is another reason that compels poor parents to deprive their girl's from education and restrict them to home, to take care of younger siblings when their parents go to work.
- Unsafe environment in educational institutions.
- According to medieval perception women need just household education and this perception of medieval India still persists in villages of India even today.
- Although scenario in urban areas has changed a lot and women are opting for higher education but majority of Indian population residing in villages still live in the medieval times.
- Another reason is far-off location of schools. In Indian society virginity and purity is given utmost importance during marriage and people are afraid to send their girl child to far-off schools where male teacher teach them along with the boys.
- In India, a large percentage of women do not have decision power. They cannot take decisions independently not even related to their own life. They have to take permission of male members for each and every issue.
- Low enrolment of girl child in the schools, engagement of girl child in domestic work, and high drop-out rates are major obstacles in the path of the women education.

Suggestions

- Adult education and non-formal education can be interlocked for solving the educational problems of females.
- The distance education can be utilized as one of the element for bringing equality in education system for women.
- The organization, who are already working for the women's upliftment can contribute towards women education.
- The organized sectors where women are working can support the women education by providing facilities like permission for further studies.
- The society should give encouragement to the women teacher and support them in their teaching carrier.

- Further new colleges and courses should be introduced for the women which would give them a chance in the demand market.
- The Governmental and Non-Government Organization can work for disseminating the inequalities in education.
- There should be collaborative efforts by the government and NGOs for the women's education.
- Through adult and non-formal education, the mindset of the society towards the women's education can be changed or reformed.

Conclusion

The statistics shows that in the world female literacy rate is 77.6 per cent whereas in India it is 58 per cent. Female school enrolment in the world is 62 per cent and in India it is 47 per cent. But in recent years India has world's largest number of professionally qualified women. As well as India has largest population of working women in the world. India has more number of doctors, surgeons, scientists, professors than the United States. Women enjoyed equal status and rights during the early Vedic period. However, after the 500 B.C., the status of women began to decline. The Islamic invasion played a vital role in restricting freedom and rights of the women. Women education in medieval India further deteriorated with the introduction of *Purdah* system. Various customs and traditions of the Islam, Hindu and Christian society worsened the condition of Indian women. But importantly enough, the interest of the Women education in India revived with the coming of the British and with the advent of Bhakti Movement. Various socio-religious movements contributed to the growth of women literacy. Many leaders took various initiatives to make education available to the women of India. The structured form of education was incorporated for women in the early centuries of the Christian era.

The period and after 1948 in India, highest priority was given to women education. As Women Education in Modern India became the major concern for both the government and civil society as educated women could play a vital role in the development of the country. Thus, there was a great upsurge in awareness regarding women's rights among all sections of the society..Various developmental programmes and policies were introduced in order to improve the social status of women. Education is creditable for women as this reduces female infant mortality and child mortality rates and it is beneficial for overall development.

In India, the educational system was modified and three-tier instruction process was developed. All citizens of India are offered the right to education and Women Education in Modern India was opened to a new vista. The structure of Indian education system came into being. Two important structures came into being: Formal and Non-Formal Education programme. Various other educational programmes such as online education and distance education were also launched. The main aim of all the educational programmes is to make every girl child of the society literate.

At present, Women Education in Modern India has achieved a new height. Currently, entrance of women in engineering, medical and other professional colleges is overwhelmingly. Most of the professional colleges in the country keep thirty per cent of the seats reserved for females. In urban India, girls are opened to a far wider scope than the rural girls. The status of Women in Modern India is a sort of a paradox. If on the one hand, she is at the peak of ladder of success, on the other hand, she is mutely suffering the violence afflicted on her by her own family members. As compared with past women in modern times have achieved a lot but in reality they have to still travel a long way. Their path is full of roadblocks. The women have left the secured domain of their home and are now in the battlefield of life, fully armoured with their talent. They had proven themselves. But in India they are yet to get their dues. The sex ratio of India shows that the Indian society is still prejudiced against female. There are 933 females per thousand males in India according to the census of 2001, which is much below the world average of 990 females. There are many problems which women in India have to go through daily. These problems have become the part and parcel of life of Indian women and some of them have accepted them as their fate.

References

Chelladuri, A. (2009). "Women's Empowerment and Economic Development", *Social Welfare*, Vol. 55 (12), March.

Khan, S. and Pandey, G. (2008). "Education: A Dignity for Women's Life in Indian Scenario", *Women's Link*, Vol. 14 (4), October-December.

Patil, P. (2009). "An Enlightened Women is the Source of Infinite Power", *University News*, Vol. 47 (18), May.

Tripathi, A. (2008). "Domestic Violence Against Indian Women", *Women's Link*, Vol. 14 (2), April-June.

Yrroju, B., Rani, S. and Surendra, G. (2003). "Community Education and Social Responsibility", *Social Welfare*, Vol. 49 (12), March.

14

Environment: Issues and Concerns

Udit Digal and *M.N. Parmar*

Everyone certainly knows that, in some parts of the world there is an imbalance between the amount of arable land and the size of the population, and, in other parts, between the fertility of the soil and available farm implements. Natural resources are limited; some are not, as it is said, renewable. Using them as if they were inexhaustible, with absolute dominion, seriously endangers their availability not only for the present generation but, above all, for generations to come. We all know that the direct or indirect result of industrialization is, ever more frequently, the pollution of the environment, with serious consequences for the health of the population. It is evident that development, the planning which governs it, and the way in which resources are used must include respect for moral demands. One of the latter undoubtedly imposes limits on the use of the natural world. The dominion granted to man by the Creator is not an absolute power, nor can one speak of a freedom to "use and misuse" or to dispose of things as one pleases.

We seem to be increasingly aware of the fact that the exploitation of the earth, the planet on which we are living, demands rational and honest planning. At the same time, exploitation of the earth not only for industrial but also for military purposes and the uncontrolled development of technology outside the framework of a long-term authentically humanistic plan often bring with them a threat to man's natural environment, alienate him in his relations with nature and remove him from nature. Although people are rightly worried though much less than they should be about preserving the natural habitats of the various animal species threatened with extinction, because they realize that each of these species makes its particular contribution to the balance of nature in general, too little effort is made to safeguard the moral conditions for an authentic "human ecology". In this context, mention should be made of the serious problems of modern urbanization, of the need for urban planning which is concerned with how people are to live, and of the attention which should be given to a "social ecology" of work.

Environment: Definition and Meaning

The word "environment" is most commonly used for describing "natural" environment and means the sum of all living and non-living things that surround an organism, or group of organisms. The Oxford definition of Environment is the natural world in which people, animals and plants live. Environment includes all elements, factors, and conditions that have some impact on growth and development of certain organism. Environment includes both biotic and abiotic factors that have influence on observed organism. Abiotic factors such as light, temperature, water, atmospheric gases combine with biotic factors (all surrounding living species). Environment often changes after some time and therefore many organisms have ability to adapt to these changes. However, tolerance range is not the same with all species and exposure to environmental conditions at the limit of a certain organism's tolerance range represents environmental stress. Environmentalism is very important political and social movement with goal to protect natural environment by emphasizing importance of future's role in protection of the environment in combination with various actions and policies oriented to nature preservation.

Environmental Issues

1. Air Pollution

Air pollution is the introduction of chemicals, particulate matter, or biological materials that cause harm or discomfort to humans or other living organisms, or damages the natural environment into the atmosphere. The atmosphere is a complex dynamic natural gaseous system that is essential to support life on planet Earth. Stratospheric ozone depletion due to air pollution has long been recognized as a threat to human health as well as to the Earth's ecosystems. Indoor air pollution and urban air quality are listed as two of the world's worst pollution problems in the 2008. Blacksmith Institute World's Worst Polluted Places report that Indian cities are polluted by vehicles and industry emissions. Road dust due to vehicles is also contributing up to 33 per cent of air pollution. India has emission standard of Bharat Stage II (Euro II) for vehicles since 2005. One of the biggest causes of air pollution in India is from the transport system. Hundreds of millions of old diesel engines continuously burning away diesel which has anything between 150 to 190 times the amount of sulphur out. Of course, the biggest problems are in the big cities where there are huge concentrations of these vehicles.

Table 14.1: List of Top 20 Countries by Carbon Dioxide Emissions (2010)

S. No	Country	Total Emissions (Million metric tons of CO_2)	Per Capita Emissions (Tons/capita)
1.	China	6017.69	4.58
2.	United States	5902.75	19.78
3.	Russia	1704.36	12.00
4.	India	1293.17	1.16
5.	Japan	1246.76	9.78
6.	Germany	857.60	10.40
7.	Canada	614.33	18.81
8.	United Kingdom	585.71	9.66
9.	South Korea	514.53	10.53
10.	Iran	471.48	7.25
11.	Italy	468.19	8.05
12.	South Africa	443.58	10.04
13.	Mexico	435.60	4.05
14.	Saudi Arabia	424.08	15.70
15.	France	417.75	6.60
16.	Australia	417.06	20.58
17.	Brazil	377.24	2.01
18.	Spain	372.61	9.22
19.	Ukraine	328.72	7.05
20.	Poland	303.42	7.87

2. Ozone Depletion

Ozone depletion describes two distinct, but related observations: a slow, steady decline of about 4 per cent per decade in the total volume of ozone in Earth's stratosphere (the ozone layer) since the late 1970s, and a much larger, but seasonal, decrease in stratospheric ozone over Earth's polar regions during the same period. The latter phenomenon is commonly referred to as the ozone hole. In addition to this well-known stratospheric ozone depletion, there are also troposphere ozone depletion events, which occur near the surface in Polar regions during spring. Depletion of Ozone layer causes increase in ultra violet rays creating warmthness in the atmosphere resulting to various chemical reactions. The main public concern is biological effects regarding the ozone hole has been the effects of increased surface UV and microwave radiation on human health. It has direct effects on human life by causing Basal and Squamous Cell Carcinomas, Malignant Melanoma, Cortical Cataracts and it badly affects the biotic and abiotic beings along with the crops.

3. Freshwater Shortages and Water Pollution

We all are familiar with the image of Earth as the "Blue Planet" when seen from space. It gives the impression that water is plentiful and indeed it is. However, pictures can be deceiving. Freshwater only accounts for 2.15 per cent of all the Earth's water. But even that percentage is deceiving because 99.5 per cent of all surface freshwater is locked away in continental ice. The present state of freshwater mainly includes the following problems: freshwater augmentation, wastewater and storm water, eutrophication of lakes and reservoirs, sewage and public health problems. Freshwater, therefore, is a scarce resource, often a limiting factor for development, and one which we should take great care to protect. We have 97.5 per cent saltwater, e.g., oceans, seas and 2.5 per cent is freshwater (54.65 million km^3). Freshwater comes from different sources. The greater portion of the freshwater (68.7%: 37.4 million km^3) is in the form of permanent ice (Arctic, Antarctic, Alpine mountain ranges, etc.). 29.9 per cent of the freshwater (16.24 million km^3) is groundwater, mostly deep seated. Only 0.26 per cent (or, 64,000 km^3) of the total freshwater is in lakes, river systems, etc. and it is accessible for our needs. In fact, the total water withdrawal worldwide is less than 5000 km^3 or about one-tenth of the total river discharge a mere drop of Earth's waters.

4. Ocean and Coastal Threats

Human activity has finally pushed oceans to their limit. For centuries people have regarded them as an inexhaustible supply of food, a useful transport route, and a convenient dumping ground—simply too vast to be affected by anything we do. But human activity, particularly over the last few decades, has finally pushed oceans to their limit. Overfished, polluted, and taken for granted, carelessly abused and destroyed, and much more fragile and complex than we once thought the largest living space on Earth is fast deteriorating. This doesn't just threaten marine habitats and species—many of which have only recently been discovered—but also our own health, way of life, and security. Large and small craft significantly pollute both inland and coastal waters by dumping their untreated sewage. Oil spilled accidentally or flushed from tankers and offshore rigs (9,00,000 metric tons annually) sullies beaches and smothers bird, fish, and plant life. In 1989, in one of the world's worst single instances of water pollution, the Exxon Valdez spilled 11 million gallons of oil in Prince William Sound, Alaska, causing great environmental destruction. In 1997, the 22 oil spills reported worldwide involved a total of 15 million gallons (57 million litres) of oil. In addition to its direct damage to wildlife, oil takes up fat-soluble poisons like DDT, allowing them to be concentrated in organisms that ingest the oil-contaminated water; thus such poisons enter the food chains leading to health hazards for sea mammals and people.

5. Shrinking Wetlands

Wetlands are at risk because half of the world's wetlands have been destroyed over 100 years. Conversion of swamps, marshes, lakes and floodplains for commercial development, drainage schemes, extraction of minerals and peat, overfishing, tourism, siltation, pesticide discharges from intensive agriculture, toxic pollutants from industrial waste, and the construction of dams, an attempt for flood protection, are major threats to wetlands everywhere. Military action, too, can be a significant factor in wetland decline. Exercises frequently causes immense damage, while wars create the kind of havoc to people and the environment that is being witnessed in the marshes of southern Iraq. Another major threat to wetlands is human overexploitation of the undergroundwater table for agriculture, housing, industry, and tourist development.

6. Forest Destruction/Deforestation

About 30 per cent of the global total land area is covered by forests, these amounts to just under 40 million km^2. But it is unevenly distributed. Mainly conversion of forests to agricultural land is continuing at an alarmingly high rate. Forest area decreased worldwide by 0.22 per cent per year in the period 1990-2000 and 0.18 per cent per year between 2000 and 2005. However, the net loss of forest is slowing down as a result of the planting of new forests and of natural expansion of forests. Native forests in India are disappearing at a rate of up to 2.7 per cent per year. The figures, published is an analysis of the country's forest cover, stand in stark contrast to those of a 2009 survey by Indian Governmental Organization, which said that forests have expanded by 5 per cent over the past decade. India is among the most densely forested countries in the world, and in 2008 the government announced goals to increase forest cover by nearly 10 per cent by 2012. The India State of Forest Report (2009) by the Forest Survey of India (FSI) indicated that the outlook was good. The main causes of total clearance are agriculture and in drier areas, fuel-wood collection. The main cause of forest degradation is logging, mining, industrial development and large dams also have a serious impact. Tourism is becoming a larger threat to the forests. Poverty and overpopulation are believed to be the main causes of forest loss. It is believed that the problem can be solved by encouraging development projects along with imparting environment education and trying to reduce population growth.

7. Desertification

It is the loss of biological or economic productivity and complexity in croplands, pastures, and woodlands. It is mainly due to climate variability and unsustainable human activities. The most commonly cited forms of unsustainable land use are overcultivation, overgrazing, deforestation, and poor irrigation practices. Seventy per cent of the world's dry lands (excluding hyper-arid deserts), or some 3,600 million hectares, are degraded. While drought is often associated with land degradation, it is a natural phenomenon that occurs when rainfall is significantly below normal recorded levels for a long time.

The study reveals that 105.48 m ha area of the country is undergoing processes of land degradation (32.07% of the total geographic area of the country). Area undergoing desertification is 81.4 m ha. India occupies only 2.4 per cent of the world's geographical area, yet supports about 16.7 per cent of the world's human population;

it has only 0.5 per cent of the world's grazing land but supports 18 per cent of the world's cattle population. Thus, there is tremendous pressure on our land-based natural resources. India is endowed with a variety of soils, climate, biodiversity and ecological regions. About 50.8 m ha land area (15.8% of the country's geographical area) is arid, 123.4 m ha (37.6%) is semi-arid and 54.1 m ha (16.5%) area falls in the dry subhumid region. All put together, about 228 m ha area, i.e. 69 per cent of the geographic area of the country is dry land (arid, semi-arid and dry subhumid). Appropriate action plan for arresting land degradation and desertification requires information on the area and the spatial distribution of the land undergoing different processes of degradation.

8. Nuclear Weapons and Nuclear Power

Nuclear weapons pose a vast threat to our society and to the global environment. They are indiscriminate in nature and enough warheads exist to threaten human existence. The use of nuclear weapons on Hiroshima and Nagasaki clearly demonstrated the horrifically destructive powers of nuclear weapons. Most nuclear weapons deployed today have a destructive capacity many times greater than those used in 1945. India now envisages to increase the contribution of nuclear power to overall electricity generation capacity from 4.2 per cent to 9 per cent within 25 years. As of 2009, India stands 9th in the world in terms of number of operational nuclear power reactors and is constructing 9 more, including two EPRs being constructed by France's Areva. Nuclear power is the fourth-largest source of electricity in India after thermal, hydro and renewable sources of electricity. As of 2010, India has 20 nuclear power plants in operation generating 4,560 MW while 4 others are under construction and are expected to generate an additional 2,720 MW. India's nuclear power industry is undergoing rapid expansion with plans to increase nuclear power output to 64,000 MW by 2032. The country is involved in the development of nuclear fusion reactors through its participation in the ITER project and is a global leader in the development of thorium-based fast breeder reactors. A series of recent scientific studies done at U.S. universities predict that the detonation of even a tiny fraction of the global nuclear arsenal in urban areas will cause catastrophic damage to the Earth's climate and environment. This smoke would engulf the entire planet within 10 days. Because the smoke couldn't be rained out, it would remain in the stratosphere for at least a decade and have profoundly disruptive effects. Specifically, the smoke layer would heat the upper atmosphere, and cause massive destruction of the protective stratospheric ozone, while simultaneously blocking warming sunlight and creating Ice Age weather conditions on Earth. Average surface temperatures would become colder than experienced in the last 1000 years. Real security requires an environmentally sustainable, socially equitable world, empowering the majority to live a healthy, dignified, and productive life.

9. World Hunger: Growing Food Crisis

There are 925 million undernourished people in the world today. That means one in seven people do not get enough food to be healthy and lead an active life. Hunger and malnutrition are in fact the number one risk to the health worldwide—greater than AIDS, malaria and tuberculosis combined. Among the key causes of hunger are natural disasters, conflict, poverty, poor agricultural infrastructure and over-exploitation of the environment. Recently, financial and economical crises have pushed more people into hunger. As well as the obvious sort of hunger resulting from an empty stomach, there is also the hidden hunger of micronutrient deficiencies which make people susceptible to infectious diseases, impair physical and mental development, reduce their labour productivity and increase the risk of premature death. Hunger does not only weigh on the individual, it also imposes a crushing economic burden on the developing world. Economists estimate that every child whose physical and mental development is stunted by hunger and malnutrition stands to lose 5-10 per cent in lifetime earnings. India has a mixed scenario of food crisis.

The following are the major emerging trends in regard to Indian food crisis:

- Decline in investment in agriculture and slow agricultural growth.
- Farming provides livelihood to nearly 60 per cent of India's 1.1 billion people even though farm produce comprises only 18 per cent of the India's current GDP.
- India is largely insulated from food prices due to huge stocks, but has challenges like inefficient distribution system and poor storage facilities.

- 70-80 per cent of the net agricultural land is rainfed thus based on monsoon.
- Future food production is uncertain.
- Bumper wheat and rice crops are being expected.
- Record procurement of wheat by Food Corporation of India and other agencies.

The present decade is going to be one in which our food security will be under stress, the Prime Minister had told the National Development Council while finalising the Eleventh Five Year Plan (2007-2012). Since 1987, there has been a yearly increase of two million tons in domestic foodgrains productivity against the requirement of seven million tons. The gap will spiral out of control if timely interventions are not made.

10. Endangered Species and Biodiversity Loss

Till 2010, about 23 per cent (1,130 species) of mammals and 12 per cent (1,194 species) of birds were considered as threatened by human activities. As Global biodiversity is being lost much faster than natural extinction due to changes in land use, unsustainable use of natural resources, invasive alien species, climate change and pollution among others. Land conversion by humans, resulting in natural habitat loss, is most evident in tropical forests and is less intensive in temperate and Arctic regions. Pollution from atmospheric nitrogen deposition is most severe in northern temperate areas close to urban centres; and the introduction of damaging alien species is usually brought about through patterns of human activity. Species loss is also compounded by:

- The ongoing growth of human populations and unsustainable consumer lifestyles
- Increasing production of waste and pollutants
- Urban development
- International conflict.

Human activity has been causing massive extinctions, "the current extinction rate is now approaching 1,000 times the background rate and may climb to 10,000 times the background rate during the next century, if present trends continue [resulting in] a loss that would easily equal to those of past extinctions." Is this the kind of world we want? After all, our lives are inextricably linked with biodiversity and ultimately its protection is essential for our very survival.

Environmental Concerns

1. State of Our Environment

A country's environmental problems vary with its stage of development, structure of its economy, production technologies in use and its environmental policies. While some problems may be associated with the lack of economic development (e.g. inadequate sanitation and clean drinking water), others are exacerbated by the growth of economic activity (e.g. air and water pollution). Poverty presents special problems for a densely populated country with limited resources.

2. Land/Soil Degradation

Most of the land areas in the country show evidence of degradation, thus, affecting the productive resource base of the economy. Out of the total geographical area of 329 million hectares, 175 million hectares is considered degraded. Erosion by water and wind is the most significant contributor to soil erosion with other factors like waterlogging, salination etc. adding to the *in situ* degradation. While soil erosion by rain and river in hill area causes landslides and floods, deforestation, overgrazing, traditional agricultural practices, mining and incorrect plans of development projects in forest areas have resulted in opening up of these areas to heavy soil erosion.

Statistical Data of Soil Erosion and Land Degradation in (Million Hectares)

1. Total Geographical Area—328.7
2. Area Subject to Water and Wind Erosion—141.3

Area Degraded through Special Problems

1. Waterlogged Area—8.5
2. Alkali Soil—3.6

3. Acid Soil—4.5
4. Saline Soil including Coastal Sandy areas—5.5
5. Ravines and Gullies—4.0
6. Area subject to Shifting Cultivation—4.9
7. Riverine and Torrents—2.7.

3. Deforestation

Forests are a renewable resource and contribute substantially to the economic development by providing goods and services to forest dwellers, people at large and forest based industries, besides generating substantial volume of employment. Forests also play a vital role in enhancing the quality of environment by influencing the ecological balance and life support system (checking soil erosion, maintaining soil fertility, conserving water, regulating water cycle and floods, balancing carbon dioxide and oxygen content in atmosphere etc.). The country has very diverse forest vegetation ranging from the moist evergreen forests in the North-East, along the West Coast and the Andaman and Nicobar Islands to the temperate and alpine vegetation in the Himalayas. However, this forest wealth is dwindling due to overgrazing, overexploitation, encroachments, unsustainable practices, forest fire and indiscriminate plan of development projects in the forest areas. Withdrawal of forest products, including fuelwood, timbers etc. are much beyond the carrying capacity of our forests. The current annual withdrawal of fuelwood is estimated at 235 million cubic metres against a sustainable capacity of about 48 million cubic metres. The annual demand for industrial wood is about 28 million cubic metres against the production capacity of 12 million cubic metres. The area affected by forest fire range from 33 per cent in West Bengal to 99 per cent in Manipur.

4. Atmospheric Pollution

Air pollution is widespread in the country and a high level of Suspended Particulate Matter (SPM) is the most prevalent form of air pollution. High concentration of Sulphur Dioxide (SO_2) and SPM occur in about 20 per cent of the cities so monitored. High domestic use of coal or biomass fuel is still a serious problem in high human exposure to SO_2, SPM and carcinogenic agents. The main factors contributing to urban air quality deterioration are growing industrialization and increasing vehicular pollution. It has been aggravated by developments that typically occur as countries industrialize: growing cities, increasing traffic, rapid economic development and industrial growth, all of which are closely associated with higher energy consumption. Industrial pollution is concentrated in industries like petroleum refineries, textiles, pulp and paper, industrial chemicals, iron and steel and non-metallic mineral products. Small scale industries especially foundries, chemical manufacturing and brick-making are also significant polluters. In the power sector, thermal power which constitutes bulk of the installed capacity for electricity generation is an important source of air pollution.

Table 14.2: Level of Air Pollution in the Metro Cities

Name of the Metro city	*Levels of Air Pollution (micrograms/m^3)*	
	SO_2	*NO_2*
1. Ahmedabad	5.4 – 110.9	3.6 – 70.0
2. Bhopal	8.1 – 22.0	12.2 – 32.4
3. Calcutta	6.0 – 122.0	6.0 – 73.1
4. Chennai	2.4 – 161.6	1.8 – 55.5
5. Coimbatore	0 – 8.9	0.3 – 19.1
6. Delhi	10.1 – 85.1	20.1 – 104.5
7. Hyderabad	5.1 – 70.7	7.5 – 124.13
8. Indore	2.6 – 10.2	4.4 – 17.4
9. Jaipur	6.1 – 53.7	4.0 – 64.3
10. Kanpur	8.2 – 22.4	7.7 – 63.0
11. Kochi	3.2 – 54.3	1.7 – 137.0
12. Lucknow	23.2 – 37.4	23.0 – 34.4
13. Mumbai	6.1 – 111.7	5.4 – 115.8
14. Nagpur	4.3 – 18.8	3.2 – 43.2
15. Patna	12.7 – 46.4	8.5 – 55.7
16. Pune	17.1 – 29.0	10.1 – 34.0
17. Surat	22.4 – 304.0	10.0 – 135.7
18. Varanasi	18.3 – 27.1	10.6 – 28.8
19. Visakhapatnam	5.5 – 80.8	5.1 – 92.0

5. Water Pollution

According to an analysis of water quality over 12 years (1986-97) by CPCB, the Biochemical Oxygen Demand (BOD) values, in a sample of 4500 observations, below 3mg/l were above 60 per cent during 1986 to 1991, the values gradually declined down to 54 per cent in 1994-95 but rose to 58 per cent in 1997. This indicates that the water quality which had gone down during 1986-91, improved during

1991-95. The rising industrial and domestic wastes have resulted in heavy stress of pollution of water bodies such as lakes, rivers, coastal areas and underground sources. A 1994 survey of groundwater quality at 138 sampling locations in 22 industrialized zones indicated that water was unfit for drinking due to high bacteriological and heavy metal contamination. The water quality monitoring results indicate that organic and bacterial pollution continue to be predominant source of pollution in our aquatic resources. A large part of municipal sewage is allowed to flow in untreated form to nearby receiving water bodies, thereby reducing dissolved oxygen required for supporting aquatic life, increasing the pollution load in terms of BOD.

6. Solid Wastes

Unregulated growth of urban areas without necessary infrastructural services and proper collection, transportation, treatment and disposal of solid wastes has resulted in increased pollution and health hazard from these wastes. Urban Municipal Wastes (MSW) is a heterogeneous mixture of paper, plastic, cloth, metal, glass, organic matter etc. generated from households, commercial establishments and markets. The plastics waste alone has increased tremendously over the last few years. The mode of waste disposal predominantly remains through land-filling, which is a conventional but unhygienic method. Alternative modes like composting and other scientific approaches are sparsely used. An inadequate collection/disposal of such wastes pollutes and degrades land and water resources, besides being a health hazard. Fly ash, phospho-gypsum and iron and steel slags are the main forms of industrial solid wastes generated in India. It is estimated that 35-40 million tons of fly ash is generated annually by the thermal power plants of which only 2-3 per cent is currently being utilised. Besides, around 5 million tons of hazardous wastes is generated annually with very little infrastructure for proper disposal of these wastes.

In India, the signs already back-up forecasts that as the mercury rises the Indian subcontinent, home to one-sixth of humanity, will be one of the worst-affected regions. The Himalayan glaciers have started to melt and the average rate of retreat is almost twice (34 metres) per year as compared to the 1971 levels of 19 metres. The melting glaciers will cause temperatures and sea-levels to rise and there will be a cascading effect on the crops and the monsoons. Worse—whole islands are expected to vanish! In fact, two have already gone under—two islands in the Sunderbans, an area which India shares with Bangladesh. Temperatures in the group of islands have already gone up by one degree centigrade. Rising sea levels have submerged two islands in the Sunderbans, where tigers roam through mangrove forests in the Ganges River delta, and a dozen more islands are under threat...official records list 102 islands on the Indian side of the vast Sunderbans but scientists found that two have been swallowed up. While some climatologists say that sea levels will increase by just 4-35 inches from 1990 levels in another hundred years some feel that the range could be higher—20-55 inches. That's a lot and will affect human habitat in a big way.

7. Global Warming

After the Industrial Revolution, through fossil fuel combustion, changing agricultural practices and deforestation, the natural composition of gases in the atmosphere is getting affected and climate and environment began to alter significantly. Over the last 100 years, it was found out that the earth is getting warmer and warmer, unlike previous 8,000 years when temperatures have been relatively constant. The present temperature is 0.3-0.6 °C warmer than it was 100 years ago. The key Green House Gases (GHG) causing global warming is carbon dioxide. CFCs, even though they exist in very small quantities, are significant contributors to global warming. Carbon dioxide is one of the most prevalent green house gases in the atmosphere.

The impact of global warming is already being seen around the world. Record temperatures in many parts of the world this summer point to more than just localised temperature fluctuations, but to the more global trend that has been observed over the last 3 decades. Despite efforts on behalf of some countries to reduce green house gas emissions, such as the Kyoto treaty, the world as a whole is pumping out more and more carbon dioxide every year. Yes, countries like Norway and Holland are meeting their goals to reduce emissions, but this is small fry when countries such as China and India are pumping out more and more every year.

8. Loss of Biodiversity

Biodiversity refers to the variety of life on earth, and its biological diversity. The number of species of plants, animals, micro-organisms, and the enormous diversity of genes in these species, the different ecosystems on the planet, such as deserts, rainforests and coral reefs are all a part of a biologically diverse earth. It is now believed that human activity is changing biodiversity and causing massive extinctions. Rapid global warming can affect ecosystems chances to adapt naturally. Over the past 150 years, deforestation has contributed an estimated 30 per cent of the atmospheric build-up of CO_2. It is also a significant driving force behind the loss of genes, species, and critical ecosystem services.

Biodiversity is under threat worldwide. For example, the global mammalian extinction rate of 0.35 per cent of species lost per century since 1600 is calculated to be between 17 and 377 times the mammalian background extinction rate during the past 65 million years, that is, since the mass extinction that removed the dinosaurs, India has considerable biodiversity that is under threat as the Table 14.3 indicates which deals only with animals.

Table 14.3: Biodiversity under Threat

Sr. No.	*Biodiversity*	*Number of Indian species*	*% of Indian species evaluated*	*Species threatened in India as per cent of those evaluated*	*Number extinct (% of those evaluated)*
1.	Mammals	386 (7%)	59%	41%	4(1.8%)
2.	Birds	1219 (12%)	—	7%	Unknown
3.	Reptiles	495	73%	46%	Unknown
4.	Amphibians	207 (4%)	79%	57%	Unknown
5.	Freshwater fish	700	46%	70%	Unknown

Biodiversity, as measured by the number of plant and vertebrate species is greatest in the Western Ghats and the north-east. This is because of the presence of tropical rainforest that are typically the richest habitats for species diversity. Both these areas are included in the world's list of hotspots of biodiversity: small geographic areas with high species diversity. Of the two, the Western Ghats have more endemic species, those that are found nowhereelse.

9. Climatic Change

Have you ever sat down and wondered what is happening to our weather pattern on this side of the globe. We have heard a lot about climate change, food crisis, global warming, and extreme weather patterns. There is a concern that human activities are enhancing the natural green house effect, which can have serious consequences on human settlements and ecosystems. The fact remains that the recent shifts in weather pattern have affected our agriculture to the extent that the seasonality and productivity of certain crops has been severely altered. The whole earthly cycle is changing and it would seem that all of creation is groaning and yearning for a return to those bountiful years. Precisely at a time when India is confronted with development imperatives, we will also be severely impacted by climate change. Like other developing countries, several sections of the Indian populace will not be able to buffer themselves from impacts of global warming. With close economic ties to natural resources and climate-sensitive sectors such as agriculture, water and forestry, India may face a major threat, and require serious adaptive capacity to combat climate change. As a developing country, India can little afford the risks and economic backlashes that industrialized nations can. With 27.5 per cent of the population still below the poverty line, reducing vulnerability to the impacts of climate change is essential.

Need for Sustainable Development

Sustainable development is often defined as 'development that meets the needs of the present, without compromising the ability of future generations to meet their own needs'. Sustainable development encompasses three basic and interrelated objectives:

- Economic security and prosperity
- Social development and advancement
- Environmental sustainability

Sustainable development demands that we seek ways of living, working and being that enable all people of the world to lead healthy, fulfilling, and economically secure lives without destroying the environment and without endangering the future welfare of people and the planet.

Impact on India

Climate change will make monsoons unpredictable. As a result, rain-fed wheat cultivation in South Asia will suffer in a big way. Total cereal production will go down. The crop yield per hectare will be hit badly, causing food insecurity and loss of livelihood. Changes in climate around the globe are expected to trigger a steep fall in the production of cereals, says R.K. Pachauri, Chairman of the IPCC. He estimated that a rise of 0.5 degree Celsius in winter temperatures could cause a 0.45 tons per hectare fall in India's wheat production. The average per hectare production in India is 2.6 tons. Total agricultural land will shrink and the available land may not remain suitable for the present crops for too long. Farmers have to explore options of changing crops suitable to weather. He also pointed out that climatic changes could lead to major food security issues for a country like India. India's economic growth would "necessarily involve increase in (green house gas) emissions from the current extremely low levels." Any constraints on such emissions by India, whether direct, by way of emission targets, or indirect would reduce growth rates, the report stated. It is very important to impart environment education so that we prevent further damage to occur.

Environment Education

Environmental Education is a process of recognizing values and clarifying concepts in order to develop skills and added tools necessary to understand and appreciate the interrelationship among humans, their culture and their bio-physical surrounding. It creates an overall perspective, which acknowledges the fact that natural environment and man-made environment are interdependent. It should consider the environment in its totality and should be a continuous lifelong process beginning at the pre-school level and continuing through all stages. It should be interdisciplinary and examine major environmental issues from local, national and international points of view. It should utilize various educational approaches to teach and learn about and from the environment with stress on practical activities and first-hand experience. It is through this process of education that people can be sensitized about the environmental issues. Thus, Environment Education and awareness assume critical importance. The 'Environmental Education, Awareness and Training' is an important aspect for enhancing the understanding of people at all levels about the relationship between human beings and the environment and to develop capabilities/skills to improve and protect the environment. People must know about issues related to environment, which can help them to take care of environment. In fact, environment education needs to be imparted since childhood or school days. It should be taught at all levels of formal education as well as through non-formal education. Suggestions for some of the areas related to environment education are:

- Sensitizing youth for environment
- Involving community in environment savvy programme
- Reducing Package Waste at the Grocery
- Earth for Energy: Eliminate Power Bills
- Installing Solar Panels at Home
- Introducing Basics of Environmental Education Job
- Looking into the Role of Media in Environmental Education
- Seeking Grants for Environmental Education
- Defining the Ethics of Environmental Education
- An Insight into Environmental Education Activities
- Procuring Environmental Education Jobs
- Analyzing the Need for Environmental Education
- Looking into the Institute for Environmental Education
- By Knowing the Ethics of Environmental Education
- Opportunities of Environmental Education Specialist Jobs
- Environmental Education Specialist Role and Specifications
- Learning about Environmental Education in Schools
- Scope of Environmental Education Grants
- Learning from Environmental Education Games
- Correlation of Environmental Education and Computer Games
- Looking into an Environmental and Education Training Centre
- Basics of Education in Environmental Field

Conclusion

Environmental protection has become a major issue in and around the world and the law is increasingly playing a central role in this regard. There are many principal laws, as well as regulations and standards which supplement the common law in regulating the activities that have an impact on the environment. New policies, laws and approaches are being adopted at a global and national level in order to strengthen the environmental protection regime. The key environmental concerns of the country that have been identified are land degradation, water pollution and scarcity, urban air pollution, loss of biodiversity, and impacts of natural disasters on economy and livelihood systems. There are sectoral policies to address these issues, but a lack of integration and overlapping of responsibilities prevails among the agencies. There is a lack of coherence among policies, and no holistic approach to mitigate environmental degradation and conserve resources. However, this can be resolved through inter-ministerial decision and coordination. Various policies are now under preparation by the relevant ministries that aim for a sustainable approach towards environmental management and development. It is important that everyone, especially those persons whose activities may have impacts on the environment, to acquaint themselves not only with existing laws and regulations but also of the emerging policies and trends in environmental protection so that when these are also translated into law, they are not caught unaware, with the need to restructure their business practices this can be done by educating people.

References

Goel, A. (2003). *Environment and Ancient Sanskrit Literature*, Deep and Deep Publication (P) Ltd., New Delhi.

Parikh, J. (2003). Editor, *Sustainable Management of Wet lands: Biodiversity and Beyond*, Sage Publications (I) Pvt. Ltd., New Delhi.

Monga, G.S. (1988). *Environment and Development*. Deep and Deep Publications (P) Ltd., New Delhi.

Verma, S.B. and Sing, S.K. (2001). *Environmental Protection and Development: Emerging Issues, Reforms and Strategies*, Deep and Deep Publications (P) Ltd., New Delhi.

www.en.wikipedia.org

www.envfor.nic.in

www.greenteacher.org

www.india.gov.in

www.indiatogether.org

www.fsdinternational.org

www.em-ea.org
www.indiabudget.nic.in
www.unep.or.jp
www.panda.org
www.greenfacts.org
www.wfp.org
www.standford.edu
www.neoncarrot.co.uk
www.indiaenvironmentportal.org.in
www.sprep.org
www.thehindubusinessline.com
www.world-nuclear.org
www.ias.ac.in
www.nature.com
www.nationmaster.com

15
Nutrition Health Education among Tribal Adolescent Girls in Jhagadia Taluka, Gujarat

Anee Kurvilla and *Shivani Bhatt*

> *"The adolescent girl still remains a young plant that neither gets light nor water. She remains the flower that could have blossomed but didn't..." (CEDPA)*
>
> —Kamla Bhasin from "Our Daughters"

There are 1.2 billion adolescents aged 10-19 yrs., in developing nations, making up one-fifth to one quarter of the country's population (WHO, 2006). Adolescents have typically been considered a low risk group for poor health and often receive few healthcare resources and scant attention (Adolescent Nutrition, June 2003). They are a significant human resource that needs to be given ample opportunity for holistic development towards achieving their full potential. Not only are the needs of the adolescents related to their physical development, but also to their emotional and psycho-social development.

Tribal Adolescents

In India, tremendous changes have taken place since the independence in 1947. The life of the inhabitants by and large has become easier and better due to the development in science and technology which have raised the standard of living. In spite of these positive gains for many of the Indian citizens, it is alarming to note that a high percentage of Scheduled Castes and Scheduled Tribes population is still living below the poverty line. It is well-known that in most of the tribal areas the struggle for life is very hard and people lead a hand to mouth existence and thus the life of the tribals is very tough.

India has several socially disadvantaged communities among which Scheduled Tribes are the most deprived ones. Indian tribal people play a major part in constructing the cultural heritage of India. They occupy a major part in the history of India as they are considered as the true inhabitants of India. The tribal people are scattered in different parts of India and they form a considerable number of the population of India. The traditional and cultural distinction of each tribal community has made them distinguishable from each other.

According to the 2001 census conducted by the Government of India, India has more than 84 million tribals that constitute 8.2 per cent of India's population. The tribal population is characterized by widespread poverty, illiteracy, malnutrition, lack of safe drinking water and hygienic conditions (Reddy, *et al.*, 2000). Although, health is one of the crucial parameters of development of a community, researchers have not paid much attention in studying the growth and nutritional status of the tribal communities in India. In fact, most of the works carried out in India on growth and nutritional status only deal with urban and rural population. Among the tribal population, the studies are limited. According to the article 342 of the Indian Constitution, at present, there exists 697 tribes as notified by the Central Government. More than half of the Indian tribal population is concentrated in the states of Madhya Pradesh, Chhattisgarh, Maharastra, Orissa, Jharkhand and Gujarat.

Tribes of Gujarat: The tribal belt in Gujarat consists of the districts of Dang, Surat, Bharuch, Baroda, Panchmahals, Sabarkantha and Banaskantha. Approximately, 8 million persons comprising 15 per cent of Gujarat's population is tribal. Health of the Scheduled Tribes in Gujarat is significantly worse than other population groups. They are economically and socially backward and they have their own way of living and different socio-cultural and eco-geographical settings (USAID, 2009).

Adolescence

Adolescence is a "Transition Period" between childhood to adulthood with specific physiological, psychological, social, emotional and cognitive

Table 15.1: Areas and Population under Tribal Area

District	*Taluka/ Pockets/ Cluster*	*No. of Villa-ges*	*Area Covered (sq.km.)*	*Population (1991 Census) Total*	*Population (1991 Census) ST*	*Population (1991 Census) %*
Vadodara	Chhotaudepur	278	1379	304275	269642	88.62
	Nasvadi	219	535	107435	90825	84.54
	Pavijetpur	213	806	199632	163193	81.75
	Vadail	53	172	33145	22187	66.94
	Bhatpur	61	250	42426	21779	51.33
	Total	824	3142	686913	567626	82.63
Bharuch	Valia	96	514	116265	88973	76.53
	Jhagadia	168	813	151335	99536	65.77
	Ankleshwar	38	226	68612	30016	43.75
	Utraj (Hansot)	13	92	10941	5434	49.67
	Amod (Mada Pocket)	16	85	11935	6204	51.98
	Total	331	1730	359088	230163	64.1

Source: Gujarat Forest Statistics, 2003.

changes which places additional requirements for nutrition. It is a phase during which many life patterns are learnt and estimated. The term youth encompasses ages 10 to 24 years, while the term adolescents as defined by WHO (1986) includes persons aged 10 to 19 yrs.

According to UN definitions,

Child: 0-17 yrs.; Adolescent: 10-19 yrs.;
Youth: 15-24 yrs.; Young people: 10-24 yrs.

According to Journal of Adolescent Research (1991), adolescence may be divided into 3 developmental phases based on physical, psychological and social changes. They are:

Early adolescence: 11 to 13 yrs.
Mid-adolescence: 14 to 16 yrs.
Late adolescence: 17 to 19 yrs.

Adolescent Girls

Currently, it is estimated that there are about 69.7 million adolescent girls constituting about 7 per cent of the total population. Adolescence is often described as a phase of life that begins in biology and ends in society (Sharma, 1996). Girls up to the age of 19 comprise about one-quarter of India's population. The majority is out of school and therefore does not receive services from school-based health programmes. Within the family, girls—especially older ones—receive less health care and education, nutrition and fewer opportunities for employment than boys. There are limited choices available for the future and girls are caught in the cycle of early marriage, pregnancy and childbearing. There are an estimated 105 million adolescent girls in the age group of 10-19 in India. Despite the improvements in the economy and provision of basic services in India, the ratio of females to males has been deteriorating from 972 females to 1000 males in 1991 to 933 females to 1000 males in 2001 (Census, 2001). Discouragingly, between the 1991 and 2001 census, the sex ratio has declined in Gujarat, Punjab and Haryana. The 1991 census found that in the 0-14 age group there were an estimated 7.8 million fewer girls than boys and in the 0-19 age group the number of "missing" girls was 13-34 million (CEDPA, 2001).

Adolescent girls have their own developmental needs, which are peculiar to them and need to be addressed separately. In many countries, the concept of a transitional period between childhood and adulthood is relatively new. During this period, known as adolescence, individuals move towards physical and psychological maturity and economic independence and acquire their adult identity.

Growth and Development in Adolescence

Adolescence is a time of rapid growth and maturation in human development. Physical growth at adolescence occurs earlier and is more rapid than during pre-adolescence. Nutrition is important during adolescence because during this age, an adolescent gains. 25 per cent of adult height; 50 per cent of adult weight; 40 per cent of adult bone mass.

Nutritional adequacy is one of the key determinants of the quality of human life. In the Indian sub-continent, female nutritional stress begins in childhood and continues through adolescence into adult. Attention to nutrition is therefore called for throughout the lifecycle of females. Seasonal and climatic changes determine the agricultural cropping pattern and vary the production and availability of local food stuffs, thus affecting the household food security, dietary practices and in turn the nutritional security (S. Deepa *et al.*, 2004). As adolescence is a time of rapid growth and maturation in human development, this change leads to an increased need for micronutrients such as iron, calcium, iodine, Vitamin A, C etc. Nutritional requirements are significantly higher during this stage to meet the physiological demands of rapid growth and development. Many causative factors leading to serious diseases in adulthood have their roots in adolescence like micronutrient deficiencies, undernutrition, poor eating and exercise habits (WHO, 2009). The nutritional status of adolescent girls, contributes significantly to the nutritional status of the community. It is only recently that efforts, although small, have been made to include adolescent girls as beneficiaries in some of the health and nutrition intervention programmes.

There is very little information about diet and nutritional status of adolescents, particularly from rural and tribal areas of India. Therefore, there is a need to develop a database on these subjects from different parts of the country to enable the governments and other non-governmental agencies to formulate policies and initiate strategies for the well-being of tribal adolescent children. They comprise a high demographic section of the population, even more in developing countries. Investing in adolescent's nutrition behaviour is an investment in adult health. They have a potential for correcting nutritional adequacies and catch up growth. Adolescence is a time period for adoption and consolidation of sound dietary habits. Nutritional intervention for adolescent girls contributes to breaking the intergenerational malnutrition cycle.

Issues Faced by Tribal Adolescents

As majority of the tribal groups living in remote forest-areas remain isolated, untouched by civilization, they are largely unaffected by the development processes going on. Therefore, these groups remain backward, particularly in health, education and socio-economic aspects. Some of the health problems of the tribal population are as follows:

1. Deficiency of essential nutrients leading to malnutrition, protein-calorie malnutrition and micronutrient deficiencies (Vit. A, iron and iodine) are common. Goiter of various grades is also endemic in some of the tribal areas.

2. Water borne and communicable diseases, Gastrointestinal disorder, particularly dysentery and parasitic infections are very common, leading to marked morbidity and malnutrition. Malaria and TB still remain a problem in many tribal areas.
3. High prevalence of genetic disorders mostly involving red blood cells, Genetically transmitted disorders like Sickle cell anemia, glucose-6-phosphate dehydrogenase deficiency and different forms of thalassaemia are also common. All these defects lead to early destruction of red blood cells and add to the overall anemia.
4. Excess consumption of alcohol: The brewing of alcohol from Mohua flower and fruits has been practiced traditionally. However, the switch over to commercially available liquor is likely to be a major threat.
5. Superstitions particularly related to health problems.
6. Extreme poverty.
7. Inadequate and improper health facilities.
8. Early marriage: In India, the proportion of adolescents getting married before completion of their growth is very high (23%; Agarwal *et al.*, 1974). If these young girls become mothers, their growth ceases, exposing them to the consequences of cephalo-pelvic disproportions.

Nutritional Problems among Tribal Adolescents

Nutritional problems, especially in adolescent children, continue to be widely prevalent in the country in spite of many nutrition oriented programmes being implemented by the Government of India. Adolescents who are not properly educated in nutrition will make less healthy choices and their diets may be compromised. In doing so, they may begin to cultivate poor eating habits which can result in chronic diseases when they become adults. The main nutritional problems among tribal adolescents include undernutrition, micronutrient deficiencies like iron deficiency anemia and genetic disorder like sickle cell anemia.

Sickle Cell Anemia

This is a hereditary blood disorder due to defective hemoglobin structure. Hemoglobin is a tetramer consisting of two pairs of nonidentical globin polypeptide chains, each chain being associated with one heme group. The heme group is an iron containing pigment responsible for oxygen transport in red blood cells. There are four polypeptide chains (alpha, beta, gamma and delta) in the globin portion. HbA consists of 2 alpha and 2 beta chains; HbF consists of 2 alpha and 2 gamma chains and HbA2 consists of 2 alpha and 2 delta chains. The alpha chains consist of 141 amino acids with specific sequences, while beta, gamma and delta chains consist of 146 amino acids. The sequences of amino acids in the alpha, beta, gamma and delta chains are different from each other and very specific for that particular chain. Sickle cell hemoglobin is a mutant form of normal adult hemoglobin. A single nucleotide base in the beta globin gene is mutated from adenine to thymine producing the corresponding change in the sixth amino acid of the protein from glutamic acid to valine. Under low oxygen concentrations, the mutant deoxyhemoglobin polymerizes and eventually leads to changes in the red cell shape. The phenomenon is called sickling and hence the mutant hemoglobin is called sickle cell hemoglobin (HbS). This disease is seen commonly in tribal areas. It is one of the most common hereditary diseases occurring worldwide, which may affect any organ or system of the human body. It is an irreversible, untreated health problem predominately seen amongst various tribes. In sickle cell anemia, the hemoglobin is clustered together and forms long, rod-like structures. These structures cause the red blood cells to become stiff and to assume a sickle shape. Unlike normal red blood cells, which last about 120 days in the blood stream, sickled red cells die after about 10-20 days. Because they cannot be replaced fast enough, the blood is chronically short of red blood cells, a condition called anemia. With its present rate of spread, in another 25-40 yrs., over 150 lakh children will suffer and die of sickle cell disease, and over 300 lakh persons will inherit the abnormal hemoglobin trait (Govt. of Gujarat, 2007). Six core outcomes for Children with Special Health Care Needs under the federal Healthy People 2010 Objectives provide guiding principles for the care of children with sickle cell disease:

1. All children with sickle cell disease will receive regular and ongoing comprehensive care within a medical home.
2. All families of children with sickle cell disease should have adequate private and/or public insurance to pay for the services they need.

3. All children with sickle cell disease will be screened early and continuously for special health care needs.
4. Services for children with sickle cell disease and their families should be organized in ways that families can use them easily.
5. Families of children with sickle cell disease will participate in health care decision-making at all levels and will be satisfied with the services they receive.
6. All youth with sickle cell disease will receive the services necessary to make appropriate transitions to all aspects of adult life, including adult health care, work, and independence.

Iron Deficiency Anemia (IDA) is uncommon in individuals with Sickle Cell Disease (SCD) because of availability of an adequate iron source potentially from increased red cell turnover and from blood transfusions. Also, iron deficiency anemia can often go unnoticed because the sickle cell disease patients are already anemic. Iron deficiency in sickle cell patients may result in lowering the intracellular hemoglobin concentration and this may ameliorate sickling (Indian J Med Res 127, April 2008).

Undernutrition

Undernutrition is a lack of food energy and nutrients. It can be divided into PEM and micronutrient deficiencies. But in real life they generally go together. It includes being underweight for one's age, too short for one's age (stunted), dangerously thin for one's height (wasted) and deficient in vitamins and minerals (micronutrient malnutrition) (UNICEF, 2006).

Undernutrition often starts in uterus and may extend throughout the lifecycle. Undernutrition occurs during pregnancy, childhood and adolescence and has a cumulative negative impact on the birth weight of future babies. Poor nutrition during adolescence can impair the work capacity and productivity of adolescent boys and girls in their later years. Further, an undernourished girl is at the risk of developing complications during pregnancy and the chances of her giving birth to a low birth weight baby increases, thus perpetuating a vicious cycle of malnutrition and ill-health. Excessive physical activity patterns and infections may also contribute to undernutrition. Undernutrition is not a simple problem with a single, simple solution. Multiple and interrelated determinants are involved and intricate series of approaches, multifaceted and multisectoral are needed to deal with it.

A factor that largely keeps malnutrition from being properly treated is lack of education in many developing countries. This lack of education allows cultures of superstitions and food taboos to persist. Food taboos are mainly observed in tribal areas. They generally don't allow girls to eat eggs and they believe that due to egg consumption, the girl will suffer from reproductive problems, as they considered eggs and jaggery as hot foods and will harm the reproductive organs. WHO (2005) has highlighted the health consequences of undernutrition in adolescence as:

1. Delays physical growth and onset of puberty
2. Reduces work capacity
3. Other widespread micronutrient deficiencies like iron deficiency anemia, Vitamin-A deficiency and iodine deficiency disorders are associated with undernutrition.

Iron Deficiency Anemia

The need for iron increases with rapid growth and expansion of blood volume and muscle mass. As boys gain lean body mass at a faster rate than girls, they require more iron than girls. The onset of menstruation imposes additional needs for girls. Adolescents should be encouraged to consume iron rich foods along with a Vitamin-C source to compensate for menstrual blood loss. Iron deficiency is the most prevalent micronutrient deficiency among adolescents. Iron deficiency and anemia are associated with impaired cognitive functioning, lower school achievement and most likely lower physical work capacity. WHO estimates that 27 per cent of adolescents in developing countries are anemic; the ICRW studies documented high rates in India (55%), Nepal (42%), Cameroon (32%) and Guatemala (48%).

Stages of iron deficiency anemia: IDA is the end stage of a relatively long drawn process of deterioration in the iron status of an individual, which may be divided in 3 stages:

1. Iron stores diminish: Measures of serum ferritin reflects iron stores and are most valuable in assessing iron status.
2. Transport iron decreases: Total iron binding capacity increases and per cent transferring saturation decreases.

3. Hemoglobin production falls: Hemoglobin precursors, erythrocytes protoporphyrin begin to accumulate as hemoglobin and haematocrit values decline. This stage is known as frank iron deficiency anemia. (Whitney *et al.*, 1999).

Strategies to Combat Iron Deficiency Anemia

1. Food Based Approach
2. Control of infection
3. Supplementation with Medicinal iron
4. Nutrition Health Education
5. Dietary intake.

This study focuses on two strategies from the above list—they are Supplementation of medicinal iron and Nutrition Health Education.

Justification of the Study

Lack of knowledge and awareness pertaining to health and nutrition aspects, limited education, and deprived of adequate health care, good nutrition and good schooling, the tribal adolescents are a disadvantaged lot, facing a slow pace of growth. They lag behind nutritionally, have higher morbidity rates especially due to various infections. There is paucity of documented data on nutritional status and health profile of tribal adolescents, especially in the tribal regions of Gujarat. In order to bring down nutrition related problems of adolescent population, one of the recommendations of WHO is "Mass informative and awareness programmes needed to alert government and communities about importance of health and nutrition". With this background, an attempt was made to assess the nutrition-health and impact of NHE (Nutrition Health Education) and IFA tablet supplementation on Hb values and KAP (Knowledge, Attitude and Practices) among tribal adolescent girls aged 10-19 yrs. in Jhagadia taluka, Bharuch district, Gujarat. This study was carried out in consultation and co-ordination with an NGO—SEWA rural, working for the development of the socio-economically disadvantaged population in Jhagadia taluka, Bharuch district, Gujarat.

The period of adolescence comprises nearly half of the growing period. With the profound growth, there is also an increased demand for nutrients like protein, energy, vitamins and minerals. One way of enhancing the adolescent nutrition would be to improve their nutrition knowledge and practices. As behaviour change is an effective tool, it should form an integral part of any nutrition intervention programme to bring the changes among tribal girls.

Thus, this study seeks to fill the information gap by discussing the primary issues relating to adolescent nutrition and growth by mapping the prevalence of malnutrition, anemia and sickle cell anemia and evaluating the impact of IFA supplementation and NHE intervention. The present study was planned with the following objectives:

Phase I: Situational Analysis

1. To study the socio-economic status of the subjects.
2. To measure the growth pattern of tribal girls in terms of anthropometric measurements.
3. To assess the prevalence of anemia in the subjects (10-19 yrs.) by estimating blood Hb levels.
4. To assess prevalence of sickle cell anemia using DTT and electrophoresis method.
5. To assess the diet intake pattern and food taboos and to determine the intake of macro and micro nutrients.
6. To assess the knowledge and perception with regard to their health, nutrition and dietary needs.
7. To assess their personal hygiene and sanitation practices.
8. To assess the prevalence of morbidity.

Phase II: Intervention Period for 3 Months

1. To plan and develop IEC materials and translating it to local language with the aim of improving the nutrition and health, knowledge and awareness of the subjects.
2. To supplement Iron Folic Acid tablets (100 mg of elemental iron and 0.5 mg of folic acid) weekly with deworming tablet i.e. Albendazole (400 mg) once at the beginning.
3. To conduct weekly NHE sessions for continuous three months.

Phase III: Impact Evaluation

1. To study the impact of NHE sessions on Knowledge Attitude and Practice of the subjects.

2. To assess the impact of IFA tablets on Hb levels of the subjects.

Sampling Frame and Sample Selection

The study was carried out in the tribal areas of Jhagadia taluka of Bharuch district in the state of Gujarat, India. From these four places, two schools from two villages were randomly selected. Medium of instruction in both the schools was Gujarati, while rest two villages were Khariya and Nana-Anadra. Since the study focuses on adolescents—10 to 19 years of age, subjects selected from Dariya School were of 8th, 9th and 10th standards and from Malpor School of 6th and 7th standards (since it was a primary school only), while from the villages they were selected age-wise and were enrolled in the study for anthropometric measurements. The total sample size was 133 (including drop-outs) from the four selected places.

Data Collection

The anthropometric measurements: height, weight and BMI were taken using standard methods. The information on adolescents as regards food choices, morbidity profile, nutrient intake, food frequency, perception on health and diseases, knowledge attitude and practices was collected using self-administered questionnaire under guidance.

Data Analysis

Both the qualitative and quantitative data was first entered in CSpro 4 software and was verified by the statistician. The data was analyzed using Statistical Package for Social Sciences (SPSS) software version 17.

Major Findings of the Study

Background Information

The study includes subjects aged 10 to 19 years having nearly the same family background. The maximum study subjects were in their mid-adolescence (62%). 8 per cent of the subjects were first born and 47 per cent were second in birth order. Most of them completed their primary education. About 83 per cent of the subjects were studying in schools and 16 per cent were drop-outs with different reasons. Only 35 per cent of the girls had attained menarche. 30 per cent of the girls (n = 14) attained menarche at the age of 13 years. The mean age at menarche of the present subjects was 13.4 years.

SES Profile

Out of 70 per cent of schoolgoing girls, 47 per cent of girls were from Dariya School and 23 per cent from Malpor School while out of 30 per cent of village subjects, 16 per cent were from Khariya and 13 per cent from Nana-Anadra village. About 72 per cent of the families were nuclear, while 26 per cent were in joint families. The average family size was 6. Family income of 26 per cent of the subjects was less than Rs. 500 and very few had income above Rs. 1000. 57 per cent mothers were illiterate and majority of them (47%) were marginal farmers. 25 per cent fathers were illiterate but about 47 per cent of them completed their schooling till primary section (7th std). Most of them lived in huts. 97 per cent had their own houses out of which 81 per cent lived in *kuchcha* houses, 10 per cent in semi-*pucca* houses. Around 83 per cent of the subjects were having their own land for farming.

Open defecation was seen among 79 per cent of the subjects. Majority of the households (96.2%) had electricity while chairs (79%) and beds (86%) were common. Most of them (78%) had bicycles also. 83.5 per cent of children were aware that they were having BPL cards.

61 per cent of the subjects belonged to medium living index and 30 per cent were in the low living index group.

Majority (62%) of them had cows and buffalos and 17 per cent had goats which they used for agricultural purposes and for their milk which they sold to generate income. Only 11 girls (8%) had poultry at their place.

Anthropometric Data

The girls of ages 10-19 years had height which was 89 to 95 per cent of WHO (2007) standards. The mean height of the girls was 143.7 cms. The overall prevalence of stunting was 44 per cent while 56 per cent were normal. By looking at the per cent prevalence of stunting, it was clear that stunting was more in late adolescence (50%). The girls of ages 10-19 years had weight which was 61 to 76 per cent of the NCHS standards and the mean weight was 33 kgs. In all of the age groups, girls had their BMI values between 76 to 84 per cent of WHO (2007) standards.

The overall prevalence of undernutrition was 55 per cent, out of which 47 per cent had grade-II undernutrition while 7.5 per cent had grade-I undernutrition. Majority (57%) of the mid-adolescents had severe degree of undernutrition followed by early (54.5%) and late adolescents (44.5%).

The overall prevalence of anemia was 95 per cent. Majority of girls (60%) had mild anemia. Severely anemic girls were less (2%). The prevalence of anemia was 98 per cent in early adolescents, 96 per cent in mid-adolescents and 89 per cent in late adolescents. Early adolescents (10-12 years) were more anemic. Only 7 per cent of the girls were suffering from sickle cell trait.

The sanitation and hygiene practices in tribal areas under study were satisfactory. They were clean and kept their surroundings also clean.

Very few percentage experienced morbidity in the last 15 days from the date of survey (22.5%). The morbidities experienced were cold and cough, fever and malaria and diarrhoea, vomiting, lose motions were not common.

Only 8 girls (6.6%) had addictions and the only addiction was consuming tobacco in different forms. Prevalence of addiction was more in late adolescent girls.

General Meal Pattern

It was observed that all the subjects had similar and monotonous meal pattern. Generally, the main meals cooked for lunch include *rotla/roti* with vegetable or *dal* with rice. Alternative meal pattern was seen at dinner time. From the study, it was very clear that total food intake was far below the daily consumption of normal healthy adolescent girls. Though, this tribal belt was known for its green leafy vegetables and cereals (jowar and bajra), it was found in the study that they were not consuming it as they could not afford it.

The staple cereals of the subjects were wheat, jowar and rice. Red gram *dal* was consumed daily though in less quantity (15 gms.). Despite the fact that the study site was an agricultural area, consumption of GLVs like fenugreek leaves (*methi*), shepu (*suvani bhaji*) and spinach (*palak*) by the subjects was rare. Frequency of consumption of Vitamin-C rich foods like lemon, tomato and guava was also very less (30%). A majority of the subjects consumed fruits either once in a week or less often. Consumption of milk was only 10 per cent even though they had domestic animals (cows, buffalos and goats). Poor availability and not cost-effective are the reasons for the poor consumption.

Determinants of Anemia

Statistical association was calculated between anemic status with different factors, i.e., education of mother and father, occupation of mother and father, birth orders, family size, type of family, age at menarche, source of drinking water, SLI, stunting, BMI, intake of Vitamin-C, iron and calories. No statistical association was found between any of the above factors except family income. This shows that higher the family income, lower the prevalence of anemia.

Impact Evaluation of Nutrition Health Education Intervention

The intervention was given for 3 months to the tribal adolescent girls by way of lectures, discussions and demonstrations through IEC materials. Post-testing was done and the impact was evaluated.

There was an increase in the knowledge, attitude and practices among the tribal adolescent girls after the intervention. A positive statistical association was observed between, before and after intervention for many of the variables.

Impact of IFA Supplementation on Hb Levels

The mean Hb was 10.13 gm/dl before intervention and 10.40 gm/dl after intervention with an increment of only 0.3 gm/dl. The increment was not statistically significant. There was no visible change in overall prevalence of anemia but a positive shift was seen from moderate to mild levels. 32 per cent of moderate anemia decreased to 14 per cent whereas 61 per cent of mild anemia increased to 78 per cent. Instead 2 more severely anemic subjects were reported, probably due to non-compliance of IFA tablets and/or any morbidity experienced during this intervention phase.

Conclusion

- The total food intake of the tribal adolescent girls was inadequate due to large family size and low purchasing power.
- The mean age at menarche of the girls was 13.4 years. A positive relationship was observed between family income and BMI with age at menarche. The reason could be that high family income contributed to adequate food purchasing and intake, indirectly affecting nutritional status. As nutritional status improves, the age of menarche is lowered.
- Faulty eating habits, superstitious beliefs and wrong perceptions play a major role in the prevalence of malnutrition.
- The growth pattern in terms of anthropometric measurements reflects on the prevalence of current undernutrition (wasting) and chronic undernutrition (stunting).
- Stunting was higher among late adolescents. As stunting is an indicator of chronic undernutrition which might have initiated at early adolescence but manifested during late adolescent age.
- Wasting was more among mid-adolescents.
- As age increases nutritional demands are raised to meet rapid physiological development which has to be fulfilled through adequate diets. Due to poor economic conditions these needs would not have been met leading to poor nutrient intake contributing to undernutrition.
- The prevalence of morbidity was only 22.5 per cent and all had taken treatment. Due to satisfactory sanitation and hygiene practices morbidities like diarrhoea, loose motion, vomiting was less common.
- Late adolescents tend to be more prone to tobacco chewing.
- Statistics proved significant association of family income with prevalence of anemia while rest determinants like education and occupation of father and mother, ordinal position, family size, family income, type of family, age at menarche, source of drinking water, nutritional status, intake of iron, energy and Vitamin-C were not statistically significant.

- From the Nutrition Health Education intervention, it was observed that awareness was created among the girls and knowledge attitude and practices had improved significantly at different levels.
- Before intervention, it was found that nearly all the adolescent (95%) were anemic in this study area, but there was no change in post analysis.
- The dietary intake was lower in all the nutrients except fat which was more than the RDA and impact of Nutrition Health Education was seen in consumption of milk and milk products (93%).

Recommendations

- Long-term continuous nutrition health education is needed to bring about behaviour changes among adolescent girls for adoption of healthy diets.
- There was no motivation or encouragement from elders and parents, to sustain the impact of the intervention so there is need to educate them through effective counselling and communication strategies.
- To improve nutritional status of adolescents, there is a need to involve both adolescents and their parents in nutrition health education.
- Food taboos and superstitious beliefs were the major setbacks for the poor nutritional status of the girls. Continuous and strong messages regarding various food taboos need to be provided to the community as a whole to stop them from further degradation.
- For late adolescents or drop-outs, teenage friendly nutrition education training centres should be initiated.
- There is a need to evolve comprehensive programmes for the overall development of the tribal adolescent girls.
- Effective and sustainable supplementation programmes implemented on a larger scale would reduce the present malnutrition.
- Promoting kitchen gardens near the neighbourhood would make the girls more involved in the cause of reducing malnutrition thereby motivating them to change their dietary habits.

References

Anand, K.K. and Kapoor, S.K. (1999). "Nutritional Status of Adolescent School Children in Rural North India", *Indian Pediatr*, Aug; 36 (8): 810-5.

Bonnie, A.S. (2002). "Adolescent Growth and Development", *J. Am. Dietetic Association/March, Supplement*; Vol. 102, No. 3.

Funke and Olunakaiya (2008). "A Matter of Concern Among Adolescents in Osum State, Nigeria," *Pakistan Journal of Nutrition* 7 (3)L: 503-508.

F. Ahmed, M.R. Khan, M. Islam, I. Kabir and G.J. Fuchs (2000). "Anaemia and Iron Deficiency Among Adolescent Schoolgirls in Semi-Urban Bangladesh", *European Journal of Clinical Nutrition,* 54, 678-683.

Government of Gujarat (2006). *Integrated Population and Development Project.*

Goel, S., Gupta, B.P. (2007). "Low Anemia Prevalence among Adolescents of An Urban Hilly Community", *Indian Journal of Community Medicine,* Vol. 32.

Hong, S.M., Hwang HyeJin, Kim HyunHee (2004). "A Study on Iron Nutritional Status and Anemia of Middle School Girls in Ulsan Metropolitan city", *Journal of Community Nutrition.*

Jayatissa, R., Ranbanda, R.M. (2006). "Prevalence of Challenging Nutritional Problems Among Adolescents in Shri Lanka", *Foods and Nutr Bull*; Jun; 27(2:153-60).

Karkar, P.D. and Kotecha, P.V. (2004). "Prevalence of Anemia Among Students of Nursing School of Vadodara", *Nursing Journal of India.*

Kurz, K.M. (1996). "Adolescent Nutritional Status in Developing Countries", *Proceedings of the Nutrition Society*, 55:32-331.

M. Mitra, P.V. Kumar, R. Ghosh and P. Bharati. (2002). "Growth Pattern of the Kamars—A Primitive Tribe of Chhattisgarh", *India Coll. Antropol.* 2: 485-499 UDC 572.512:612.65(540) Original Scientific Paper.

P. Deshmukh, B.S. Garg, N. Garg, N.C. Prajapati and M.S. Bharamb (2006). "Prevalence of Sickle Cell Disorders in Rural Wardha", *Indian J. Community Med.* 31:26-7.

UNFPA State of World Population (2005). "The Promise of Equality: Gender Equity", *Reproductive Health and the MDGs.*

WHO (2007). *Micro Nutrient Deficiencies* www.who.int/nutrition/topics/ida/en/

16
Computer Literacy: An Action Project

Rameshwari Pandya and *Chandani Jhadav*

Computer education is the most powerful tool for change and hence it must train the mind of those educated to cope with the change. Those who are thinking about education must realize that in the fast changing world of today no education is complete without the knowledge of computer education. The education environment is changing as a result of the computer and will continue to change (Rayed, 1993). The world of modern day is often called as the "Age of communication and information", for which computer is playing a very important role. A computer is an electronic media that helps us to solve problems. Those problems that can be solved with the aid of computer are wide and varied. They can be problems relating to industry, medicine, education, law, social science or arts. In fact, any problem that can be solved through a step-by-step procedure can be solved by a computer.

The computer is one of the most powerful forces in present society. As it is being increasingly used in all aspects of social life in the country and no one can doubt about that. During the last twenty years, information and communication technologies have provided a wealth of new technological opportunities, with the rapid development of both the internet and cellular technology has changed our life. Computers are extremely versatile. In fact, they are universal information processing machine. Early electronic computers were the size of a large room, while smaller computers designed for individual use are called personal computers. A computer is a device that accepts information and manipulates it for some result based on a programme or sequence of instruction on how the data is to be processed.

Thousands of educational programmes are available in such category as reading languages, Science etc. It depends on the individuals, how he can make best use of such an important, dynamic and modern device to update one's knowledge and add to the education provided into the formal set-up. The computer programme is a set of detailed, minute and explicit instruction that direct the operation of a computer. As human body has many parts like the head, hands and legs, each part performs a different action or work. In the same way, a computer system is made up of different parts like the screen, C.P.U., keyboard and mouse and each part of the computer does different work.

The computer can do several things, few of them are listed below:

- The computer can store data in binary form.
- The computer can receive data from various types of inputs media.
- The computer can output data into various media.
- The computer can make logical decisions.
- Communication for people with special needs.
- Computers with appropriate key-board and other device to teach literacy and writing.
- Develop special awareness and psycho-motor control.
- E-mail to support collaboration writing and sharing of resources.
- Communication technology to exchange of administrative and assessment data.

More and more, different hardware as well as software courses are coming now-a-days and are running successfully as it is new for people they want to use it as a tool to learn, express creativity and also increase productivity. The computer is one of the most powerful forces in society. It is being increasingly used in all the aspects of social life in the country and no one can doubt about that. The following are some of the benefits of using computers at home or at workplace or even for business—

1. Speed

Computers work at an incredible speed. This can be gauged from the fact that the speed of the computers is measured in the terms of milliseconds, microseconds, nanoseconds or picoseconds, i.e. one thousandth, one millionth, one billionth, one trillionth of a second, respectively chances are there, that the computer you are presently working on, would be processing information at the speed of a couple of a million instructions per second, also called MIPS in computer jargon. This helps to deal with lot of data and work with more speed and efficiency.

2. Accuracy

In addition to being fast, the computers are also very accurate. It gives the correct answer, however it must be remembered that the computer is capable of doing only what it is instructed to do. If faulty instructions are provided for processing the data, obviously faulty answers will be given. This is also called GIGO, i.e. Garbage In Garbage Out. Hence the only possibility of an error occurring is due to inaccurate instructions or faulty data. This further helps the people using computers to do their jobs accurately.

Consistency

Unlike human beings, computers being machines are highly consistent. They never get bored. We are yet to meet a computer complaining of a monotonous job! Hence, they are ideal machines for carrying out repeatative and voluminous work, with consistent results.

Storage Capacity

Today's computers can store huge amounts of data. Once recorded, a piece of information is never forgotten and any information can be retrieved almost instantaneously. CD ROM of a computer can contain the entire Encyclopedia, Britannica and more. This helps the computer users to store large and extensive data on their machine, i.e. computers.

Flexibility

Computer is a versatile machine and its use is limited only by your imagination. In today's fast developing technology world, it would be very difficult, in some cases inconceivable, to find an area where computers are not being used to a great advantage. This is more so because they offer lot of flexibility to their users.

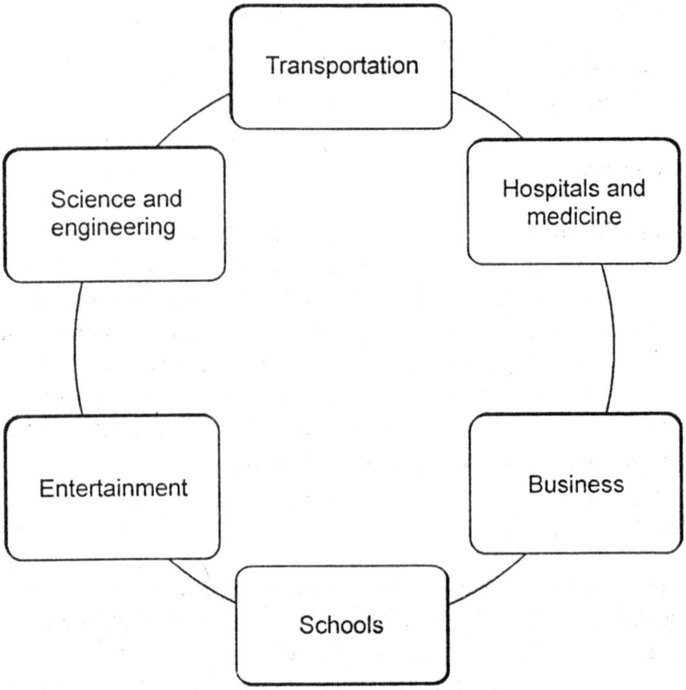

Fig. 16.1

Source: Mahalingan S.,1994.

Some Other Uses of Computers

1. Computer Used for Entertainment

Do you know computers can play games with you? There are many games which computers can play. Though computers cannot play games with you on the playground, they can play with you inside your home. Using computers you can draw pictures of different shapes, size and colours. People can make music on them and do many more things.

2. Computers Used in Science and Engineering

Scientists always think of doing something new. For this they need to do a lot of calculations, store a lot of details like results of experiments, complex calculations, findings of other scientists in their work. They cannot only calculate fast, but can also store large amount of details as well.

3. Computers Used in Transportation

People need to travel from one place to another. They use any of the means of transport available like cycle, car, train or plane. Computers help in designing vehicles, controlling the vehicles, and also test their parts and their working. Computers are also used for booking tickets of passengers, preparing list of people travelling, storing details of trips made by trains and many other details which are required.

4. Computers Used in Hospitals and Medicine

In hospitals many people come for treatment. Computers are used to maintain record of patients. Computers also help doctors to find out the disease of patient, and help doctors in treatment. There are special computers made to help doctor to test part of the body. They also help in finding new medicines for diseases.

5. Computers Used in Business

Businessmen need to prepare a lot of documents, collect money from and pay money to people. Computers help them in many ways in keeping records and in networking as well as in advertisements.

6. Computers Used in Schools

Children can have a lot of fun with computers; they can also be used to learn lessons. Computers are used in classrooms to solve many problems, play games and for many other things like collecting fees and keeping exam records.

Computer Literacy

Computer literacy is the knowledge and ability to use computers and technology efficiently. Computer literacy can also be referred to the comfort level of learners to use computers for all their benefits, i.e. speed, accuracy, consistency, storage and flexibility in systematic and scientific manner. Someone who is using computer programme and other application those are associated with computers. Another valuable component of computer literacy, knows how computers work and operate. Having basic computer skills is a significant asset in the developed countries especially when the computers are a tool used practically in all walks of life and all purposes in homes, at work and business from simple ticketing to buying products. We see computers being used by big business houses to small business offices for storing data and for the ease of work. Hospitals, hotels, travel agencies, educational institutions, all use computers for various tasks and jobs. Today, students and teachers use computers to save time for convenience and further this will lead us to paper free offices, work places, business houses and educational institutions.

The precise definition of "computer literacy" can vary from group to group. Generally, literate are one who can read any arbitrary book in their native language, looking up new words as they are exposed to them. Likewise, an experienced computer professional may consider the ability to self-teach to be central to computer literacy. As computers become more widely used in schools, educators have invented many different ways to use them. The different uses of computers are based on quite diverse models of what the purposes of computer education should be. Computer literacy introduces learners to technology skills such as word processing, graphics, spreadsheets, multimedia and internet research. As computers are widely used today, acquiring computer education is the need of all age groups including youth and women. Thus, the computer literacy will cross the digital divide and will make people computer literate.

Importance of Computers in Daily Life

The computer technology is spreading all-over the world! Could we have ever imagined back in the 1980s that computer would play such a huge role in our lives? Computers have become an integral part of day to day life. They have become an integral part of the education system also having computers as a part of one's education can prove very helpful. Being good in studies and computers can secure better job prospects, in this age and time computer knowledge is a must. Computers have helped a lot in compiling a lot of data which is used to be in hard records. One of the uses or benefits of computers is that they are able to provide and retrieve information quickly thus they have increased the pace of our work. The increase in the speed of work has helped us to do many things with less resource. Each day something new comes out which makes technology a better friend to humans and a computer literate should at least be abreast with the information.

This is one of the use of computers in our lives other than that computer has helped us to work with machine which have the ability to produce the best quality of products with maximum speed and efficiency. In today's world it is necessary that to cater big population with things that are made at a higher pace with best quality, it is possible with the help of computer that we are able to cater the need of quality and quantity of product required in daily life. Computer today is in every walk of life, and is helping us a lot in developing at a fast pace. Today, computers are no longer specialized tool only by scientists or engineers. They do not hum behind sealed, glass walls in climate-controlled environment. Computer systems are everywhere. They are a fact of life, a common thread that ties together our education, work and home life. Computer is an essential part of business, in most places of business, a computer is standard. In the bank they use computers to look in your account information. You cannot find books in the library by looking in a card-catalogue; you must use a computerized database. The point is this no matter where you find employment, there is a good chance a computer will be a basic tool you will have to use. It will help you to get a job and it will help you to advance in career. Computer literacy does not mean you need to know how to use every single piece of software you may encounter. It does not mean you need to know how to write programme or network computers, you just need to know some basics, it means having some sort of level of comfort around computers rather than a look of fear. Computers are not only storage devices and processing units, but also are excellent communication media. They are the means to access the internet and get connected to the world. They are an effective audio-visual media. They are solving the purpose of entertainment by providing functions like listening to music, playing views, playing games and so on. The word processing applications of a computer serve as an effective means of documentation. The database management software that is a part of computer system serves as the means of managing large amount of data. The networking capabilities of a computer network these days have a powerful impact on the ways which individuals and private organizations can communicate with each other. Computers are the future, whether we like it or not. Some people dislike computers, because of the complications it takes to understand the basics. Computers are not exactly the easiest tools to work with, but they are the future. Computers find a wide variety of applications in different spheres of life. With an increase in their widespread use and their ever-increasing popularity, computer education has become the need of the day.

Need for Computer Skill among Learners

Laehrmann (1984) emphasized that literacy in mathematics means the ability to do mathematics to do essential arithmetic, solve algebraic equation and so on. A newer area in which the knowledge and skills needs to decoded and understood message delivered by means of electronic media like TV, video, film etc. Here computer literacy is the ability to get hold of equipment, know how to operate it, gather information and understand the strength and limitation of the message. Skills on the computer have become as basic as those of reading and writing. Its impact is so much that the public ignorance of the subject constitutes as real crisis. Today, when one can seek job from any agency, institution or organization, many employers are looking for prospective candidate with computer literacy which further makes it important that today's candidates seeking jobs should be well versed with and have ease in using the computer specially *vis-à-vis* using word for typing, using excel for making data sheets. Thus, looking to the present scenario, computer is essential of life in an inevitable growing technological society and the learners cannot be an exception to this. The learners must have minimum knowledge of computers.

Justification for Computer Literacy Project

With reference to the potential of computers, the Seventh Five Year Plan described the following as a priority measures: "Extension of computer literacy programme to cover all the schools and institutions by 1991." In accordance with this policy recommendation, the

Department of Education, Ministry of Education and Culture and NCERT, New Delhi in close co-ordination with the Department of Electronics, Government of India and IIT Delhi launched a project called CLASS (Computer Literacy And Studies in School) similarly in 1992, CABE report highlighted that, "computer literacy needs to be given special emphasis. In the emerging technological paradigm, computer literacy and numeracy". It is with this background and justification that today we are thinking of a nation or world with all its citizens having the basic knowledge of using computers for ease of living, work and excellence.

Justification for Selection of the Learners

To plan and implement strategies to minimize the gap between the computer illiterate and literate a comprehensive examination of computer use in work places like office, shopping malls and home and community settings is required. The extent to which learners have access to computers may be an indicator of how well prepared participants will be to enter into technological workplaces which demands computer literacy. It is with the help of this project that learners would be able to keep pace with the job world. This was the reason for selecting 15 participants as learners who wanted to use computer literacy as a basic tool for seeking jobs in the marketplace, example—Bank, Shopping malls, Hospitals and so on.

Justification of the Project in the Department of Extension and Communication

The Department of Extension and Communication was started in 1953 at the Faculty of Home Science, the Maharaja Sayajirao University of Baroda, Vadodara. The Department has expertise in the area of education, research and extension under the component of extension education and many training programmes are conducted successfully. Useful reference material is available in the Research and Documentation centre of the department, as it is being used by the undergraduate students for the computer literacy projects in the schools where they are conducting their urban extension programmes.

The students of the department undertake various training programmes under the field experience course. The department also holds seminars and workshops to spread awareness and information among adolescents in particular and in general masses about the communication technology. Computer literacy and working for computer jobs is the most pressing demand in the communities belonging to Low Socio-Economic status and Middle Socio-Economic status families. This makes them more prepared for computer related jobs in all areas of work. Moreover, many projects have been undertaken in the department on computer training programme in relation to various groups of people like children, women, handicapped and senior citizen. The present project can further contribute in training the women in using computer and making them computer literate.

Objective of the Project

- To Promote Computer literacy amongst the women of Sevasi village.

Planning the Project

The first step in implementing the project successfully is to plan the activities. The plan of the activities includes the list of work to be completed for a particular period of time. Plan of activities helps in execution of the project and it answers the major questions as to where, when, who and how regarding the project. The project of Computer Literacy was well planned in order to make the entire project systematic and successful. The steps of the project were planned in order to be successful in conducting the project. The steps were:

1. Finalizing the programme
2. Forming the group of learners for the project
3. Estimating the budget for the project
4. Plan for daily activities for computer literacy
5. Deciding venue and time for training
6. Preparing Teaching Aids
7. Finalizing the content of computer literacy
8. Planning for Evaluation

Fig. 16.2: Planning the Project.

Finalizing the Programme

The village selected for conducting the project was—Sevasi village, Vadodara. As the village authorities as well village women of Sevasi, were keen to have the project in their village. Moreover, this village has good infrastructure, facilities in terms of place, furniture, light, ventilation for conducting various educational activities.

Forming the Group of Learners for the Project

Learners were identified and selected through the publicity which was done by the project worker. The women who wanted to learn, showed keen interest and had actually demanded to learn computer were given the first preference. The learners were selected on the recommendations of Teachers and Sarpanch of the village. Some of the learners had no knowledge about computer but were very keen to learn computers they were also selected. The project worker selected all those women who wanted to get computer related jobs, finally a group of fifteen learners was formed and finalized.

Estimating the Budget for the Project

The budget was estimated for various heads of expenditures to be carried out under the Computer Literacy Project.

Plan for Daily Activity for Computer Literacy

To conduct the activities smoothly, the daily activity schedule was planned. The plan for computer literacy training programme was planned to teach the following topics:

- Introduction of computer

Table 16.1: Budget was Estimated according to the following Heads

S. No.	*Items/Particulars*	*Amount in Rupees*
1.	Budget for the reference material for the learners	850
2.	Guajarati Typing and formatting	850
3.	Typing and art work and computer jobs	2500
	Total	**4200**

- Paint
- Note pad
- Microsoft Office Excel

Deciding Venue and Time for Training

The project worker and learners along with the resource person decided to have all the sessions of training at the Milk Dairy which is at the entrance of the Village, as it was convenient for all. The project worker and the learners decided that 12:30 p.m. to 2:30 p.m. would be the convenient time for the training sessions, for the teacher, project worker and the learners.

Preparing Teaching Aids

Teaching Aids helps the learners to understand the concepts easily. Several experiments have shown that Teaching Aids can be helpful in making programme successful, so project worker also prepare teaching aids like charts, posters, flip book and pamphlets for different lessons on computer. The project worker felt the need for developing a booklet in the form of ready to use reference material which could be used by the learners, even after completion of the action project. This booklet can also be used by the school teachers and the community volunteers imparting computer education in the schools and communities.

Finalizing the Content of Computer Literacy

The content of the computer literacy programme was finalized after discussing with the teacher from the village as well as taking into consideration the need, interest and level of the learners. The Project worker also referred previous action projects of Computer Literacy which were carried out in the Department.

Planning for Evaluation

A reaction scale was planned to elicit the reactions of learners regarding the computer literacy project. Evaluation of the project would be helpful for finding out how far the project was successful. This would also give feedback for planning computer literacy project in future.

Executing the Project

For the execution of any action project, it is important to execute or implement the activities in systematic and scientific manner. The steps of the execution were as follows—

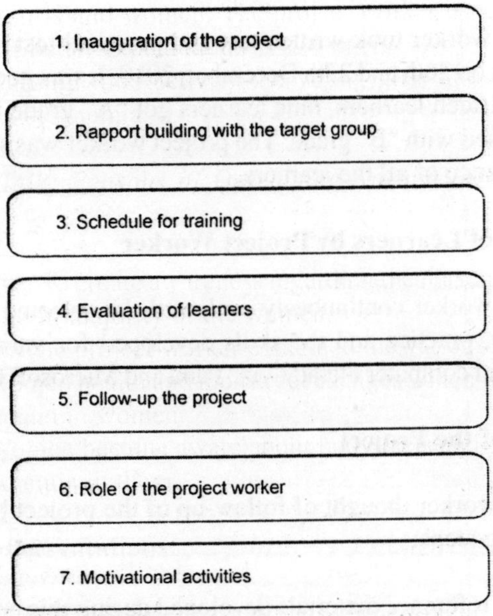

Fig. 16.3: Executing the Project.

Inauguration of the Project

This Action project on computer literacy was inaugurated on 9th November, 2010 at Sevasi village, Vadodara wherein the project worker, guide, invited people of Sevasi village and learners inaugurated the project by lighting the lamp in a very formal manner.

Rapport Building with the Target Group

First time when project worker met the beneficiaries she introduced herself and discussed with them about the project which she had in mind. Informally during discussion she found out their names and interest in learning 'computer literacy' gradually rapport was built. They shared their experiences during the introduction classes. It was a good time for building rapport with them.

Schedule for Training Programme

The execution of the project was as shown in Table 16.2.

Evaluation of Learners

The project worker took written test and practical test of the fifteen (15) learners on 26th and 27th December, 2010. It was good to observe that out of fifteen learners, nine learners got "A" grade whereas two learners passed with "B" grade. The project worker was satisfied with the performance of all the learners.

Evaluation of Learners by Project Worker

The project worker continuously evaluated the selected learners for their activity, practice and the skills developed for various selected components of computer literacy, viz., Paint and Microsoft Office Excel.

Follow-up of the Project

The project worker thought of follow-up of the project by taking up the following steps:

1. The reference materials developed during this project can be used by the undergraduate and postgraduate students of the Department of Extension and Communication, Faculty of Family and Community Sciences for urban and rural outreach programmes.
2. The project worker would also make efforts towards distributing the booklet in different schools. So that it can be used by the government and local schools of Baroda city or nearby rural schools.

Role of the Project Worker

A successful action project requires the project worker to be very systematic and organized while undertaking the project. The following activities and involvements in various activities was the major role of the project worker for smooth, systematic and flawless execution of the Action Project.

Table 16.2: Schedule for Training on Computer Literacy

S. No.	*Date*	*Content*
1.	9-11-10	–Introduction of computer History
2.	10-11-10	Characteristics Usage
3.	11-11-10	Exercise Typing practice
4.	12-11-10	–Typing practice
5.	13-11-10	–Introduction to paint Usage
6.	15-11-10	Characteristics Paint menu
7.	16-11-10	Exercise Paint menu
8.	17-11-10	Drawing practice Exercise
9.	18-11-10	Exercise
10.	19-11-10	Exercise Typing
11.	20-11-10	Drawing practice Exercise
12.	22-11-10	Exercise
13.	23-11-10	–Introduction of Microsoft Excel History
14.	24-11-10	Characteristics Usage
15.	25-11-10	Excel Spreadsheet Making Graphs
16.	26-11-10	Making Graphs Exercise
17.	27-11-10	Exercise
18.	29-11-10	Uses of Formulae Exercise
19.	30-11-10	Practice of Different Formulae Exercise
20.	1-12-10	Exercise
21.	2-12-10	–Revisions of Microsoft Excel and Paint Solution of Queries.
22.	3-12-10	–Revisions of Microsoft Excel and Paint Exercise
23.	4-12-10	–Practice of Microsoft Excel and Paint Exercise Solution of Queries.
24.	6-12-10	–Theory Test
25.	7-12-10	–Practical Test
26.	8-12-10	Motivational Activities Akshar Pushtak Sentence making

1. The project worker helped the experts during identification of learners.
2. The project worker prepared well in advance all the reference material for learners for better understanding of the topic.
3. The project worker made the learners realize the importance of computer literacy and interrelatedness of computer related jobs and importance of computer in daily life.
4. The project worker made her learners realize the importance of Microsoft Office Excel and Paint through practicals on computer, illustrative talks, and expert talks for making them understand the simple ways in which they could contribute in computer related jobs.
5. The project worker helped expert during the sessions. The topic of the expert talk would be introduced by project worker. Introducing the expert and facilitating the expert talk and show practicals on computer without any problems was facilitated and organized by the project worker.
6. The project worker introduced and summarized the topics for the sessions
7. The project worker supervised during the exams of the learners.
8. The project worker had to guide, supervise and monitor all the activities like practical exam, written exam and seek their suggestions and co-operation.
9. The project worker organized small valedictory programme and distributed the booklet on computer literacy as ready reference material.
10. Reference material was developed and designed by the project worker, taking validated content from school books.

Motivational Activities

The project worker had planned variety of motivational activities so as to make the teaching learning experience more interesting.

1. Akshar Pustak

This game focused on reinforcing capability to construct meaning word from alphabets.

2. Sentence Making

The game on sentence making focused on reinforcing skills of making sentences. Motivational activity helped in developing rapport with the group.

Evaluation of the Project

Evaluation of any programme or project is essential to understand the achievements and shortcomings in the entire programme or project. Evaluation is the last major step of any project, which is very crucial as it gives an idea about our achievements and shortcomings and thus for follow-up. The learners' reaction scale was intended to collect the background information, their opinion and reactions regarding the project worker and methods used during the project and finally to collect suggestions for organizing the projects in future. The present Action Project to promote computer literacy amongst selected learners of "Baroda city in collaboration with Sevasi Village, Vadodara in 2010-2011" was mainly conceived under the following steps:

- Planning
- Execution
- Evaluation
- Follow-up

The project worker, therefore, decided to evaluate the implementation of this particular project on computer literacy with learners using a Reaction scale.

Background Information of the Learners

This section deals with Background Information of the learners of Sevasi village, Vadodara, who were the target group for the present for the computer literacy project.

Table 16.3 reveals that out of fifteen learners, three each were between fifteen years to twenty years and thirty one to thirty five whereas five learners were between twenty years to twenty five years, while two learners were between twenty six to thirty years and thirty six years and above.

Table 16.3: Frequency Distribution of Learners According to the Age

N = 15

S. No.	Age(in years)	Frequency
1.	15 years–20 years	3
2.	21 years–25 years	5
3.	26 years–30 years	2
4.	31 years–35 years	3
5.	36 and above	2

N = 15

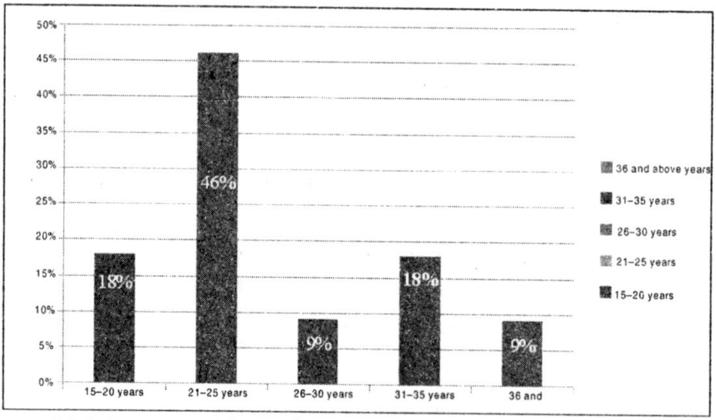

Figure 16.4: Frequency Distribution of learners according to their Age.

Table 16.4: Frequency Distribution of Learners according to their Present Status

N = 15

S. No.	Present Status	Frequency
1.	Studying	4
2.	Housewives	8
3.	Working	3

Table 16.4 reveals that out of fifteen learners, four learners were still studying, eight learners were housewives and another three learners were working in school and private offices.

Table 16.5: Frequency Distribution of Learners according to their Type of Family

N = 15

S. No.	Type of Family	Frequency
1.	Nuclear	7
2.	Joint	8

N = 15

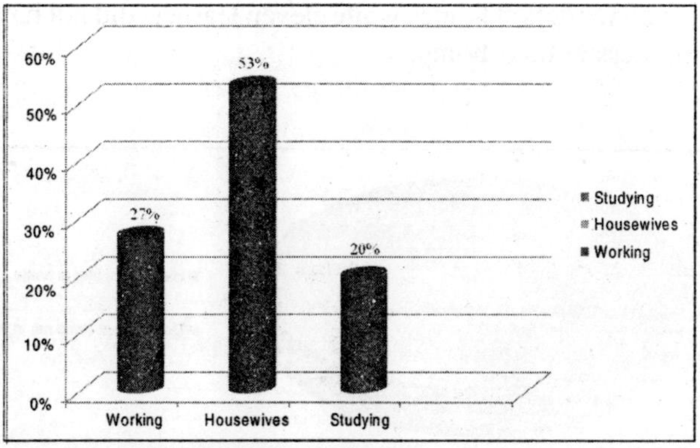

Figure 16.5: Frequency Distribution of Learners according to their Present Status.

Table 16.5 reveals that out of fifteen learners, seven learners belonged to nuclear and eight learners belonged to joint families.

N = 15

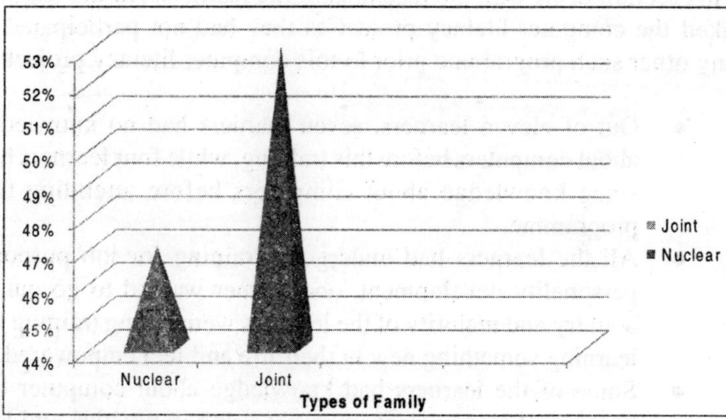

Figure 16.6: Frequency Distribution of learners according to their type of family.

Table 16.6: Frequency Distribution of Learners according to access to Computers at Home

N = 15

S. No.	*Type of Family*	*Frequency*
1.	Have Computer at home	4
2.	Do not have Computer at home	11
	Total	**15**

Table 16.6 reveals that out of fifteen learners, four learners had access to computers at homes while eleven learners did not have access to Computers at their home.

N = 15

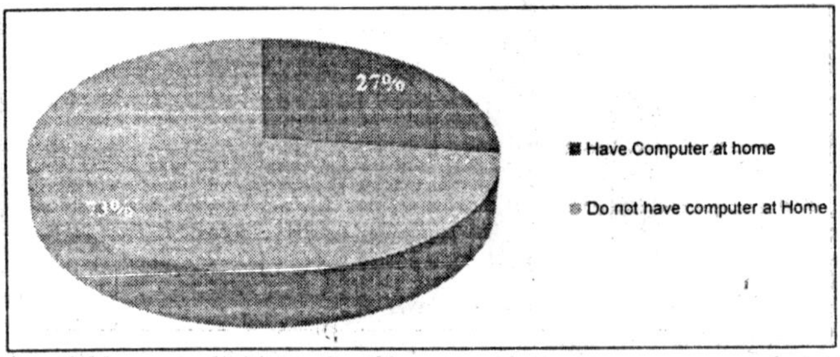

Figure 16.7: Frequency Distribution of Learners according to access to computers at home.

Reactions for the Computer Literacy Project

This section deals with the reactions of the learners. All the learners liked the computer literacy project as they had not participated in any other such programme prior to this computer literacy project:

- Out of eleven learners, seven learners had no knowledge about computers before this training, while four learners had some knowledge about computers before attending this programme.
- All the learners had undergone training for job purpose, personality development, one learner wanted to go out of country and majority of the learners were taking training for learning something new in their life and feel empowered.
- Some of the learners had knowledge about computer but because of some reasons like not being in practice and less of knowledge, not getting good training in other institutes and majority of the learners had earlier left the computer class in between because of some dissatisfaction. So, they felt a need to attend the computer training again, as per the job market demanded computer knowledge.
- All the learners found the physical facilities good and place and time convenient. They did not face any problem during the project, in this regard.

- All the learners liked the content of computer literacy, however, four learners liked Microsoft-Excel more than other components of computer literacy. All the learners were satisfied with the topics covered, explanation skills, teaching methods and behaviour of the project worker. The learners did not face any problem with the project worker, or with the project.

Conclusion

Computer Literacy today has become important in everybody's life. Need for computers is increasing day by day. Computers are useful and are being used to a large extent, in Railway stations, Airports, Schools, and so on. Computer Literacy becomes necessary for seeking jobs in many places. In developed countries, many schools are using online examination for development of children; many jobs are also given on the basics of online tests and examinations. Learners of the project can be key leaders for "Computer Literacy" as they can further educate their peers, siblings, parents, grandparents, relatives and colleagues. The present Action Project on "Computer Literacy" covered various topics on basics of computer. It gave effective, systematic and proven result. The project helped the learners to learn practically what computer is and also got the platform and opportunity for seeking jobs. Computer Literacy programme focused on bringing the change in attitude of learners towards seeking jobs which needed computer skills. Department of Extension and Communication has conducted successful computer literacy projects at undergraduate as well as postgraduate level in various communities and schools of Baroda city. Department has adopted participatory approach to make students learn about computer literacy, in government schools. This Action Project will help the undergraduate and postgraduate students for the Department of Extension and Communication for strengthening Computer Literacy programmes in Outreach and Extension programmes.

Problems Faced during the Project

Although taking an action project on imparting Computer Literacy amongst learners was very interesting but there were some problems faced at various stages of the project:

- Some learners were irregular thus project worker found it

difficult, since she had to repeat the previous topic again for them.

- Some of the computers, had old version, so, project worker had to teach both the old and the new versions which took more time.

Suggestions

1. A similar action project with adolescent boys, girls, differently abled people, senior citizens can be carried out in other villages of Baroda.
2. A similar type of action project can be conducted with 'TALLY' and other programmes of computer.
3. Research for the effectiveness of Computer Assisted Multimedia Package (CAMP) for teaching other subjects may also be carried out.
4. As the coming century is surely of computer age, so, Computer Literacy project for school and college teachers can be taken up in future.
5. Teachers have to make pupils aware to get computer education. An Action Project with trained teachers can be taken up for further dissemination of computer literacy.
6. The learners could start earning by taking up computer jobs, if any financial institute provide them loan facilities for buying computers.
7. The learners could use computer for job purpose and for helping their children to learn basics of computers and in their school projects.

References

Archthan, S. (1983). *Computer Technology on Higher Education*, Vol. II, An Indian Experience, Concept Publishing Co., New Delhi.

Basu, D.K. Nasipuri, M. Kundu, M. (1997), *Computer Systems and Data Analysis*, Narosa Publishing House, New Delhi.

Bhojwani, L. (2006). "Education in a Corporation Primary School of Vadodara 2004-06". Dissertation Master of Education. Center of Advanced Study in Education, Faculty of Education and Psychology. The M.S. University of Baroda, Vadodara.

Desai, F. and Pandya, R. (2002). "Computer for School Education", *National Journal of Education*, VII (2).

Dubey, S. (2007). "Effectiveness of Computer Assisted Multimedia Package for Teaching Science to GSEB Standard IX Students." *Faculty of Education and Psychology*, Department of Education, The M.S. University of Baroda, Vadodara.

Gerald, C. (1972). *Computers and the Art of Computation*, Addison Wesley Publishing Company, California.

Lakhar, I. (2005). "An Action Project to Promote Literacy in the Primary School of Baroda through the Use of Games", Dissertation (M. Sc.), Department of Home Science Education and Extension, *Faculty of Home Science*, The M.S. University of Baroda, Vadodara.

Malhotra, S. (2004). "A Study of the Usage of Computers by 6th Standard Students of the Selected Schools of Baroda City", Dissertation (M. Sc.), Department of Home Science Extension and Education, *Faculty of Home Science*, The M.S. University of Baroda, Vadodara.

Mistry, Pooja (2010). "An Action Project on 'Adobe Photoshop', amongst differently abled People of Vadodara city", Department of Home Science Extension and Communication, *Faculty of Family and Community Sciences*, The M.S. University of Baroda, Vadodara.

Roger, H. and Shelly J., (1984). *Computer and Commonsense*, Prentice Hall of India Pvt. Limited, New Delhi.

Sahasrabudhe, S. (1994). "A Study of Computer Education in the Secondary Schools of Baroda city". Center for Advanced Study in Education, *Faculty of Education and Psychology*, Department of Education, The M.S. University of Baroda, Vadodara.

Saxena, S. (2004). *Basic of Computer*, Sterling Publication Pvt. Ltd., New Delhi.

Shah, R. (2002). "The Survey of Computer Education in Secondary School Affiliated to GSEB in Vadodara City". Dissertation *Faculty of Education and Psychology*, The M.S. University of Baroda, Vadodara.

Shah, K. (2009). "An Action Project to Promote Computer Literacy Amongst Selected Learners of Baroda city in Collaboration with Jan Shikshan Sansthan, Vadodara, Department of Extension and Communication", *Faculty of Family and Community Sciences*, The M.S. University of Baroda, Vadodara.

Shah, M. (2009). "An Action Project on Promoting Basic Computer Literacy Course with Jan Shikshan Sansthan Among Senior Citizens of Vadodara City", Dissertation (M.Sc.), Department of Extension and Communication, *Faculty of Family and Community Sciences*, The M.S. University of Baroda, Vadodara.

Solanki, T. (2002). "Study of Computer Literacy of Teachers of the M.S. University of Baroda", Dissertation, *Faculty of Education and Psychology*. The M.S. University of Baroda, Vadodara.

Index